Relational-centred Research
for Psychotherapists

Relational-centred Research for Psychotherapists

Exploring Meanings and Experience

By Linda Finlay and Ken Evans

WILEY-BLACKWELL

A John Wiley & Sons, Ltd., Publication

This edition first published 2009
© 2009 John Wiley & Sons, Ltd.

Wiley-Blackwell is an imprint of John Wiley & Sons, formed by the merger of Wiley's global
Scientific, Technical, and Medical business with Blackwell Publishing.

Registered Office
John Wiley & Sons Ltd, The Atrium, Southern Gate, Chichester, West Sussex, PO19 8SQ, UK

Editorial Offices
The Atrium, Southern Gate, Chichester, West Sussex, PO19 8SQ, UK
9600 Garsington Road, Oxford, OX4 2DQ, UK
350 Main Street, Malden, MA 02148-5020, USA

For details of our global editorial offices, for customer services, and for information about how
to apply for permission to reuse the copyright material in this book please see our website at
www.wiley.com/wiley-blackwell.

The right of the editors to be identified as the authors of the editorial material in this work has
been asserted in accordance with the Copyright, Designs and Patents Act 1988.

Library of Congress Cataloging-in-Publication Data

Finlay, Linda, 1957–
    Relational-centred research for psychotherapists : exploring meanings and experience / by
Linda Finlay and Ken Evans.
        p. ; cm.
    Includes bibliographical references and index.
    ISBN 978-0-470-99776-5 (cloth) – ISBN 978-0-470-99777-2 (pbk.)   1. Psychotherapy–
Research.   2. Qualitative research.   I. Evans, Kenneth (Kenneth Roy), 1947–   II. Title.
    [DNLM: 1. Psychotherapy.   2. Interpersonal Relations.   3. Qualitative Research. WM 420
F511r 2009]
    RC337.F56 2009
    616.89′140724–dc22

                                                                                    2009021006

A catalogue record for this book is available from the British Library.

Set in 10.5/13 pt Minion by SNP Best-set Typesetter Ltd., Hong Kong
Printed in Singapore by Fabulous Printers Pte Ltd

1   2009

Contents

About the Editors

Linda Finlay is an academic and therapist. She is currently an Associate Director of the Scarborough Psychotherapy Training Institute and is working to complete the requirements for registration as an Integrative Psychotherapist with UKCP. She also teaches qualitative research at several psychotherapy training centres across Europe. Linda describes herself as belonging to three distinct professional communities: psychology, occupational therapy and phenomenology. In the psychology field she teaches (social) psychology and qualitative research methodology with the Open University. In occupational therapy, she was a mental health practitioner and is known for her textbooks on psychosocial occupational therapy and group work. But it is in the world of phenomenology, that she has found a home. Here she is able to bring her professional identities together using relational-centred research to explore the lived experience of disability. She is currently researching with Virginia Eatough the lived experience of discovering a kindred spirit connection.

Linda has published widely. Since 2003 she has published three books: *The Practice of Psychosocial Occupational Therapy* (Nelson Thornes); *Qualitative Research for Allied Health Professionals* (John Wiley & Sons), a volume co-edited with Claire Ballinger; and *Reflexivity: A Practical Guide for Researchers in Health and Social Science* (Blackwell Publishing), a volume co-edited with Brendan Gough.

Ken Evans is registered as a Gestalt Psychotherapist and as an Integrative Psychotherapist. He is also a supervisor and a visiting trainer at several centres across Europe. He is currently Co-Director of the European

Institute for Psychotherapeutic Studies based in France and an Associate Director of the Scarborough Psychotherapy Training Institute. Ken describes himself as a radical, Buddhist-influenced, Anglican Priest who has completed 135 parachute jumps. He has a 30-year commitment to the creation of psychotherapy as an independent profession which is reflected in his work for a number of professional associations. He was President of the European Association for Gestalt Therapy (EAGT) and Chair of the EAGT Human Rights and Social Responsibility Committee. In this latter capacity, in 2006 he participated in a cross-cultural dialogue in Tel Aviv with Israeli Jews and Arabs and Palestinian Arabs. He is Registrar of the European Association for Integrative Psychotherapy and a former President of the European Association for Psychotherapy (1994) and Chair of the UKCP Training Standards Committee (1998–2001).

Ken is the co-founder and Senior Editor of the online *European Journal for Qualitative Research in Psychotherapy*. He has written numerous articles and he has co-authored two books with Maria Gilbert: *Psychotherapy Supervision: An Integrative Relational Approach* (OUP) and *An Introduction to Integrative Psychotherapy* (Palgrave Macmillan). His current research interests include exploring intersubjectivity and the use of self in therapy as well as the application of relational-centred practice in research.

Contributing Authors

Virginia Eatough is a lecturer in psychology at Birkbeck, University of London, UK where she teaches qualitative research and phenomenological psychology. Her primary research interest is the lived experience of emotion and emotion-related phenomena. At the heart of this interest is a focus on emotion's embodied feeling dimension. Current research projects include exploring the experience of adult tears, living with Parkinson's disease and kindred spirit connections, the latter with Linda Finlay.

Darren Langdridge is a senior lecturer in social psychology at The Open University, UK, a visiting lecturer at the New School of Psychotherapy and Counselling (London) and a UKCP accredited existential psychotherapist working in private practice. He has written/edited several books, including *Phenomenological Psychology: Theory, Research and Method* (Pearson Education), and numerous papers on sexualities, families and psychotherapy. His primary research interest involves the application of the philosophy of Paul Ricoeur to better understand the construction of identities.

Maria Luca is Head of the School of Psychotherapy and Counselling Psychology, Regent's College, London, UK. She is a UKCP registered integrative psychotherapist using phenomenological and psychodynamic constructs to inform her practice. She has extensive clinical experience in the NHS and lectures widely. Her research interests include embodiment in grounded theory, and bodily phenomena, the subjects of her PhD. She is past books review editor of the *European Journal of Psychotherapy, Counselling and Health*.

Anna Madill is a senior lecturer in psychology at the University of Leeds, UK. She is co-founder and current chair of the Qualitative Methods in Psychology Section of the British Psychological Society and Associate Editor of the *British Journal of Clinical Psychology*. Her research interests are in qualitative methodology, particularly in the evaluation of qualitative research and promoting understanding between researchers specializing in different methods. She has published in the areas of health and psychological therapies.

Susan L Morrow is a professor and psychologist in the Counseling Psychology Program at the University of Utah, USA. A qualitative researcher, methodologist, and educator, she brings her early activism in civil rights, the women's liberation movement, and the lesbian/gay/bisexual movement to her social justice perspectives in her research and teaching. She is also a psychotherapist specializing in work with women, trauma and lesbian/bisexual issues.

Preface

This book was born out of an intertwining of the different backgrounds and experiences of Linda and Ken. Linda is a mental health therapist and qualitative, phenomenological researcher; Ken is registered both as a Gestalt Psychotherapist and as an Integrative Psychotherapist. When we met, we each saw a kindred spirit in the other. In our respective fields we had both, over many years, talked of the importance of the relational–dialogic context and the need for reflexivity. We were both committed to research that was fully relational in practice and spirit. Such an approach, we thought, could be twinned seamlessly with the practice of many psychotherapists and counsellors, helping them to engage and deliver the relevant and resonant research so needed in the current climate.

This book aims to provide psychotherapists and counsellors with an accessible, practical introduction to carrying out qualitative, relationally focused research. (When relational dimensions between researcher, participants and their wider social fields are fore-grounded, qualitative research is 'relational-centred'. Relational-centred research can be considered a *facet* of the qualitative research diamond.)

The growing demand for evidence-based practice and the professionalization of psychotherapy (where courses are now seeking accreditation and university-level validation) means that psychotherapists and counsellors are increasingly being called upon to do research. As members of a relatively young profession, psychotherapists often lack the confidence to engage with the world of research and find it hard to know where to start. Their difficulties are compounded by the gap – chasm even – that exists between academic theory/research and clinical practice. The research that is carried out tends to focus on meeting formal academic requirements (and never sees the light of day beyond academic institutions); alternatively, research results published in articles often seem to bear little relationship to the concerns of practising therapists. In fact, the pool of relevant, resonant research relevant to psychotherapy is growing rapidly.

In this book we seek to address the gap between research and practice by providing numerous practical examples of small-scale research based firmly in clinical experience. We hope to show how psychotherapists can carry out research that is meaningful and enables them to find answers to questions raised in their practice. In taking a relational-centred approach which mirrors relational-centred practice – we value the idea of doing research *with*, as opposed to *on*, participants and we celebrate the co-creation of knowledge within the relationship between researcher and participant. We also hope to impart our own commitment, passion and enthusiasm for what we believe is offered by qualitative relational-centred research.

A key assumption of this book is that both therapy and research involve a journey of evolving self-other understanding and growth. Both therapy and research are relational activities which confront all parties (be they practitioners, clients or participants) with moments of struggle, uncertainty and confusion. Many of the familiar skills, values and interests of therapists are, in fact, directly transferable to the research domain. Interviewing skills, reflexive intuitive interpretation, inferential thinking and a capacity for warmth, openness and empathy are all qualities needed in both practice and research. We believe that a competent, relationally oriented therapist, equipped with an appropriate introduction to qualitative research methods will be a competent researcher. By the same token, we argue that qualitative research will be enriched considerably by the professional competencies and emotional literacy expected of a relational-centred therapist.

We are targeting this book primarily at practising psychotherapists, counsellors and students. Members of the allied therapeutic professions (such as clinical psychology, social work, occupational therapy and mental health nursing), who seek to integrate research into their practice, should also find this book useful.

*   *   *   *   *   *

In the spirit of relational research, the writing of this book was a *co-creation*. Ken's teaching and practice of relational psychotherapy inspired Linda to articulate more clearly the relational approach she had been striving for in her research practice. Linda's writing and phenomenological research experience gave voice to Ken's intuitive though less formed research approach. As we witnessed each other's work in both therapeutic and academic contexts, we saw the magic in the other's practice and we have tried to bring this alchemy into this book.

We have particularly appreciated the preparedness of the other to be open and non-defensive as our ideas evolved through emerging chapters. We challenged each other through successive drafts and valued the way the other set aside ego and shame processes, as we struggled to articulate our vision for relational-centred research.

Many other people have also helped with the evolution of this book. We would first like to acknowledge our spouses Mel and Joanna: without their extraordinary support, forbearance, personal and professional challenge, and loyal encouragement we could not have sustained the project from beginning to end. Secondly, our friends in the human science research and psychotherapy worlds have provided their own amazing insights and nourished us with dialogue over the years. A few deserve extra special mention: Steen Halling, Bob Shaw, Maria Gilbert, Paul Barber, Diana Shmukler, Peter Ashworth and Barbara Payman. We are also grateful to the contributing authors for adding their remarkable expertise. Their voices have enriched the book and demonstrate the art of our research.

Finally, our thanks need to be extended to Andrew Peart (Commissioning Editor), Karen Shield (Project Editor), Ruth Jelley (Production Editor) and the rest of the publishing team for seeing the manuscript through to publication.

Linda Finlay and Ken Evans
January 2009

Part I

Engaging Qualitative Research and the Relational-centred Approach

Introduction

In this first part of the book, we distinguish between the idea of 'qualitative research' in general and 'relational-centred research' specifically. *Qualitative research* is that which uses more subjective, impressionistic, interpretive, holistic and contextual methods, going beyond the 'facts and figures' gathered by quantitative researchers. *Relational-centred research*, on the other hand, can be considered a type of qualitative approach – a facet of the qualitative diamond as it were. In foregrounding the co-created relationship between researcher and participant (co-researcher), relational approaches can be applied in different guises to many different qualitative methodologies.

In these five initial chapters, we invite you to reflect on the nature of the qualitative research project. In *Chapter 1*, we suggest qualitative research can be likened to going on a voyage of discovery – a voyage which promises excitement and uncertainties on the way. We describe what that voyage involves; what qualitative and relational-centred research means in theory and practice.

If qualitative research is a voyage, qualitative methodologies offer us our maps and guides for different routes. In *Chapter 2*, we describe some of these different methodological 'routes'. Using examples from research practice, we show how the initial choice of methodology can have radical consequences for the type of research conducted and the way in which the data is understood.

Chapter 3 puts the spotlight on relational-centred research highlighting its underpinning theory and values. The concept of embodied co-creation is especially important. When we relate to an 'Other' in a research encounter, each person touches and impacts on the other and that effects how the research unfolds. Relational-centred researchers believe that much of what can be known about another arises in that mysterious but powerful intersubjective space *between*.

In *Chapter 4*, we take a step outwards and look at the wider field and context of qualitative research. Specifically, we critically challenge prevailing preoccupations of the evidence-based practice movement which favours relying on the quantitative evidence such as randomized controlled trials (RCTs). We suggest that relevant research may also be achieved through collecting smaller scale, *practice-based qualitative evidence* focused on therapy processes, not just outcomes.

Chapter 5 continues to explore the question of what comprises good, useful research. Good research, we say, is not only rigorous but it resonates and enriches our work as practitioners. The special contribution and strength of qualitative relational-centred research is the way it can capture the ambiguity, ambivalence and richness of lived experience while touching the complexity of meanings in the social world.

Chapter 1

Qualitative Relational-centred Research: A 'Voyage of Discovery'

Qualitative relational-centred research can be likened to going on a voyage of discovery, a journey into unknown territory which promises excitement and surprises on the way as well as frustrations and uncertainties. As with the practice of psychotherapy where we find ourselves drawn into our clients' worlds, our research venturing brings us face to face with the unfamiliar and the challenging. In research, as in therapy, we seek to build a bridge to the Other, using our own special awareness, skills, experience and knowledge. We reflect on the Other's stories while simultaneously analysing our own responses and the dynamics of the evolving relationship between us.

There are, of course, major differences between psychotherapy and research (be it qualitative research in general or relational-centred specifi-cally). In research we aim to understand individuals and their social world with an eye to producing knowledge. Our contact with those we research may well be short-lived, involving perhaps just a couple of hours of con-versation. In psychotherapy, on the other hand, we aim to understand and also enable another in some way, influenced by the goal or purpose of our modality. What links psychotherapy and research are the elements of mutual discovery and the sense of being in a 'process' which calls to be engaged and examined. In both psychotherapy and research there is poten-tial for the experience to be transformative.

Relational-centred Research for Psychotherapists: Exploring Meanings and Experience
Edited by Linda Finlay and Ken Evans
Copyright © 2009 John Wiley & Sons, Ltd.

In this book, we (Linda and Ken) set out ways to do qualitative relationally orientated research which mirror our practice, values, skills and concerns as psychotherapists (McLeod, 1999). We argue that many of the familiar clinical skills and interests of psychotherapists (such as interviewing skills, empathy, reflexive or intuitive interpretations and inferential thinking) are directly transferable to the research domain. As we use these skills we can find that our co-researchers (participants) may experience the research process as empowering or healing in some way. We are also of the view that knowledge of the research process and awareness of the findings (of both qualitative and quantitative studies) can enhance the practice of psychotherapy. As we see it, research can provide us with vicarious therapeutic experiences (Polkinghorne, 1999), broadening our understanding of clients' worlds as well as challenging our assumptions and beliefs about therapy (Cooper, 2004). Psychotherapists have much to give and much to gain when it comes to relational-centred research.

In this introductory chapter we start by outlining the purpose and process of the qualitative research voyage of discovery. We explain how the qualitative approach in general is different from the traditional view of science embraced by quantitative research. We then move on to define 'relational-centred research' and describe what it specifically involves.

The Qualitative Research Voyage

One way of conveying the purpose and process of qualitative research is to tell a story …

> In 1492, Christopher Columbus set out from Spain with three ships in the hope of finding India. There were times during the voyage when a fair wind caused them to make good progress but at other times the wind fell away, the sea turned to glass and the ships floated rudderless, without purpose. Worse, were the times when thunder roared, lightening flashed and huge waves threatened to overwhelm ships and crew. After over two months of sailing into the unknown land was eventually sighted!

Columbus had set out to discover a new route to India but instead discovered a new world.[i] Like Columbus, as qualitative researchers we embark on an 'adventure' (Willig, 2001), fired by the vision of a rich and tantalizing land ahead. Like Columbus, we make careful preparations for the expedition, despite our uncertainty about what will happen *en route* and where we will finally end up. And as with the late 15th-century adventurer, the significance of any discoveries we make will not be properly understood until later.

Unlike Columbus, however, as qualitative researchers we avoid making predictions (hypotheses): there are no declarations that 'India' will be discovered. Instead, we keep ourselves open to unfolding encounters and celebrate the possibility of landfalls. The new worlds that open up, both during and at the end of the voyage will almost certainly be beyond what we could have imagined when first setting forth.

What are these new worlds that open up? How do we keep our senses open? And what is it, exactly, that qualitative researchers do? How does qualitative research differ from quantitative?

Qualitative researchers[ii] study the social world of subjective meanings. This is a point of contrast with the research conducted by quantitative researchers which generally focuses on quantifiable, objective measures and behaviours. Qualitative researchers aim to offer rich, textured, nuanced descriptions of emotions, thoughts, experiences and/or discourses in order to highlight personal experience or taken-for-granted social practices.

Qualitative research is inductive and exploratory rather than deductive. Researchers start with open research questions rather than seeking to test a hypothesis. We aim to understand the social world rather than predict, explain and control behaviour. The focus is on the 'hows' and 'whats' rather than the 'whys' and 'whethers'. For instance, when investigating whether a treatment intervention is effective, the qualitative researcher would not proceed by comparing a treatment group with a control group. Instead, we would pose the question: '*How* does this client experience this treatment?' Rather than asking participants to answer a questionnaire whose responses are quantifiable, the qualitative researcher poses open-ended questions such as: '*How* do you understand…? *What* do you mean by…?'

Qualitative research takes place in natural, real-life settings and attempts to capture people's experiences in context. 'Qualitative researchers study things in their natural settings, attempting to make sense of or interpret phenomena in terms of the meanings people bring to them' (Denzin & Lincoln, 1994, p. 2). Qualitative researchers also recognize that we are influenced by what's in the field – including wider social relationships and our historical and cultural 'situatedness' in the world; this recognition is subsumed into our work. Being extra sensitive to issues around cultural diversity and anti-discriminatory practice, we try to be conscious of our own social location and how this may impact on participants and on the research in progress.

Qualitative researchers understand that meanings are fluid – subject to interpretation and negotiated within particular social contexts. Qualitative researchers are aware that multiple meanings can be inferred and that interpretations can be made according to chosen frames of reference. Whereas a researcher who is a psychotherapist may interpret a participant's responses as 'being defensive' or 'being resistant' or 'engaging substitute projection for retroflection', a lay person would be unlikely to derive such specialist understandings.[iii] Researchers therefore acknowledge that different re-searchers with their different backgrounds, using the same data, are likely to unfold different meanings.

Qualitative researchers accept that the researcher is a central figure who influences (and actively constructs) the collection, selection and interpretation of data. Researcher subjectivity – called 'bias' in quantitative research – is celebrated rather than shunned; it is considered an opportunity rather than a problem. In addition, as qualitative researchers we recognize that research is dynamic and co-created. It is a joint product of researchers and participants (and readers), and the relationships they build.

In qualitative research, the world is understood as too chaotic to be represented in unambiguous, clear-cut ways, or in straightforward cause-and-effect terms. As a result, researchers tend to eschew unduly rigid methodologies and prefer to work flexibly and creatively in response to the situation at hand. Data may be collected, and then presented in all manner of ways including employing creative art forms to deliver ironic or evocative presentations to maximize impact. As Braud and Anderson (1998, p. xxvii) playfully suggest, 'We need an imaginative, even outlandish, science to envision the potential of human experience … not just tidy reports.' Qualitative findings are typically complex and messy, reflecting the ambivalent, uncertain world of life experiences. They can be raw, painful and resonant; researchers can be deeply moved by the stories they encounter.

To illustrate the ideas above and show some of the different ways they play out in practice, consider the following four examples of qualitative studies.

Example 1.1   Exploring psychotherapists' experiences of erotic transference

Aim of study: to explore psychotherapists' own experiences of erotic transference

Methods: Semi-structured interviews conducted with 10 psychotherapists which are analysed using 'grounded theory' methodology.

Findings: Emergent themes identified from therapists' descriptions of their 'process' highlight issues around attachment including emotional inhibition, passionate experience and obsessive love (Josselson, 2003). A provisional theory is developed showing how past developmental deficits (such as lack of intimacy) are replayed in currently experienced needs and issues (such as the search for intimacy).

Example 1.2   Explicating a mother's grief

Aim of study: to explore the lived experience of a mother coming to terms with the death of her child

Methods: Three in-depth interviews plus communications through letters/emails over the course of a year are transcribed and analysed 'phenomenologically' in dialogue with the co-researcher-participant.

Findings: A narrative of the mother's lived experience is created revealing powerful themes concerning the bereavement process and describing existential issues of loss, death, the meaning of life and identity issues of being a parent. The research process itself is shown to have played a part in this mother's healing.

Example 1.3   Evaluating an art group

Aim of study: to contribute to the pool of evidence-based practice by evaluating an art psychotherapy group, run by two co-therapists who aim to support individuals dependent on alcohol as they engage their rehabilitation

Methods: (1) A questionnaire is given to group members at the end of the group evaluating how useful and supportive members found it. (2) Participants' artwork is analysed thematically for significant qualitative themes arising in the group.

Findings: The mixed methodology employed offers both quantitative and qualitative findings which demonstrate the value and limitations of the group as well as offering insights into change processes and the concerns of the group members.

Example 1.4   Examining relationships in a group home

Aim of study: to examine how relationships between staff and residents are managed in a group home for people with learning disabilities

Methods: 'Participant observation' is used as the researcher is both a support worker in the group home and a researcher.

Findings: Findings explore the researcher's own involvements with the residents as well as examining broader interactions and relationships that take place in the home. The analysis focuses on how power and control are enacted in complex and subtle ways by both staff and residents. Analysis also highlights dominant discourses and the ways in which the wider social, political and cultural context influences relationships in the home.

The four examples above show something of the diverse range of qualitative research possible. (*See Chapter 2: Competing Qualitative Research Traditions* for a more in-depth discussion of the range of methodologies at our disposal.) Which study appeals most to you, and why? If you are about to engage in research, your choice here may indicate which approach best suits your own values and interests.

Whatever methodology qualitative researchers choose, they know they are embarking on a potentially transformative exploration of relationships and meanings within our social world; a voyage whose capacity to open fresh horizons alerts us to how much more lies waiting to be discovered. As Braud and Anderson (1998, p. xxvii) put it,

> When the inquiry proceeds further than the sketchy maps left by others, following the surprises and 'chance' occurrences of the inquiry will guide the way to more gratifying insights and far-reaching conclusions and understanding.

The Relational-centred Research Voyage

If qualitative research refers to voyages of discovery in general, then 'relational-centred research' might be usefully seen as a particular type of expedition.

At one level, of course, all qualitative research inevitably contains relational elements in much the same way as all psychotherapy contains relational elements. Both attempt to analyse the impact of the social world on individuals. Not all qualitative research is specifically relational-centred, just as not all therapy is relational-centred.

Qualitative research can only be considered *relational-centred research* if relational dimensions between the researcher and co-researchers, and/or their wider social context, are foregrounded in some way. All four of the examples above have the potential to come under the category of relational research in that they all focus on aspects of social relationships. However, our (Linda's and Ken's) definition of relational-centred research goes further. We would say that qualitative research is 'relational-centred' when the research relationship between researcher and co-researchers is explicitly examined. Using this more precise definition, only Examples 2 and 4 mention the researcher/co-researcher relationship as a specific focus, so only these two are fully relational-centred in our view.

In practice, relational-centred research comes in many shapes and forms. Pick up any qualitative research book or journal and you will almost certainly come across relevant examples. There are, for instance, a range of approaches which foreground active collaboration between researcher and co-researcher, such as *Participatory Action Research* or PAR (Reason, 1994), *Co-operative Inquiry* (Heron, 1996) and the *Collaborative Narrative Method* (Arvay, 2003). In these methods participants take part in the analysis of data as well as generating data becoming 'co-researchers' in the fullest sense. *Feminist Research* (for example, see Fonow & Cook, 1991) also aims to ensure that research is collaborative and egalitarian, with particular attention paid to gender, power and emancipation issues. In the phenomenology and existential fields exploring lived human experience, much research can be considered relational though the *dialogal approach* (Halling, Leifer & Rowe, 2006) stands out as, here, the researchers dialogue as a group until they reach consensus. Broadening the focus of both phenomenological and feminist inquiry to include spiritual dimensions, *Transpersonal Research* methods (Braud & Anderson, 1998) also foreground researchers' qualities and their relationship with co-researchers.

Central to all these versions of relational research is the understanding that the research relationship involves an interactional encounter in which both parties are actively involved. Relational research – like relational forms of psychotherapy – does not involve a participant talking to a passive, distanced researcher who receives information. Rather it involves a constantly evolving, negotiated, dynamic, co-created relational process to which both researcher and co-researcher contribute (Evans & Gilbert, 2005). Relational dynamics between researcher and co-researchers are explored 'reflexively' (i.e. in a self-aware way) (Finlay & Gough, 2003), mirroring the kind of work therapists do. For one thing, the research relationship may help co-researchers to feel listened to and valued, in potentially profound and transformative ways, and this impacts both co-researcher and researcher. The reflexive process also includes taking into account dimensions of power, control and inequality, with the researcher attending to issues of gender, class, race, ethnicity, age, sexuality and so forth that may be impacting on the evolving relationship with the co-researcher. The researcher's negotiations with their co-researcher can involve considerable 'emotional labour' (Hoffmann, 2007).

An example of relational-centred research in practice comes from Lewis' (2008) grounded theory study of social workers' narratives about critical incidents in their practice. Describing how she identified with one male practitioner who had distanced himself from the pain of his client's suicide, Lewis acknowledges her struggle to keep focused on her participant's experience. To give another example, Gilbert (2006) describes feeling some shame when she undertook her research on the impact of the death of a child on Social Services staff:

I was aware of carrying the feelings of shame, that we should not be talking about C's death and that in raising the issue I was breaking a taboo ... co-researchers may not have been aware of its presence, projecting it outwards so I carried the feelings for them. (2006, p. 6)

We explore these kinds of relational dimensions further in *Chapter 3: Embodied Co-creation: Theory and Values for Relational Research* and in Part II of the book. Then, in Part III, four particular examples of relational research are discussed in depth.

Reflections

Our ... journey requires us to be touched and shaken by what we find on the way and to not be afraid to discover our own limitations ..., uncertainties and doubts. It is only with such an attitude of openness and wonder that we can encounter the impenetrable everyday mysteries [of our world]. (van Deurzen-Smith, 1997, p. 5)

We (Linda and Ken) see qualitative relational-centred research as an adventure into uncharted territory. We enjoy the excitement, challenges and 'unknowing' involved. We like the fact that qualitative research is both science and art; that it requires researchers to act from both mind and heart; and that it can touch both intellect and soul. When qualitative research is at its best, we appreciate its transformative power and resonance. We particularly cherish the possibilities opened up by relational-centred research, which acknowledges our complex and multifaceted links with others.

We believe that a competent, relationally oriented therapist, equipped with an appropriate introduction to qualitative research methods, can be a competent researcher. Psychotherapists, with their professional competencies and emotional literacy, have a great deal to offer the research world and also much to gain. Like du Plock (2004, p. 32), we believe that good research 'should leap off the page to revitalize some aspect of our way of being as therapists.'

If you are new to research, we hope this book will encourage you to take that first bold step into the unknown. If you already have research experience, we hope you will be inspired to engage more deeply and reflexively with the relational processes involved. Whatever your experience, the following chapters are offered as your compass, providing guidance and support as you venture into the intriguing, perplexing, endlessly exciting world of qualitative research ...

Notes

[i] This story has been adapted from one told in Evans and Gilbert (2005). In this, a psychotherapist (Ken) uses the story of Columbus to introduce and explain the process of psychotherapy to a client.

[ii] With the kind permission of John Wiley & Sons, Ltd. the following account of qualitative research has been developed from the description offered by Finlay (2006a) on pp. 6–7 of '"Going exploring": the nature of qualitative research', in *Qualitative Research for Allied Health Professionals: Challenging Choices*, edited by Linda Finlay and Claire Ballinger.

[iii] It is unlikely that researchers will offer in-depth psychoanalytic interpretations (for example, about deep structures of personality) on the basis of an interview lasting an hour or two. However, there will be some opportunities to probe latent meanings and the researcher's own responses, including possible projections and transferences, might offer valuable clues.

Chapter 2

Competing Qualitative Research Traditions[i]

Qualitative researchers today face a baffling range of choices of research traditions (Cresswell, 1998). Just as psychotherapists need to grapple with many competing theoretical and practice traditions, so too do researchers. Pick up any qualitative research book and it will emphasize different qualitative research approaches. Sometimes the methodologies discussed in one book will not even overlap with those in another. Navigating the qualitative research territory can be distinctly confusing.[ii]

While the array of qualitative research traditions at our disposal testifies to the richness and dynamism of the field, it also presents challenges for conducting research. Novice researchers, particularly, can be confused about how to start. The temptation is to engage simplistically with 'methods' (such as interview or qualitative thematic analysis) instead of 'methodology' (which includes methods but also encompasses certain philosophical and theoretical commitments). We would argue that it is critical to engage with the fuller methodology. If qualitative research is a voyage, methodology helps us understand the type of trip we are embarking on, and offers maps and guides. Engaging just with methods in the absence of a methodological context is a bit like packing before we know where we're going!

This chapter discusses some of the competing research traditions available to qualitative relational researchers. In the first half of the chapter, we contrast a few methodological traditions commonly used and offer some

Relational-centred Research for Psychotherapists: Exploring Meanings and Experience
Edited by Linda Finlay and Ken Evans

guidelines for choosing between them. The second half focuses on broader philosophical questions to do with epistemology and you are invited to consider your own commitments here.

As you read through this chapter, we hope you will not tune out when you come to any unfamiliar jargon. Philosophical concepts like epistemology can be distinctly off-putting, yet they are also important to learn about as they are commonly referred to in the qualitative research literature. We ask you to bear with us. Hopefully by the end of the chapter you will have a clearer idea about what such concepts mean and how knowing them can help you to approach your research.

Choosing between Methodological Traditions

'Mapping' the territory

The examples in Box 2.1 show how six researchers, each of them adopting a different methodology (i.e. philosophy + methods), set out on projects that all involve interviewing co-researchers about how they live and cope with depression. Because they are using different methodologies, the six researchers all have different aims for their research and they depart in completely different directions to explore different areas. Their contrasting aims impact not only on how the interviews are carried out and analysed but also on the nature of the research relationship and the research as a whole (Finlay, 2006b).

Box 2.1 highlights the different researchers' intentions emphasizing the point that although all six researchers chose to do interviews, their

---

Box 2.1   Researching the nature of depression through interviews: six contrasting methodologies

Sharon chooses to take a 'phenomenological' approach, aiming for rich description of individuals' lived experience of their depression. She asks her co-researchers to describe, as concretely as possible, a typical day when they have been particularly depressed and she focuses on what it means to them personally. She analyses this data in terms of existential themes, exploring her co-researchers' sense of embodiment, identity and self-other relations.

Lee takes a 'psychodynamic' case study approach to explore how six individuals' experience of managing their depression links back to childhood patterns. Specifically he wants to examine the defence mechanisms used such as particular introjects and internalized messages the individuals carry or the way they disown parts of themselves as a defence against shame. Focusing his questions on the 'here and now' and the 'then and there', he is alert to the ways the individuals' past experiences may colour the way they view themselves in the present. He also looks reflexively at his own interpretations of various transferences and counter-transferences which seem to be in action.

Will opts to do a 'grounded theory' study where his interview questions are focused analytically on the process of 'coping with' depression. When and how does coping happen? What disrupts coping? He sees the co-researchers' responses as a reasonably accurate reflection of their thoughts and feelings. He aims to categorize systematically their types of coping and show how coping occurs in particular social situations at different levels.

Novak undertakes an 'ethnographic' study geared to understanding the culture and characteristics of a day hospital as a social setting designed to help clients with their mental health problems, including depression. His interview questions are focused on how the clients perceive their mental health needs and their rehabilitation. He is interested in how the clients are positioned in the setting and how they interact with each other and the professionals. He aims to develop a story of these clients and how this particular social and cultural context enables clients to live positively with their mental health problems.

Katie undertakes a 'discourse analysis' (DA). She aims to examine the way the diagnosis of 'depression' is both constructed and performed by individuals in terms of the subject positions they adopt. She views the 'text' (her transcripts) as a manifestation of discursive resources which the participants are drawing upon to construct their versions. She is alert to the presence of cultural scripts – for instance, the use of particular narratives and metaphors. She takes her reflexive analysis seriously by recognizing the power of her role as interviewer and the entirely co-constructed nature of the text.

Meena chooses to do some 'participatory action research' (PAR) to help a group of British Asian women who speak little English cope with their depression and isolation. Specifically, she aims to study the effect of a new community outreach initiative designed to encourage these women to take up counselling support offered. Meena aims to interview each co-researcher both prior to the project and after six months. In addition, she will run an ongoing group to offer support and to monitor their changing needs. After a period of four months, she hopes the women themselves will take on the running of this group.

underlying philosophies, theories and methods employed to collect and analyse their data differ quite sharply. Being clear about their preferred methodologies will have helped these researchers select the most appropriate research methods (techniques and procedures). How would they know what kinds of questions to ask and how to approach the analysis without having a broader sense of the methodological route they were taking?

Choosing between Routes

Of course, in practice, methodologies are often not so clearly differentiated or spelt out. It would be possible, for instance, to simply take a therapy session and analyse its content descriptively and thematically, and to publish this as an empirical article. Dallos (2004), for instance, offers an in-depth case study which illustrates (with extracts from the therapy sessions) the four-stage approach to family therapy offered to a young woman with an eating disorder, and her family. Landy and Hadari (2007), to give another example, offer an account of a gestalt drama-therapy workshop they ran on the topic of destruction and renewal. Jacobsen (2007) offers a psychoanalytic case study of parallel processes based on two psychotherapy sessions and the supervision session between.

Sometimes researchers will straddle methodologies, for instance, blending phenomenological and psychoanalytic approaches as part of focusing on individuals' subjective worlds. One good example of this is Hollway and Jefferson's (2000; Hollway, 2007) work using their research method they call FANI: free association narrative and interview method. They draw largely on psychoanalytic concepts (in particular, the work of Klein) while also identifying relevant social discourses and trying to describe lived experience – in other words, they straddle psychoanalytic, discursive and phenomenological approaches. For example, they speak of the 'defended subject' who invests in 'discourses when these offer positions which provide protection against anxiety and therefore supports to identity' (2000, p. 23). In their view, anxiety and the defences which it precipitates are complex responses to events and people in the social world, both present and past.

The other complication when thinking about methodology is that often significant variants exist signalling the likelihood of intense academic debates around the favoured way to carry out that methodology.[iii] Diploma and Masters' level students might conveniently ignore these subtle distinctions. However, they are important to acknowledge at PhD level.

Faced with so many competing methodologies and different options of methods, how do you, the researcher, choose which one to use?

Often the choice comes down to practicalities. For instance, if you are doing research as a practitioner or for a Diploma or MSc, your time will be limited. The prudent choice here would be to opt for a more straightforward, established methodology. It is likely that your supervisor will guide you towards doing a 'case study' of a session (or a course of sessions) which you reflexively analyse theoretically, narratively and/or thematically. Alternatively, you might research someone's lived experience of a problem or issue using a variant of phenomenology like interpretative phenomenological analysis (IPA) or another relational-centred approach. These would be relatively straightforward options given the time available and your existing skills and knowledge. If you are doing a PhD you will need to examine different methodologies more critically and perhaps even evolve your own.

As you strive to make a decision about which methodology, you may find it useful to reflect on some key questions. What are your particular beliefs and values? What are you especially interested in as far as research is concerned? Do you have any specific goals? What resources do you have at your disposal? Do you have sufficient knowledge and skills to pursue the line of research you are interested in? Are there any academic or professional demands which concern you?

If we apply these questions to the case examples in Box 2.1, we find that Sharon, for example, is interested in the personal and emotional aspects of her participants' experience. Her background experience in the field of mental health should provide her with the knowledge and skills to carry out her research. Lee, a psychoanalytic therapist working relationally, seeks to use own his skills and experience in his research methodology. In contrast, Will chooses a study which suits his natural science background and the values that accompany this. He wanted a research method which was more objective and clearly anchored in empirical data. Novak, who manages a unit similar to the one he is researching, hopes to learn something about how the culture of a unit can be a positive influence. Katie believes in the power of societal factors to influence an individual's experience and she chooses a methodology to reflect this position. Meena's goal is to make a practical difference to the British Asian community to which she herself belongs.

Looking across the six methodologies outlined here, is there one to which you feel particularly drawn? Psychotherapists and counsellors are often attracted to doing phenomenological and/or psychodynamic *case study* research into individual lived experience. Perhaps this is not surprising given the nature of our therapy practice.[iv] There are many examples in the literature of case studies – as McLeod (1999) notes, they are the single most widely used genre of practitioner research and the clinical cases written up by Freud and his colleagues remain foundational today.

It takes time and experience to build sufficient confidence to know exactly where you stand in terms of your theoretical and philosophical commitments. In a way, you have a distinct advantage here if you are a psychotherapist or counsellor as you have had to go through a similar process as part of establishing your theoretical preferences for your therapy work. You also may well be able to use your therapeutic knowledge, skills and values to guide you towards particular research approaches, as Lee did in the example above. Where you are likely to be less confident is in working out your epistemological commitments – a concept we explain in the next section.

Engaging Epistemology

Different philosophers and researchers do not just argue about methodology, they argue about the nature of our social world and the degree to which it is open to study. Now we are in the territory of 'epistemology'. Epistemology is a branch of philosophy concerned with the theory of knowledge and the role of science. It asks 'what can we know?' and 'how can we know things?' It looks at the way we think about the nature of the social world and our being (i.e. our 'ontology'). In research terms, it asks how we conceptualize the nature and status of our research enterprise. It poses such questions as: What understanding am I aiming for? What kind of knowledge can I possibly gain? How do I understand the role of the researcher?

Answers to these questions are hotly contested between researchers. However, they are fundamental to your research preferences and choices so it is well worth looking at them in more detail. While you may be put off initially by the dense, abstract philosophical language that can sometimes be used, it is worth getting to grips with the basic concepts so that you can be sure to make coherent, consistent choices.

• *What understanding am I aiming for?*
One way of identifying the aims of your research is ask whether it falls into the positivist or the interpretivist tradition.[v] Positivists aim for 'truths' while interpretivists explore multiple meanings and interpretations.

'Positivists' are optimistic about the possibility of gaining true knowledge about an independently existing 'real' world. Positivist epistemology argues that there is a relatively straightforward relationship between the world (objects/events) and our perceptions and understanding of it. The goal of research is objective knowledge gained through the labours of the researcher as an impartial observer who stands outside the phenomenon or process under investigation. Positivists believe that it is possible – at least to a degree – to describe and explain what is going on in the world, and that such understandings can be reached by researchers working independently of one another: in other words, the findings of one researcher can be replicated by another.

'Interpretivists', on the other hand, deny the possibility of capturing 'truth' which they regard as relative. There is not one 'reality', they argue, but many; what is true for you may not be true for me – it all depends on our perspective. Different realities result from 'construction and negotiation deeply embedded in culture' (Bruner, 1990, pp. 24–25). Interpretivist epistemology states that people's perceptions and experiences are socially, culturally, historically and linguistically produced: in other words, that our situatedness determines our understanding. Interpretivist researchers argue that it is impossible to be objective as the researcher's identity and standpoint shape the research process and findings in a fundamental way: two researchers studying the same phenomenon are certain to interpret and understand that phenomenon differently. Interpretivists see themselves as part of the world they are studying, rather than external to it. In their view, any understanding they gain from research informs them simultaneously about the object of study and about their own preoccupations, expectations and cultural traditions. Understandings gained from research remain provisional, partial and entirely dependent on context. Interpretivist researchers, with their poststructural and postmodern commitments, argue that positivist methods are only one of many ways to tell stories about our social world and, further, that this one way may actually silence too many voices (Denzin & Lincoln, 2005).

From the above description, you can see that quantitative research (based on the tenets of natural science) rests on positivist epistemological assumptions, while most qualitative research – in particular relational research – draws on interpretivism. That divide is just the starting point, however. Of the numerous qualitative research methodologies, some rest on assumptions closer to those of positivism (for example, postpositivist) while others are more thoroughly interpretivist. Some grounded theory researchers, for instance, pride themselves on being so rigorous and systematic in their effort to categorize the social world that they emulate natural scientists' procedures which minimizes subjective bias. They would proudly own the postpositivist label. Other grounded theory researchers prefer more subjectivist versions of grounded theory and are explicitly interpretivist in flavour (for example, see Charmaz, 1994).

The next time you read a qualitative research article look out for signs indicating where the authors stand on the positivist-interpretivist continuum. They may not explicitly state their position but they will give it away when they use phrases like, 'in order to ensure the reliability of my analysis' (a classic positivist phrase) or 'the impact of researcher's own subjectivity' (a clear interpretivist line).

• *What kind of knowledge can I possibly gain?*
Linked to the positivist-interpretivist debate is the one between 'realists' and 'relativists'.

The 'realist' position maintains that the world is made up of structures and objects which have cause-effect relationships with each other. Phenomena are seen to be made up of essential structures which can be identified and described. The aim is Newtonian in spirit: to study and measure that real world out there. For instance, realists argue that illnesses are objectively real and that when studying them we should carefully examine their effects on people.

The 'relativist' position takes issue with the realist notion of simple cause-effect relationships. It emphasizes the diversity of interpretations that can be applied, accepting a postmodern, poststructuralist sensibility (Denzin & Lincoln, 2005). While an illness may be 'real', people experience and understand it in different ways, deriving *meanings* that may vary considerably and cannot be predicted. People may experience an illness a certain way because that is what they have been brought up to expect. An extreme relativist position would go so far as to deny the 'reality' of an illness, arguing that if there were no words for an illness, people would not see it as troublesome! In other words, experience is constructed through language.

In between the two poles of realism and relativism is a position variously called 'critical realist' (Bunge, 1993; Denzin & Lincoln, 2005) or 'subtle realist' (Seale, 1999). Here, researchers tend to be pragmatic. They accept there is a real, observable world but that it is socially constructed. They consider meanings to be somewhat fluid while accepting that co-researchers' stories of having an illness reflect their subjective perceptions and meanings of their experience (if not their actual experience). To give a specific example, in their social psychoanalytic FANI work mentioned earlier, Hollway and Jefferson (2000) argue that 'real' events in the social world are defensively (i.e. psychologically) and discursively (socially) appropriated by the individual 'subject' – person – as meanings.

Relational-centred researchers embrace interpretivist epistemology but we vary considerably on where we place ourselves on the realism-relativism continuum.[vi] Phenomenologists usually adopt a critical realist position as they seek to capture, as closely as possible, the way in which a phenomenon is experienced. The same can be said for variants of gestalt, and psychoanalytic work. Pure discourse analytic researchers and some ethnographers and feminist researchers, in contrast, often view texts, such as interview transcripts, as simply *one version* obtained in a specific social context. While the text can be examined for broader social and cultural meanings, any knowledge gained from the data is seen as relative: it is contingent, partial, emergent and co-constructed.

Applying these ideas of realism-relativism to the researchers in Box 2.1, Will's study is on the realist side in its assumptions. As he analyses the emergent themes, he works hard to stay faithful to what is contained in the data and not let personal biases intrude. His supervisor also carries out some independent coding and analysis to affirm the reliability of Will's analysis. At the same time, he recognizes that the theory he is developing is constructed and based on his interpretations of particular individuals at a particular point in time so here he moves towards critical realism. Sharon and Lee's studies are underpinned by critical realist assumptions: they assume the co-researchers' accounts reflect something of the co-researchers' subjective perceptions of their lived experience while also recognizing that their own interpretations will, inevitably, play a crucial role. Novak and Katie's research, in contrast, is more explicitly relativist as they recognize the multiplicity of voices within their data. Katie particularly acknowledges the entirely co-constructed nature of the text and how another researcher will have obtained different stories from the co-researchers.

- *How do I understand the role of the researcher?*

All qualitative research methodologies recognize, at least to some degree, that the researcher is implicated in the research process. They agree that the researcher is a central figure who influences the collection, selection and interpretation of data and that researchers' prior experience and understandings affect how they construct what they see. Qualitative researchers recognize that their behaviour, and the relationships they have with co-researchers, have an impact on co-researchers' responses, and hence the findings obtained (Finlay, 2002a, 2002b). These ideas are particularly emphasized in relational research where any outcomes are generally viewed as somewhat relative and *co-created*: a joint product of the researcher, the co-researcher and their relationship. Because meanings are negotiated within particular relational and social contexts other researchers are likely to unfold different stories.

In order to develop self-awareness of these intersubjective dynamics, relational researchers engage in a process called 'reflexivity'. This involves sustained critical self-reflection, focusing on the ways a researcher's social background, assumptions, positioning, values, feelings, unconscious processes and behaviour impact on the research process (2003a). However, *how* this reflexive analysis is done varies between researchers from different traditions. In one tradition, 'doing reflexivity' may mean providing a transparent methodological account while in another it may involve exploring the conscious and unconscious intersubjective dynamics between researcher and researched. Some researchers use reflexivity to critically examine the power of the researcher while others use it to deconstruct pretences of established meanings. (See Finlay, 2003a for a review of different variants. *See also Chapter 8: Embracing Relational Research* where reflexivity is discussed more fully and *Chapter 9: Engaging 'Process'* where it is explicitly engaged as a data-gathering tool.)

The skill of being thoughtfully and critically self-aware is expected of psychotherapists and counsellors, it is common to see therapy research being undertaken which includes reflexive components. For example, Vetere and Gale (1987) carried out an in-depth exploration of the nature of interactions in families who had presented with child-focused problems. A participant observation approach was used involving the researcher living with a family on two separate occasions for a week at a time. The researcher kept detailed notes of family members' interactions and structure plus her own reflexive notes about her own and the family experiences.[vii] A different approach is taken by Kiser (2004) in that his whole research can be considered reflexive. He offers a first person narrative and existential analysis about his experience of having a psychotic episode. To give you a flavour of this, he describes the experience as involving such internal devastation that it:

> ... leaves in its wake scars like canyons that can never be erased ... When the wasteland of nothingness came to claim me yet again, I was utterly helpless and undone. (Kiser, 2004, p. 433)

The role of the researcher, then, is open to considerable debate. Different methodologies see the researcher as either being the '*author*' or the '*witness*' of their research findings (Willig, 2001).

In grounded theory, the researcher's role is often viewed as that of a witness who faithfully records what the participant is saying and what is going on. Here, the researcher aims to be relatively neutral and to avoid unduly importing biases or assumptions into the analysis. The researcher's role is to represent, in as systematic a way as possible, the participants' world and perspective. To give a specific example, Meena, in Box 2.1 shares many feelings and responses with her co-researchers as she, too, is British Asian. She strives to work extra hard to ensure that her research findings reflect the experiences of the women and not herself. She thus keeps a research diary to record her own subjective responses and brings this to her research supervision to begin to work through these issues.

In contrast, heuristic researchers and (auto)ethnographers are usually explicit about being authors of their reflective, creative and sometimes autobiographical work.[viii] Similarly, when discourse analysts emphasize the constructive and functional nature of language they acknowledge that they are the authors of their research, playing an active role in the construction of their findings. They take seriously the need to be reflexively aware of the problematic status of their knowledge claims and the discourses used to construct them. If Meena had been drawing upon social constructionist theory she would explicitly use her reflexivity to identify those discourses, for example about race, ethnicity and the position of women, which were affecting both her and her co-researchers.

Relational-centred researchers often take a middle position. We recognize that we are part of the relational field being studied. (More on this in *Chapter 3: Embodied Co-creation.*) Often relational researchers could be said to act as both witness (in seeking to represent participants' experience) and author (in the way interpretations are made). We seek to reflexively examine our own conscious and unconscious responses to become aware of the emotional investment we have in the research. Research can be 'an arena in which conflicts and fantasies are subtly acted out to confirm unconscious assumptions the researcher seeks to verify' (Cartwright, 2004, p. 222).

Brown's (2006) psychoanalytically informed infant observation study is a case in point as it required sustained and evolving reflexive meditation. During her fieldwork, for example, she writes of her confusion about whether a mother she was visiting had heard but ignored the door bell:

> She was, however, very reassuring ... and said that she would let me know if she was going to cancel ... My experience was nevertheless an ambivalent one ... I felt simultaneously rejected and welcomed. Mother was, in fact, initially ambivalent ... (p. 185)

Brown goes on to discuss how her experience may well have involved projections from the family being visited.

To give another example, in her work on the police, Hunt (1989) identifies how her status as an unwanted female outsider raised a number of unconscious personal issues which then impacted on the research relationship:

> Positive oedipal wishes also appeared to be mobilized in the fieldwork encounter. The resultant anxieties were increased because of the proportion of men to women in the police organization and the way in which policemen sexualized so many encounters ... The fact that I knew more about their

work world than their wives also may have heightened anxiety because it implied closeness to subjects. By partly defeminizing myself through the adoption of a liminal gender role, I avoided a conflictual oedipal victory. That the police represented forbidden objects of sexual desire was revealed in dreams and slips of the tongue ... the intended sentence "Jim's a good cop" came out instead "Jim's a good cock". In those words, I revealed my sexual interest in a category of men who were forbidden as a result of their status as research subjects. In that way, they resembled incestuous objects. (1989, p. 40)

In relational-centred research reflexivity allows researchers to bring themselves into their research. They are, after all, a part of what is being studied. As Peter (in Etherington, 2004) says,

The greatest gift I have gained from reflexivity is a healing of the split between research and practice. I am the same person, with the same mind and the same heart ... [Research] doesn't need to sequester my heart. (2004, p. 231)

To summarize, you have seen that what can be understood and expected from research depends on the researcher's theoretical and philosophical commitments including their epistemological stance. These ideas are not easy and you might benefit from taking more time to dwell on them. It may help to apply them to different examples of research. Table 2.1 summarizes the different epistemological positions associated with the different methodologies used by the researchers in Box 2.1 and indicates the methods (i.e. techniques and procedures used to collect and analyse data) the researchers have employed.

Reflections

We (Linda and Ken) celebrate the messiness and multiplicity of qualitative research approaches available. It is inevitable that new methodologies are going to evolve while old ones endure or undergo change. It also seems intuitively right to us that particular traditions and methodologies are hard to pin down. Indeed, rigid categorization seems to flout the fluidity which lies at the heart of qualitative research.

That said, we would argue that qualitative research should not simply be a free-for-all where 'anything goes' and researchers make up their own methods willy-nilly. There are natural and logical affinities within the diverse traditions and between particular philosophies, theories and

Table 2.1 Distinguishing between methodologies, philosophies, theories, role of researcher and methods.

Name	Methodology	Philosophy	Theory	Primary role of researcher and reflexivity	Methods (data collection/analysis)
Sharon	Phenomenology	Critical realist, Interpretivist	Ideas from work Merleau-Ponty and other phenomenologists	Witness/Author; reflexive analysis as part of the 'bracketing' process	Interviews/Existential hermeneutic analysis of life world dimensions
Lee	Psychodynamic case study	Critical realist, Interpretivist	Ideas from Klein and other object relations theorists	Witness/Author; reflexive analysis to probe transference and counter-transference processes	Interviews/Thematic and reflexive analysis
Will	Grounded theory	Realist, Postpositivist	Theory less relevant – focus instead on published empirical work	Witness; reflexive analysis as part of methodological audit to demonstrate rigour	Interviews/Constant comparative method
Novak	Ethnography	Relativist, Interpretivist	Ideas stemming from anthropology and cultural studies	Witness/Author; reflexivity to recognize the impact of context and cultural assumptions	Interviews, participant observation/ Ethnographic thematic analysis
Katie	Discourse analysis	Relativist, Poststructuralist	Ideas from work of Foucault and other sociologists	Author; reflexive analysis focused on exploring the issue of power within the research relationship	Interviews/Discourse analysis of interpretive repertoires and subject positions
Meena	Participatory action research	Realist, Postpositivist	Theory less relevant – focus instead on published empirical work and aiming for social change	Witness; reflexive analysis to separate out her own feelings/experiences from co-researchers	Interviews, focus groups and questionnaires/ Thematic and statistical analysis

methods. For example, it makes little sense to explore personal lived experience by analysing discursive constructions. It would be better to opt for methodologies which grapple with personal meanings such as biographical, narrative, phenomenological, psychodynamic or heuristic approaches. Equally, it would be possible to take a more discursive line and explore subjectivity in a different way such as by identifying cultural assumptions underlying particular discourses.

As we noted at the beginning of the book, setting out to do qualitative research is a bit like embarking on a voyage, while deciding a methodology (with its associated philosophy/theory and methods) is like deciding the type of trip we are going to take and it offers a compass and relevant maps to guide us. When you embark on your research journey, we would urge you to have a sense of: the direction you are going in and the type of trek you have signed up for. As you select one route rather than another, be aware of the paths you are rejecting, and why. 'Awareness of competing perspectives and alternative approaches acts as a continuing – and constructive – travel companion in our quest for knowledge' (Finlay & Ballinger, 2006, p. 2).

Our own preference, you will not be surprised to hear, is: relational existential phenomenology underpinned by reflexive, dialogal, interpretivist, feminist-poststructuralist epistemology (taking either a critical realist or relativist view) and inspired by a range of relational psychotherapy theories. (Well it is an accurate description if something of a mouthful!) However, we still appreciate the diverse riches which arise from research favouring other methodologies. *Vive la différence!*

Notes

[i] With the kind permission of Wiley-Blackwell, the material in this chapter has been adapted from Finlay (2006b) 'Mapping methodology', in *Qualitative Research for Allied Health Professionals: Challenging Choices*, edited by Linda Finlay and Claire Ballinger.
[ii] If you are interested in exploring different ways of conceptualizing qualitative research traditions we can recommend you refer to classic texts such as Denzin and Lincoln (2005), *Handbook of Qualitative Research*, 3rd edition or Cresswell (1998), *Qualitative Inquiry and Research Design: Choosing among five traditions*.
[iii] Take the case of phenomenology: descriptive empirical phenomenologists inspired by Husserlian ideas (Giorgi, 1985) would attempt to study essential structures as they appear in consciousness. Other researchers following Heidegger prefer to focus on existential, hermeneutic dimensions (Ashworth, 2003; van Manen, 1990; Dahlberg, Dahlberg & Nystrom, 2008; Todres, 2007) exploring in a more interpretative way a person's sense of self, space, time, embodiment and relationships. Halling and colleagues (Halling, Leifer & Rowe, 2006) offer a more specifically *relational* version in their

dialogal approach which focuses on collaboratively negotiated understandings. The heuristic approach adopted by Moustakas (1990) highlights the researcher's role in self-reflection and creative synthesis. Two further variants of phenomenology are detailed in Chapters 13 and 15. While all these different approaches aim to describe lived experience, their specific objectives differ, as does their tenor.

[iv] If you are an existential, gestalt or humanistic therapist then you are likely to be drawn towards phenomenology, discovery-oriented research (Mahrer & Boulet, 1999) and/or heuristic approaches (Moustakas, 1990). Ethnography, participatory action research and cooperative enquiry (Heron, 1996) could also appeal. If you are committed to a psychoanalytic perspective, you may favour pursuing psychodynamic themes through case study research, perhaps studying an individual, a family, a group or an organization (Cartwright, 2004; Menzies-Lyth, 1988). If you use personal construct theory and repertory grid technique in your therapy work (Kelly, 1955), you could employ a similar approach in research (for example, see Winter and Viney, 2005). If you are a narrative therapist, you are likely to be drawn to narrative theory and research (Angus & McLeod, 2003). If you are interested in therapeutic practices across different cultures you may well choose to engage in ethnography (Marcus, 1998).

[v] There are many more detailed typologies of philosophical world views available. In their classic typology, Denzin and Lincoln (2005) recognize four major *paradigms*: positivist and postpositivist; constructivist-interpretive; critical (Marxist, emancipatory) and feminist-poststructural. Taking a similar approach and applying it to the counselling field, Ponterotto (2005) contrasts positivism, postpositivism, critical/ ideological and constructivist/interpretivist approaches. Donmoyer (2001) goes a different route and distinguishes approaches concerned with truth-seeking, thick description, development, personal essay and social change.

[vi] Many psychotherapists and counsellors may well be drawn to methodologies which favour degrees of *ontological realism* (a belief that experiences are real and that there is a real social world out there to investigate) and *epistemological relativism* (a position which acknowledges multiple perspectives, realities, understandings and interpretations). This position seems particularly suited to relational-centred research and therapy, despite it being a bit of a mouthful! We tend to believe psychological pain feels 'real' and that relationships do have a 'real' impact. At the same time, we agree that much of our understandings are based on interpretation which means that another person (including a researcher or therapist) could well understand the same story differently.

[vii] The findings showed that the family dynamics observed in the home were similar to those typically observed in family therapy, but their timescale was different (for example, arguments or sulking could last for days rather than minutes as seen in therapy). Analysis of family beliefs was attempted using repertory grid analysis which suggested that family dynamics were shaped by members' beliefs.

[viii] Autoethnography is an approach to qualitative research which has been gaining popularity across sociological fields and the humanities. It involves the researcher in systematic and reflexive introspection regarding autobiographical material (see Ellis, 1991, 1999). While most commonly seen in the written form, more recent researchers have used images, the Internet, podcasts and other media designed to break away from convention.

Chapter 3

Embodied Co-creation: Theory and Values for Relational Research

Excerpt from a research interview:

- *Linda (researcher): ... I'm seeing your travelling when you were younger in a different light now. It sounds like you were really running away from home.*
- *Pat (co-researcher): Yeah.*
- *Linda: But you've made something of yourself and you feel proud(?).*
- *Pat: [nods] Now I'm putting them together.*
- *Linda: So it is like two sides of you coming together: your childhood side and your adult side are now coming into one, instead of being split. [after a pause] I'm feeling very emotional like I'm about to start crying.*
- *Pat: And I'm the same.*
- *Linda: [after a pause] Feels profound. I think I'm beginning to understand something of your mixed feelings.*
- *Pat: You definitely have! ...When you were talking earlier I was puzzled and wondered did I say it or did she?...*

Relational-centred therapists highlight the core importance of the therapeutic relationship. Similarly, relational-centred researchers value the research relationship. In relational-centred research, data is seen to emerge out of the researcher-co-researcher relationship, co-created (at least in part) in the embodied dialogical encounter. As we relate to an Other in the research encounter, each person touches and impacts on the other and,

---

crucially, that affects how the research unwraps itself. Relational researchers believe that much of what we can learn and know about another arises within the intersubjective space between researcher and co-researcher (Evans, 2007; Finlay, 2009 *Forthcoming*). Like Pat says, in this space it can be hard to know sometimes where you end and the Other begins. *Did I say it or did she?* 'To the extent that I understand, I no longer know who is speaking and who is listening' (Merleau-Ponty, 1960/1964, p. 97).

In our opinion (Linda's and Ken's), the central significance of the relationship and the recognition of the co-created nature of the human encounter together comprise the most influential ideas in contemporary psychotherapy. These ideas do not only impact a wide range of modalities; they offer a significant point of convergence between the different schools of psychotherapy, moderating against our tendency towards isolation and competition between therapeutic modalities (Evans, 2009). Relational-centred researchers draw from across these modalities.

We believe it will be helpful to you, the reader, if we take time here to describe some of these major influences and associated values underpinning our relational research approach. In the first section we highlight significant theoretical strands that feed into our relational approach. In the section following we lay out the key values relational researchers seek to embrace and provide an illustration from research practice to give you a feel of some of these values in action.

Theoretical Influences on Relational-centred Research

'Relational theory ... is a domain of many diverse waters and much eclecticism even within defined streams of practice', says DeYoung (2003, p. 39). Four particular tributaries that feed into our relational approach to research are: dialogical gestalt psychotherapy; existential phenomenology; intersubjectivity theory; and relational psychoanalysis.[i] Ideas between these four theories overlap considerably, while also contributing their own specific riches.

Dialogical gestalt psychotherapy

The first significant influence on our approach to relational-centred research is dialogical gestalt psychotherapy. This focuses on the healing dialogue in psychotherapy and the importance of the space between therapist and client as the arena through which healing occurs. Two foundational ideas underpinning gestalt theory are that: (i) The present experiential moment (the 'now') is considered to be the most helpful focus of psychology/therapy; (ii) We only know ourselves through the web of our relational interconnections (Latner, 2000).

The philosophical base of gestalt draws primarily on existential phenomenology and Lewin's field theory. The work of the phenomenological philosopher, theologian and educator Buber (1923/2004) is also significant. Tapping into the more spiritual dimensions of human relationships, Buber talked poetically of the *I-Thou* relationship. In this relationship, each person is accepting of, and open to, the Other. The *I-Thou* relationship aspires to be free from judgment, narcissism, demand, possessiveness, objectification, greed or anticipation. Persons respond creatively to the Other, in the moment, eschewing instrumental and habitual ways of interaction found in the *I-It* relationship.

> Where the dialogue is fulfilled in its being, between partners who have turned to one another in truth, who express themselves without reserve and are free of the desire for semblance, there is brought into being a memorable common fruitfulness … The interhuman opens out what otherwise remains unopened. (Buber, 1967, p. 86)

Gestalt therapy has over some 60 years evolved and matured its understanding and clinical application of the importance of the quality of contact in the meeting between therapist and client, as exemplified in the writings of Hycner and Jacobs (1995), Staemmler (1997), Wheway (1997), Yontef (1993), and Evans and Gilbert (2005) among others. In the current view of dialogical gestalt psychotherapy, the therapist attends to his or her own empathic, authentic presence while surrendering to the relational space *between* therapist and client.

> If we take seriously the concept of the between there is a reality that is greater than the sum total of the experience of the therapist and the client. Together they form a totality that provides a context for the individual experience of both. Perhaps that is the most succinct meaning of the between. (Hycner, 1991, p. 134–5)

The therapist commits to and trusts the 'process' of whatever appears figural at the moment of the embodied dialogical/experiential encounter.

Existential phenomenology

Overlapping with gestalt theory is existential phenomenological philosophy. Existential phenomenologists are concerned to return to embodied lifeworld experience.

The phenomenological philosopher Merleau-Ponty calls our attention to the way existences (beings) are dynamically interconnected: 'I discover in that other body a miraculous prolongation of my own intentions ... As the parts of my body together comprise one system, so my body and the other person's are one whole' (Merleau-Ponty, 1945/1962, p. 354). In his later work, *The Visible and the Invisible*, he elaborates this idea by employing the radical metaphors of 'chiasm' and 'flesh'. When he writes of 'the intertwining of my life with the lives of others' (1964/1968, p. 49), he emphasizes the interpenetration of self-other, body-world. The flesh of the world and the individual as flesh are seen as enveloped in a reversible 'double-belongingness'.

In using such tantalizingly mysterious metaphors, Merleau-Ponty is calling our attention to the body which is in primordial relationship with others and the world. The body, for him, is a site full of implicit meanings and relational understandings. Applying such ideas to research, existential phenomenologists argue that it is our shared embodiment and capacity for intersubjectivity which create the possibility of real empathy and understanding of the Other. Our embodied intersubjective horizon of experience gives us access to the experiences of others (Wertz, 2005). Engaging in existential analysis in research involves examining one's embodied relations with self and others.

The embodied enquiry research approach of Todres (2007) exemplifies this focus. Drawing specifically on the work of Gendlin (1978) as well as philosophers such as Heidegger (1927/1962) and Merleau-Ponty (1945/1962), Todres (2007, p. 175) outlines his approach as four assertions:

- Embodied enquiry is a practice that attends to the relationship between language and the experiencing body.
- Embodied enquiry marries thought and feeling, 'head' and 'heart'.
- Embodied enquiry, by not relying on thought alone, opens itself to what is creative and novel – the pre-patterned 'more' of the lifeworld.
- The kind of embodied understanding that arises from the practice of embodied enquiry is *humanizing* and is much needed in a world that too easily objectifies self and other.

Intersubjectivity theory

Bridging phenomenology and psychoanalytic theory, is intersubjectivity theory. Experiencing, according to this theory, emerges out of interactions within the intersubjective field (past and present relationships) while the unconscious is seen in terms of conscious and unconscious intersubjective dynamics rather than as a container of id impulses.

Intersubjectivity theory was initially informed by Kohut's (1984) self psychology theory where he developed the idea of 'selfobject' to fill a gap in object relations theory. Kohut proposed clients suffered from deficits of the selfobject experiences that sustain self-esteem and cohesion (such as experiencing being cared for by others). The therapeutic situation forms the key intersubjective field of focus where the relationship with the therapist is the medium in which derailed self-development is reprised. However, the idea that therapists provide an empathic relationship to enable the client to use the therapist in a selfobject manner to heal past deficits or kick start the developmental momentum means that self psychology is still primarily a one-person psychology. The therapist is not an equal participant in the relationship, but rather functions to provide empathy for the client's selfobject needs.

Further extending Kohut's thinking Stolorow and Atwood (1992) along with others, have developed their intersubjectivity theory to highlight the interpersonal dimension. They conceptualize the therapeutic relationship as an interactive process of 'reciprocal mutual influence' (Stolorow & Atwood, 1992, p. 18). They write that, 'clinical phenomena ... cannot be understood apart from the intersubjective contexts in which they take form. Patient and analyst together form an indissoluble psychological system' (Atwood & Stolorow, 1984, p. 64). They use the term 'codetermination' (Stolorow & Atwood, 1992, p. 24) to describe this reciprocal process in development and in psychotherapy.

While Stolorow and Atwood argue that: 'the trajectory of self experience is shaped at every point in development by the intersubjective system in which it crystallizes' (1992, p. 18), the theory is still focused on the subjectivity of the client or therapist. It is, arguably, not as radical as dialogical gestalt psychotherapy, phenomenological philosophy or relational psychoanalysis in focusing on the relational ground *between* the therapist and client.

Relational psychoanalysis

Finally, we draw from contemporary relational psychoanalysis (where the term 'relational' was first applied by Greenberg and Mitchell in 1983). In this approach, a person's learned patterns of interactions are seen to be the root of their psychological problems.

Relational psychoanalysis arises out of interpersonal psychoanalysis (Sullivan, 1953) and object relations theory (Klein, 1952/1993; Fairbairn,

1952) while also drawing on other perspectives such as feminist theory. Ideas from traditional psychoanalysis that innate drives were the basis of psychic development were dropped in favour of the view that the individual developed in relationship with other people. Winnicott (1965), for example, thought it was impossible to think of a person as being separate from others, since from birth we are always in relation to others.

Moving away from traditional psychoanalysis,[ii] relational psychoanalysis argues against therapist neutrality as an a priori given. Instead, the therapist is acknowledged as being a major influence impacting on the client's conscious and unconscious experience. Furthermore, both client and therapist are seen to affect one another as they 'co-mingle' and mutually share a range of emotions generated in the therapeutic process (Aron, 1996). Therapist self-disclosure is increasingly being seen as a powerful intervention in the unfolding of the therapy process, especially with regard to the nature and meaning of resistance (Rucker & Lombardi, 1998).

Relational analysts argue that learned patterns of interaction are inevitably enacted in the therapy situation and so careful attention needs to be paid to what is happening in the therapy relationship. Special attention is paid to regression and transference as powerful unconscious manifestations of early trauma, while the relational analyst tries to find the best mix of safety and challenge (unsettling the client's customary way of being in that relationship) to help the client construct new meaningful narratives. In these ways, focusing on the immediate therapy relationship is thought to impact on the client's way of being in wider relationships.

A synthesis for relational-centred research

All the theories outlined above prioritize the relational world while their points of focus differ in the way they variously highlight the significance of 'dialogue', 'embodied experiencing', 'intersubjectivity' and the 'relational unconscious'.

Our own (Linda's and Ken's) relational-centred research approach combines and synthesizes these theories. Specifically, we draw on the relational and developmental components of intersubjectivity and psychoanalytic theories while retaining the gestalt and phenomenological interest in the embodied lived experience in the 'here and now'.

One way of demonstrating this synthesis in practice is to appreciate the way our relational-centred approach keeps firmly in mind co-researchers' past, present *and* future.[iii] Everyone's life is worth a novel wrote Polster (1987); the past is relevant to the story of how we have arrived in the present and where we want to go in the future. However, we suggest that a research exploration that relies too heavily on investigating a person's history loses both the immediacy of the present moment and the significance of the sociocultural context.[iv] If research only refers to immediate experience (even when investigating an issue of contemporary importance), it loses the relevance and continuity of experience over time (Melnick & Nevis, 1992).

To illustrate how we incorporate past, present and future in research practice, consider Yontef's (1993) classification of experience into four time zones which we apply to research.

- In the *Here and Now*, we investigate a person's whole self-environment field at the particular moment of the research encounter.
- In the *There and Now*, we are concerned to understand a person's life outside the research setting.
- In the *Here and Then*, we examine what has happened in the research exploration over time (a few moments ago or in preceding interviews/ observations).
- In the *There and Then*, a person's history – the background from which meaning emerges – is an ever-present horizon. (In research, an understanding of so-called 'past' issues is sometimes essential in order to understand what is going on in the here and now. However, for us there is no such thing as the past. There is history but the past is always present in the background and may become figural in the here and now, especially in times of stress.)

To illustrate and apply these ideas to actual research practice, consider the research conducted by Linda on the lived experience of someone with recently diagnosed multiple sclerosis (Finlay, 2003b). (*See* research Example 8.1 in *Chapter 8: Embracing Relational Research* for more details.) Drawing on Ann's own reflections captured in a relatively unstructured interview, Linda developed an existential-phenomenological analysis of how Ann's life was derailed with her multiple sclerosis:

> Ann's experience of having multiple sclerosis is found to be one of chronic uncertainty. Confronted by the death of the life she once had, she is forced to live a new, temporary, life. She can no longer be certain of what her physical condition will be tomorrow or six months from now and that threatens her future plans and dreams. Unable to project into the future, Ann throws herself into the 'now' of being a good wife and mother, trying to wring what she can out of every borrowed moment. Being a 'good' wife and mother (a long-held value emerging out of her own family history) gives her new life meaning.

The above description is a taster of the more extended analysis a relational-centred researcher might undertake which implicitly draws on a range of relational theories.

Ten Core Values Underpinning Relational-centred Research

While relational-centred researchers vary in their specific theoretical/ practice preferences, they are joined in their commitment to the research relationship where both parties are seen to be actively involved. Relational-centred research does not just involve a participant-subject talking to a passive, distanced researcher who receives information. Instead the research data (and possibly the analysis stage as well) is seen to emerge out of a constantly negotiated, evolving, dynamic process. It is *co-created* – at least in part. Beyond this central idea lurk a number of core values and assumptions related to the researcher, the co-researcher, the research relationship and the research enterprise respectively. In this section we lay out what some of these relational values, arising out of the theories above, involve.[v]

The list below does not constitute the 'rule book' about how relational researchers *should* behave. It is offered here to give orientation; to give a picture of the spirit of what we lean towards in our relational research encounters. Further, these values are not intended to be abstract, reified concepts like 'equality' and 'justice'. Instead, they are the values which need to be enacted in practice, in everyday research encounters (Walsh, 1995).

Values related to the researcher

1) **Owning oneself** – As researchers we need to accept our own humanness including our embodied way of being, emotions, interests, values, politics, frailties and strengths. We also need to have some understanding of where we come from in terms of our relational and social/cultural background. It is ourselves as a whole, after all, that we bring to any encounter. Levin (1985) recognizes this when he says:

> As soon as we begin to move and gesture in response to the presence of the human Other, we are held by our culture in the corresponding beholdenness of our bodies. In every human voice, there are echoes of the mother's tongue, echoes of significant teachers, respected elders, close friends; and there are accents, too, which bind the voice to the history of a region, a culture, and generations of ancestors. (Levin, 1985, p. 174)

2) **Integrity** – The relational researcher aims to be authentic, energized, active, transparent and reasonably direct in the research encounters. Unlike some versions of psychotherapy/counselling, relational researchers do not necessarily seek to be unconditionally accepting or neutral in their responses. Instead, they aim for integrity and honesty of responses; they are prepared to challenge and disagree. For instance, where values collide such as when a co-researcher makes a racist or sexist remark, you might challenge the other's view while keeping the dialogue open. The difficulty is how to be congruent with your own values while being respectful of others' different views even as you may challenge them.

3) **Reflexivity** – More than owning and sharing ourselves, we need to examine reflexively how our conscious and unconscious selves may be impacting upon the research process and outcomes. We need to be able to have enough awareness to sift through our personal experience of the relational encounter in order to decide what to respond to and what to put aside and what to take to our supervisor or research mentor. Reflexivity is:

> More than self awareness in that it creates a dynamic process of interaction within and between our selves and our participants, and the data that informs decisions, actions and interpretations at all stages of research. (Etherington, 2004, p. 32)

In particular, reflexivity exposes moral dilemmas and the relational researcher needs to try to monitor the research process for any ethical breaches such as the potential for abuse of power within the relationship.

Values related to the co-researcher

4) **Acceptance** – Relational researchers believe that the subjective experience of the co-researcher is *their* truth and this is the starting point of any exploration. The co-researcher's expressions are both accepted (that is, not morally judged) and assumed to reflect perceptions of their lifeworld. We accept (and assume) what is given is the other's reality (at least as they understand it or wish to present it). Part of this acceptance is also acceptance of the co-researcher's social/cultural background, taking seriously our respect of difference and diversity.

5) **Agency** – Relational researchers aim to honour the co-researcher's choices and capacity for agency. We understand that the other's way of being comes from their relational experience (past and present). At the same time we believe they are 'response-able' and they are able

to make choices and, to a degree at least, can determine their own behaviour. In the research context, researchers try to ensure co-researchers are as self-directing as possible, even to the point of being involved in research decisions about both content and method. Heron's (1996) use of Co-operative Inquiry is a prime example where these ideas are fully embraced. In respecting others' choices, researchers need to resist the temptation to control, direct, push or manipulate.

6) **Empathic inquiry** – The relational researcher has a responsibility to build a bridge to the co-researcher, using his or her own special awareness, skills, experience and knowledge (Evans & Gilbert, 2005). Our goal in research is to comprehend meaning from within clients' own subjective frame of reference. Researchers strive to pay close attention to the other with curiosity, empathy and compassion, encouraging them to share their perspective. At the same time, differences between researcher and co-researcher are preserved so there is sufficient distance to challenge and be critically analytical where appropriate.

> I have that quality of attention so that I may be with you, alongside you, empathizing with you; and yet not losing myself in confluence with you because the dialogue between us both bridges and preserves our differences. (Reason, 1988, p. 219)

Values related to the research relationship

7) **Mutuality** – The relational-centred research process involves reciprocal dialogue and participation during the data collection phase and possibly beyond during data analysis and writing-up phases. It involves a 'way of being with, without doing to' (Zinker & Nevis, 1994, p. 395). It may also involve some mutual self-disclosure where researchers might proactively share aspects of themselves in response to co-researcher's stories. This self-disclosure is seen as part and parcel of 'mutual creative meaning-making' (Shaw, 2003, p. 59).

While this mutuality is rarely symmetrical (and does not imply equality or sameness), it acknowledges that two people cannot be in relation without impacting on each other. The co-researcher's life experiences and ways of interacting with another will impact both consciously and unconsciously on the researcher, and vice versa. As a result, researcher and co-researcher will often find themselves going beyond understandings they had prior to their encounter. As Merleau-Ponty (1964/1968, p. 13) expresses it: 'A genuine conversation gives me access to thoughts that I did not know myself capable of.'

8) **Openness** – As we intertwine with another in a research encounter, we may find ourselves surprised, touched and awed by the connections we make and 'co-transferences'[vi] we discover. The researcher needs to be alert to the possibility that the research encounter is likely to be a thickly populated microcosm involving multiple subjectivities and various co-transferences. The 'here and now' contains something of the 'there and then' where the selves of one person elicit those of the other. As relational researchers, we aim to open ourselves to these processes and whatever layered meanings might emerge in that intersubjective space between researcher and co-researcher. It takes courage to sit with uncertainty and not-knowing, and be open to what is emerging in the 'now' of the embodied dialogical encounter.

Values related to research outcomes

9) **Impact** – The primary goal of relational research is to *understand* something of the co-researcher's experience and/or social meanings (as opposed to aiming to predict, which is what quantitative researchers are aiming for as they measure and manipulate behavioural variables). However, numerous additional outcomes may be involved – both intended and unintended. Relational-centred research has the potential to be transformative at both a proximal level (for the co-researcher) and at a distal level (impacting on others) in ways that might not be foreseen. While, relational research does not aim to change others, researchers have a responsibility to be mindful of the potential impact of the study. Any research that encourages us to reflect on ourselves and the social world around us is likely to have some (if not huge) impacts on others. If such power exists within our research, then that needs to be managed and respected. It is worth asking, whose interests does the research serve?

10) **Humility** – Relational researchers need to acknowledge their potentially powerful position as well as recognizing the potential power of their research. At the same time they need to remain humble and modest. Research is *always* partial, tentative, emergent, dynamic, evolving and subject to new insights or interpretations. Relational researchers need to try to resist the urge to make larger claims on the basis of their one project or to generalize experience from, say, one idiographic account. At the same time, relational researchers hope that their relatively small-scale study will offer particular insights and have wider resonance. The study might serve as a vignette, a pen portrait whose insights can be returned to, perhaps when readers are working with others in similar circumstances.

Embodied Co-creation

The following illustration shows some of the values related to *embodied co-creation* in action, particularly reflexivity, openness, empathic inquiry, mutuality and impact. Here, the researcher (Linda) carried out some collaborative research with Pat (her friend and co-researcher) on her lived experience of receiving a new cochlear implant (Finlay & Molano-Fisher, 2008).

Example 3.1   Tuning into the world of sounds

At the time of their research encounter Pat had been profoundly deaf for 50 years and was learning to hear once more with her new implant. Specifically, she was learning how to pick up and distinguish sounds; how to use her ears first rather than rely on lip-reading and the interpretation of visual clues. Pat found herself confronting a bewildering babble in a new noisy world. Linda's reflexive research diary entries catch something of how Pat's experience and how this experience began to colour Linda's own ways of perceiving:

> *Together we went for a walk in the woods. It was an extraordinary experience. Step by step, I found myself tuning into her world. We started playing a game. I would draw her attention to a noise: the sound of a bird singing, her dog's paws rustling up the leaves, a car passing, children laughing in the distance. It took a minute but she would eventually discriminate and hear the sound. "Oh, that's what a xxx sounds like!", she'd say. Slowly but surely as she memorized each sound, a new world opened up for her.*
>
> *Pat proved to be a quick learner. Then she turned the tables on me. "What's that?", she'd ask. Sometimes I'd be able to answer. At other times, I had no idea. I was hearing new sounds myself! Slowly, I discovered my own perception changing just as Pat's was changing. Previously I would have thought our walk in the woods had been wonderfully peaceful and quiet. Now, I was seeing/hearing the world differently. What a cacophony: [birds, leaves rustling, cars, trains, voices].... Yes, it is an incredibly noisy world!*

Reflecting on this process, Linda recognized that for a brief period while in this participant observation, it felt as though she was 'seeing' the world through Pat's ears. She was able to empathize with Pat's own colourfully raucous lifeworldly experience (Finlay, 2008).

These insights formed the basis of a comprehensive analysis of Pat's experience which Linda evolved collaboratively with Pat:

For fifty years Pat had lived her world through her senses in one particular way. Then, abruptly, everything changed. Whereas in the past she had been used to 'seeing' and thinking-through sounds, she now had to learn to *hear* sounds with her ears. This involved more than a simple cognitive-perceptual process by which Pat learned how to exercise selective attention and process new sensations. Rather, Pat found that her entire lifeworld (hitherto largely silent) had disappeared, to be replaced by a harsh, intrusive new domain of noise. Instead of being a 'deaf person who lip reads', she had become a 'person with an implant who can sometimes hear things'. As those around her began expecting different things from her – and her own expectations about herself also changed – Pat confronted the challenge of re-orientating herself to a radically new world.

The specific existential issues at stake for Pat concerned her somewhat daunting project to reconstruct a comfortable and valued self in the face of her changing lifeworld. (Finlay & Molano-Fisher, 2008, p. 261)[vii]

By attuning to Pat's world Linda began to understand Pat's experience and, together, they were able to mutually create meaning and produce their analysis. Beyond the research findings Linda was, paradoxically, enabled to go more deeply into her own embodied, grounded and emotionally present way of being. Pat, too, was enabled to become more present to the impact of her new way of being.

Embodied co-creation indeed.

Reflections

In this chapter we have outlined the general theoretical and value base of relational-centred research approaches. We have tried to highlight how both researcher and co-researcher bring to the research encounter their lifeworlds creating a highly complex relational field spanning past, present and future, that is the locus of action and analysis. Returning to our analogy of research as a voyage of discovery, we suggest that if methodology is our 'map or guide', then theory and associated values provide the orientating 'compass'.

Some of the ideas discussed in this chapter will have more relevance and resonance for you as a researcher than other ideas. As individual researchers we all have our particular preferences which colour our way of both seeing the world and *being-in-the-world*. At the same time we respect alternative choices other researchers might make providing they have been applied coherently and consistently. We also think it is fine not to be bound to particular schools and to work out your own synthesis of different relational theories. It all depends on the needs and context of your particular research project. As de Young says, 'All of us relationalists have our own ways of locating ourselves within this complex domain' (DeYoung, 2003, p. 39).

Regardless of which particular relational theory you support, the key concept across them all, where all these ideas converge, is embodied co-creation. *Did I say that or did she?* If we fully embrace this concept in our research practice, we surrender ourselves to uncertainty and not knowing. We are never going to be in a position to control or understand fully or see what is *really* going on. All we can do is simply (perhaps not so simply!) tune into the relational moment and figure things out as best we can.

Notes

[i] We could have included a number of other theories and paradigms such as humanistic theory, radical feminist theory, existentialism, personal construct theory, narrative theory, systems theory, to name a few. These theories are potentially of equal relevance to relational research approaches. They also intersect in relevant ways with the theories mentioned above. However, we had to draw the line somewhere and we decided on the 'big four' mentioned above as these were the theories most commonly cited when discussing relational psychotherapy.

[ii] Freud's early illumination of unconscious processes significantly undermined Descartes' illusion of the human being as a rational person and opened the door to the exploration of unconscious processes. However, classical psychoanalysis appears to have remained firmly entrenched in the modernist or enlightenment paradigm and still believes that relationships are shaped by individual drives while contemporary psychoanalysis (and arguably gestalt psychotherapy is also a school of psychoanalysis) acknowledges that relationships have meanings that cannot be located within the psychic processes of the individual isolated mind. Newtonian cause and effect has now given way to postmodern epistemologies such as relativism, constructivism and field theory. Contemporary psychoanalysis is very much a two-person psychology (Aron, 1996).

[iii] In phenomenological terms, all experience entails a temporal horizon where past, present and future converge. We anticipate and rush towards the future, we act and endure in the present, we reminisce or long for the past … In any one 'present', we carry with us our past memories and future hopes; the past and future speak to us in our present. We then subjectively live that time and feel it stretching endlessly into the future when we are bored, or whizzing by in the present when we are happy or we get stuck in the past when we are unhappy …

[iv] We do not believe that the past *causes* the present. However, we argue that through the original infant-primary caregivers and sociocultural field, we form patterns of relating which tend to continue (habitually and out of awareness) throughout life –

especially in times of stress or crisis. These relational patterns emerge in relationships (including therapeutic and research relationships) as resistance and often in the form of transference and counter-transference, but we believe that these relational patterns are developed primarily in order to survive and as such represent a 'creative adjustment' (Perls et al., 1951/94). From this theoretical perspective resistance is a person's coping strategy, which may be respected as the best solution they could find in the past and remains their way of being in the present.

[v] A comprehensive analysis of the values of relational therapy (rather than research) can be found in Chapter 1 of DeYoung's (2003) book *Relational Psychotherapy: A primer*. In this chapter DeYoung contrasts relational therapy against the medical model, Freudian therapy, Jungian therapy, short-term solution-focused therapy, humanistic therapy, narrative therapy and radical feminist therapy.

[vi] Donna Orange (1995) amongst others advocates the use of the idea of 'co-transferences' rather than transference and counter-transference. We adopt this term here to indicate a more mutual relational process where both researcher and co-researcher are subject to transference and counter-transference.

[vii] This extract has been reproduced from Finlay and Molano-Fisher (2008), 'Transforming' self and world: a phenomenological study of a changing lifeworld following a cochlear implant, in *Medicine, Health care and Philosophy*, 11, 255–267, with the kind permission of Springer Publications.

Chapter 4

Challenging 'Evidence-based Practice'?

Increasingly, psychotherapists and counsellors are being exhorted to carry out research. We are being pushed to provide evidence of the effectiveness of our work and to draw on evidence-based practice to improve the quality of our services (Rowland & Goss, 2000). But the term 'evidence' begs a number of questions as it comes in various shapes and forms. What kind of evidence might best show the value of the work we do? What type of evidence should service users and funders of health care rely on?

Much depends on how 'evidence' is defined. The prevailing view of the *evidence-based practice movement* is that evidence should be 'scientific' utilizing measurement and quantification. But while results derived from quantitative research have contributed enormously to developing psychological and mental health services in general, how relevant are they when it comes to therapy? How can a therapist's understanding of the ambivalence of human experience be quantified? Is it possible to measure the complex, ever-evolving, multi-layered nature of therapeutic relationships and the work we do?

In the first part of this chapter, we critique the current preoccupations and practices of the evidence-based practice movement. Yes, of course, it is important to use evidence to back up practice. Yes, of course, we want therapists more actively involved in collecting this evidence. We just challenge existing assumptions about what constitutes 'best' evidence. We take

Relational-centred Research for Psychotherapists: Exploring Meanings and Experience
Edited by Linda Finlay and Ken Evans
Copyright © 2009 John Wiley & Sons, Ltd.

issue with the over-emphasis on quantitative evidence where the use of randomized controlled trials (RCTs) is held up as the 'gold standard'. We also take issue with the evidence-based practice movement's focus on comparing the effectiveness and outcomes of various therapy modalities since research suggests differences between them are less relevant than the underlying relational processes which they share.

In the latter part of the chapter we offer our preferred form of evidence-based practice. We make the case for a special type of evidence: qualitative relational-centred, *practice-based evidence*. We advocate more research on therapeutic process (rather than just on outcomes) showing how therapy evolves in practice and over time. We believe it is important for you (as a practitioner) to feel there are things you can do in your everyday practice which can be regarded as a respectable level of 'research activity' towards making a difference to your wider profession and clients. The research activity we have in mind here involves either doing or reading research (that is to say, being a research producer or consumer).

Debating the Nature of 'Evidence'

Hierarchies of evidence

In its guidelines on managing depression, NICE (the National Institute for Health and Clinical Excellence) recommended the application of guided self-help programmes based on cognitive-behaviour therapy (CBT) for patients with mild depression and the use of a combination of CBT and anti-depressants for those presenting initially with severe depression (NICE, 2004/7).[i] NICE arrived at this recommendation after examining a good deal of evidence but it is instructive to take a closer look at the 'evidence' it consulted.

NICE worked with a hierarchy which classifies and rates evidence in terms of its supposed value. At the top of the hierarchy, Grade A evidence is that obtained from controlled experiments, particularly randomized controlled trials (RCTs).[ii] Grade B evidence is derived from well-designed quantitative studies (such as surveys and non-randomized experiments, for example, comparing the results of two groups using different treatment formats).[iii] Lower down still, Grade C evidence includes expert opinion (primarily that of doctors and psychologists) based on case reports and clinical examples.

The omissions in this version of a hierarchy of evidence are glaring. What of the opinions of service users and carers? What of the views of psychotherapists themselves? Why is there no reference to 'practice-based evidence'? Why is qualitative research – the main evidence employed in our field – left completely out of the frame? What of issues to do with therapy 'process' as well as 'outcome'? Surely what is or is not considered 'good' evidence depends on values, choice and context?

It is worth asking yourself what *your* hierarchy would look like. Would you not put psychotherapists' clinical experience and intuition, and service users' preferences and narratives high on the list? This was, in fact, the conclusion of an American Psychological Association (APA) task force that was set up in 2004 to help bridge the gap between researchers and clinicians. They recommended that research evidence be seen as constituting only one of several factors when making treatment decisions. They concluded that therapists' expertise and clients' values are co-equal inputs to be used *alongside* a range of research evidence (including and beyond RCTs). (These recommendations were accepted by the APA and formalized as policy.)

However, not all people within the evidence-based practice movement agree. Some adherents of rigorously controlled 'scientific' clinical trials go so far as to assert that only treatments which have been demonstrated to be effective via clinical trials are 'ethical'. Those practitioners who fail or refuse to use such tested treatment approaches have been called 'irresponsible' (Lebow, 2006).

Attitudes like these are pervasive and point to the political context of research, for example, the way it can be used to advance the cause of some groups over others. This then impacts on practice. For example, on the basis of the recommendations made by NICE, additional funding was made available by the United Kingdom government to address the shortage of CBT practitioners; no such extra funding was given to other modalities.

To give another example, at the time of writing (2009), the UK government (via the Health Professions Council) has begun the process of regulating counselling and psychotherapy with anticipated completion around 2011. National Occupational Standards are being produced based on a review of the effectiveness of a range of psychotherapy modalities.[iv] Considerable anxiety about the outcome is now evident across the profession because the review is going to specifically foreground RCT evidence and thus CBT. This evidence will favour CBT as outcomes of CBT are much more amenable to being tested by RCTs and that has lead to many more studies being conducted on the effectiveness of CBT. Other therapy modalities are less open to being studied using RCTs which means there is less research currently available on their effectiveness. The playing field is not level.[v]

Given the power and influence wielded by RCT evidence, it is worth evaluating its contribution further.

RCTs under the Spotlight

Some experimental and RCT evidence has been very valuable in demonstrating the value of psychotherapy as a whole: Bovasso, Williams and Haroutune (1999), for instance, conducted a 15-year follow-up study into the long-term effectiveness of therapy in a mental health service in the United States using a cohort of individuals with psychiatric problems randomly sampled from a community population and treated in the community. The participants who had received therapy had lower distress at follow up compared with those on medication or who did not take up treatment. The researchers concluded that 'psychotherapy produces changes of greater magnitude than has been previously found, which might take a long time to manifest' (1999, p. 537).

To give another example, Bolton et al. (2007) considered the impact of therapy on adolescents in war-torn Uganda by studying 314 adolescents presenting with depression-like syndromes living in camps for internally displaced persons. They randomly allocated individuals to one of three experimental conditions (group interpersonal psychotherapy, creative play, or waiting list control). The active intervention groups met for weekly sessions lasting 1.5–2 hours for 16 weeks. At the end of this period, outcomes in terms of changes in depressive symptoms were measured and compared across the three conditions. Findings demonstrated that the individuals receiving group interpersonal therapy had significantly reduced depression symptoms compared to the control group.

On the face of it, this approach of using RCTs to 'prove' the value of psychotherapy seems reasonable and entirely necessary. Certainly if you were going to study the effectiveness of a drug, you would want this kind of research to be used. After all, it is relatively straightforward to measure and evaluate the impact of a drug which has clear physical consequences, and to compare this with situations where the drug has not been administered. The question is can psychotherapy, with its layers of emotional and relational complexity, be equated to a drug treatment? Is there a *limit* to what can be studied and demonstrated using RCTs?

While RCTs are effective at measuring changes in physical health and behaviour (such as a reduction in quantifiable symptoms), they are less able to measure changes in feelings and in one's sense of being. Further, how well do RCTs address real-life practice, given they are designed to measure condition-specific efficacy in tightly controlled conditions for carefully screened patients/clients? For example, long-term treatments are rarely studied in RCTs studies (a few studies such as the one by Bovasso et al. above notwithstanding) despite the fact that research indicates therapies conducted over longer periods tend to have more successful outcomes.

With these questions to the fore, critics of the over-reliance on RCTs have highlighted a number of potential weaknesses in the way that experimental research has been applied as the sole measure of therapy effectiveness. They argue that the use of experimental designs (including RCTs) assumes that people's problems can be clearly demarcated and compared, and that techniques can be isolated and applied in the required 'dose'. Anyway, they would question whether changes in participants' symptoms can necessarily be down to the type of therapy rather than to other factors? For example, in the Bolton study above, does the reduction of depressive symptoms necessarily mean that the group members were less depressed or might they just be representing themselves in that way? Alternatively, could the improvements seen from the therapy group be down to other external factors such as having extra nurturing attention from the therapists (a factor which may not have been sufficiently controlled for in the random group allocations)? These questions emphasize the complexities and ambiguities involved in practice.

Mottram (2000) explains that the conditions created in psychotherapy RCTs represent a 'substantial deviation from usual psychotherapy clinical practice' (2000, p. 1). A gulf seems to separate the more artificially constructed RCTs from the practice of psychotherapy. The tests are wont to zoom in on disorders that rarely, if ever, exist in pure form in practice. RCTs also tend to focus on single problems, ignoring the fact that most clients have more than one clear primary problem for which they seek psychotherapy. As Westen, Novotny and Thompson-Brenner (2004) point out, much RCT research rests on the DSM diagnostic system[vi] – despite the fact that only a very small percentage of those who seek therapy do so because they have a particular DSM diagnosis. In most cases patients/clients are seeking help for the business of living. Clumping people together into groups of disorders erases the specificity of individual personalities and conceals the subtle adaptations therapists make in response to personality differences. Ramsay (cited in Bovasso et al., 1999) suggests that we need more research focused on 'free-range humans'– the people clinicians actually meet in their consulting rooms.

It would appear that, far from constituting the 'gold standard' of psychotherapy research, RCTs are a good but limited research tool, able to contribute something to the evaluation of psychotherapy outcomes when used in conjunction with other approaches. As Seligman, a former President of the American Psychological Association, concedes,

> My belief has changed about what counts as a 'gold standard' … deciding whether one treatment under highly controlled conditions works better than another treatment or a control group is a different question from deciding what works in the field. (Seligman, 1995, p. 966)

Even Professor Michael Rawlins (2008), the Chair of NICE at the time of writing, suggested in a speech to the Royal College of Physicians that RCTs have been placed on an 'undeserved pedestal'. He called for other types of research to be given more attention.

Comparing Psychotherapy Modalities: A Worthwhile Undertaking?

One of the understandable but potentially erroneous developments stemming from the evidence-based practice movement has been the push to compare the effectiveness of different psychotherapy treatments (as opposed to comparing groups who receive psychotherapy with those who receive medication, say). In the psychotherapy world, the move to find evidence to value one modality over another has proved divisive and unhelpful. Substantial and compelling research produced over a number of years reveals that relational dimensions which operate across *all* modalities are more important than specific techniques.

In 1975, Luborsky, Singer and Luborsky completed a meta-analytic study of more than a hundred research projects conducted between 1949 and 1974. The study focused on possible differential effects between one approach to therapy and another; between medication and therapy; and between one mode of therapy and another. When it came to examining patient/client improvements, the researchers found that the type of therapy a client had received had made no significant impact on the outcome. Clients undergoing *any* of the different therapies researched seemed to improve as a result of their experience. All forms of psychotherapy researched appeared equally effective when competently applied, 'We can reach a "Dodo bird verdict"' was how the researchers put it. 'It is usually true that everybody has won and all must have prizes' (Luborsky et al., 1975, p. 1003). A subsequent meta-analytic study by Smith and Glass (1977) confirmed the 'Dodo bird verdict'. As the authors noted,

> Despite volumes devoted to the theoretical differences among different schools of psychotherapy, the results of research demonstrate negligible differences in the effects produced by different therapy types. (Smith & Glass, 1977, p. 33)

While these early studies have been criticized for their simplistic methodology, similar findings have emerged from more sophisticated projects. For instance, Wampold et al. (1997) reviewed research carried out between 1970–1995 and found little or no difference between the effectiveness of different modalities. Further evidence comes from the APA's Division of Psychotherapy which published an edited volume titled *Psychotherapy Relationships That Work* (Norcross, 2002). Here, general processes which transcend theoretical orientation (such as the establishment of the therapeutic alliance) were found to have the greatest bearing on successful outcomes.

A range of research specifically demonstrates that the best predictor of successful outcomes is a high-quality 'therapeutic relationship'. This finding applies across various therapies and a range of client problems (Bryan et al., 2004; Everall & Paulson, 2002; Gershefski et al., 1996; Hubble, Duncan & Miller, 1999; Margison et al., 2000). Summarizing the findings of a body of research into the relationship between therapy and change in patients/ clients, Lambert (1992) found that only 15% of therapeutic change was attributable to factors specific to a particular therapy. In contrast, 30% of such change was attributable to factors common to all therapies, such as empathy, warmth and acceptance. A further 40% of change appeared to be linked to factors outside the therapeutic relationship, such as changes in the client's life, while 15% was attributed to the placebo effect. Wampold (2001) attributes only 8% to specific factors and 70% to general effects, with an unexplained variance of 22% (non-specific effects).

Hubble et al. (1999) offer an explanation for this lack of evidence supporting any one modality or technique over others; they suggest that clients are resourceful and can be the architects of their own change processes as they have the ability to use whatever healing processes are offered. Since all therapies provide useful structures or tools for solving personal problems, it is likely that the client creatively uses what is on offer. Different therapies thus provide alternative structures for the learning process that forms the heart of therapy. The more the therapist's own rationale coincides with the client's understanding of how problems are solved in their particular culture, the more hope the latter will have and the greater the likelihood of their benefiting from the process.

If therapy is to be effective, collaborative models which facilitate interpersonal dialogue seem to be indicated. Collaboration implies *processes*. It is these that need to be investigated further if we are to deepen our understanding of what makes therapy work. For too long research has unduly focused on therapist techniques and provision rather than on what the client brings to the therapeutic relationship. Hubble et al. (1999, p. 425) wryly quote an African proverb to underline the point: 'Until lions have their historians, tales of the hunt shall always glorify the hunter!'

At a time when the growth of qualitative methodologies is placing greater emphasis on the therapy relationship and clients' contribution to it, why is psychotherapy research still committed to efficacy studies across modalities? The pervasive culture of the market place, with its emphasis on accountability, competition and choice, offers a clue (Evans & Gilbert, 2005). Research geared to establishing the supremacy of method seems to have more to do with professional competitiveness than with the pursuit of clinical excellence. Resistance to the 'Dodo bird verdict' comes from the threat it poses for specific theories. As Bohart observes,

> If it were not so threatening ... it would long ago have been accepted as one of psychology's major findings. Then it would have been built upon and explored instead of continually being debated. (Bohart, 2000, p. 129)

One factor which highlights the challenges of comparing treatments and techniques across the different modalities is the fact that a neutral language or basic vocabulary shared by the competing therapy theories is lacking (Schmitt Freire, 2006). In a review of the literature, Goldfried and Padawer (1982, cited in Goldfried, 1995, p. 203) identify several common factors which could usefully be explored across the different psychotherapy modalities:

Hope: What Yalom describes as 'the instillation of hope', i.e. the expectation that therapy can be helpful (Yalom, 1986).

Acceptance: The provision of an accepting, caring and attentive relationship as the basic ingredient of effective therapy and often a unique experience in the person's life (Rogers, 1951).

An alternative perspective: An external perspective on oneself and the world through the feedback provided by the therapist which supports the client to consider a change in self-perception.

Experimentation: The opportunity for the client to repeatedly test reality through gaining a new perspective from external feedback, along with the opportunity to practice new behaviours and responses in the supportive and challenging environment of therapy.

A corrective emotional relationship: The provision of new corrective emotional experiences, within the session or between sessions. Such experiences appear to be a major component of therapy.

Goldfried went on to seek a common language for psychotherapy across different modalities that would enable people of different theoretical orientations to engage in clinical dialogue. For example, he used the term 'vicious cycles' to describe repetitive, destructive patterns in a client's life and the term 'virtuous cycles' to denote constructive alternatives to these (Goldfried, 1995). (The term 'vicious cycle' can be likened to the 'fixed gestalt' in gestalt psychotherapy; the 'repetition compulsion' in psychoanalysis; the 'game' in transactional analysis; and the 'core schema' in cognitive therapy.)

Despite Goldfried's impressive attempts to create a common language, psychotherapists remained polarized, seeming to prefer their own particular language, and resistant to the notion that someone from another modality might be referring to a similar premise, issue, theme or process.

We (Linda and Ken) view research into common factors as offering a route to greater collaboration among psychotherapists. We would like to see future evidence-based research focusing on core therapeutic processes rather than simply on outcomes, recognizing that these processes take place *across* psychotherapy modalities. We would like to see a research tradition which is consistent with the values and practices of psychotherapists and counsellors blossom (McLeod, 2001; Moodley, 2001).

Celebrating a 'Practice-based Approach' to Evidence

In recent years there has been a growing call for *practice-based evidence*, rather than evidence-based practice. This promotes relatively small-scale research in natural, everyday clinical settings and places service users' experiences of therapy at the core of the research (Foskett, 2001; Macran et al., 1999; Mellor-Clark & Barkham, 2003). The research described in Chapters 14 and 15, for instance, provide two good illustrations of practice-based research: in Chapter 14, Maria Luca takes one therapy session as her focus and examines the client's verbal and implicit language, along with her own therapist/researcher responses; in Chapter 15, Darren Langdridge critically explores one client's narrative and his own emerging understandings as both therapist and researcher.

In practice-based research, clinicians are often the main researchers (perhaps in collaboration with academics) and the research is integrated into the therapy programme. In such research, practitioners might offer detailed descriptions of some aspect of their clinical case work, perhaps including descriptions of the context and the patients/clients and an account of the work carried out supported by evidence of its effectiveness, as measured by standardized measures, practitioner observation and client self-reports. Both quantitative and qualitative methods can be drawn upon. For example, Conway et al. (2003) investigated the processes and outcomes of their multi-modal group therapy using standardized outcome measures (the *Inventory of Interpersonal Problems – 32* and the *Brief Symptoms Inventory*) in conjunction with a qualitative component (patient self-reports). An interesting finding was that patients' responses varied over time, a result that demonstrated the value of taking a longitudinal (studying participants over a long term) approach.

Morgan (2004) argues that practice-based evidence not only gives service users and therapists a voice but also recognizes their first-hand knowledge: for example, of what works, and what needs to change. Margison et al. (2000) see practice-based evidence as a way of resolving questions about the quality of interventions. For instance, practice-based research has been used to explore unexpected results such as early improvement (Stiles et al., 2006).

While there is no one model of how to do practice-based research, we concur with Dallos and Vetere (2005, p. 82) who consider 'experiential, theoretical and empirical evidence for our therapeutic practice as having equal legitimacy'. We would also argue practitioners are well placed to conduct research of interest and relevance (see, for instance, the range of Masters' theses available on the HIPS website). As McGuire (1999) puts it:

> Every counsellor is a researcher: for every time we form an understanding of what is going on for a client, and work with that, we are testing out a hypothesis, and altering our activity in the light of evidence. (1999, p. 1)

The following examples show something of the range of this broad category of what constitutes practice-based evidence.

Research Example 4.1   Strickland-Clark, L., Campbell, D. and Dallos, R. (2000). Children's and adolescents' views on family therapy, *Journal of Family Therapy*, 22(3), 324–41

Five children/adolescents were interviewed immediately following their family therapy sessions. They were asked about their experiences of helpful and unhelpful events during the therapy sessions. The children/ adolescents were helped to identify these significant moments through the use of video-tape cues. The interviews and the significant events were analysed using grounded theory and 'comprehensive process analysis'. Key themes which emerged included the importance of being heard; the importance of being included; coping with the challenges of therapy; how therapy brought back painful memories; difficulties of saying what you feel and think; and needing support. An important by-product of the research was that the children felt empowered by the research (and the non-judgmental researcher) and expressed their pleasure in being asked to take part.

Research Example 4.2   Qualls, P.A. (1998). On being with suffering. In R. Valle (Ed.), *Phenomenological Inquiry in Psychology*, New York: Plenum Press

The researcher investigated the phenomenon of being with suffering in the lives of nine individuals who had travelled to Eastern Europe to work as volunteers with children in a Romanian orphanage. The volunteers wrote descriptions of their internal worlds. This was then followed by a 'walk-through interview'. Data was analysed phenomenologically by the researcher, who was also a volunteer caregiver. The experience of seeing the way the children had been so inhumanely treated challenged their sense of the world and their faith in God, and drained their personal reserves. Co-researchers found themselves in various uncomfortable states arising from powerful and ambivalent emotions including feeling love, fear and disgust simultaneously. Strong supportive bonds with colleagues and a sense of community helped them cope both during the experience and for years later. 'Freedom comes from confronting one's fear of suffering, breaking through one's isolation, and being touched by the suffering of others' (Qualls, 1998, p. 353).

Research Example 4.3   Gilbert, A. (2006). A phenomenological exploration of the impact of a traumatic incident (death of a child) on Social Services Staff, *European Journal for Qualitative Research in Psychotherapy*, 1, 1–9

This research involved a phenomenological exploration of the effects of a traumatic event (the death of a child) on six Social Services personnel. The researcher, a gestalt psychotherapist, had previously been involved in offering Social Services staff support and was interested in how the staff perceived the support they received and what meaning they constructed from the death. Findings included: recognition by the six co-researchers of the scale and uniqueness of the impact; expressions of anger, self-doubt and anxiety; the development of physical symptoms; and a developing awareness of personal qualities and strengths. Participants valued support from friends, family and (most of all) colleagues. Self-support strategies were important along with the use of humour. While the participants appreciated the institutional support they were given and the availability of emotional support, they would have liked more information about what had happened.

Research Example 4.4   Elliott, S., Loewenthal, D. and Greenwood, D. (2007). Narrative research into erotic counter-transference in a female therapist–male patient encounter. *Psychoanalytic Psychotherapy,* **21(3), 233–249**

This research describes the first author's experience of erotic counter-transference during her clinical work as a trainee psychotherapist. A personal account of a therapy encounter is offered as narrative data and analysed using the 'free association narrative method' (Hollway & Jefferson, 2000).

    Elliott describes how she was deeply moved on listening to her client Ryan describe his fears of intimacy alongside his intense longings to *feel* 'touched' and to *be* 'touched' by another:

> I felt spellbound. However, within the enchantment it was as if I had drifted into an 'emotional storm'. In the silence, I felt small and powerless in front of something very large and powerful. (Elliott et al., 2007, p. 242)

Elliott goes on to explain that his expressions touched her own feelings of aloneness. She acknowledges her ambivalent desire to either flee the room or embrace her client. On the basis of Elliott's personal account, the three authors explore whether erotic-(counter-)transference is a defence against emotions and the intimacy of the therapeutic relationship or an opportunity for therapeutic transformation.

The four small-scale studies briefly described above show how elements of psychotherapy practice can be explored from practitioners' and/or clients' perspectives. These research projects, all growing out of the researcher-practitioners' own practice and experience, were shaped by their specific concerns, questions and uncertainties.

Reflections

We are saddened by the fact that, for many practitioners, research often seems to have little or no relevance to practice. This seems so ironic given that every time we engage in therapy with clients we are, in effect, engaging in a form of experiential research (Evans, 2009). It is also ironic as we see so much good, small-scale, interesting and relevant research being conducted by individuals. The conundrum is how to bridge the chasm opening up between clinical practice and academic research.

We celebrate the fact that, increasingly, both quantitative and qualitative research is being conducted. Happily much of this research demonstrates the value of psychotherapy – an argument that can be used positively by practitioners. We remain concerned, however, that RCT evidence is being *mis*-used to support one therapeutic modality over others when other evidence supports the value of relational dimensions across *all* modalities.

RCTs – couched in the language of 'hard' science and supported by the inevitable treatment manuals – tend to present human beings as objects or machines that can be measured, tested, shaped and manipulated. 'RCTs typically cast clients as passive recipients of standardized treatments rather than active collaborators and self-healers – assumptions at odds with our values as relational oriented therapists' (Elliott, 2001, p. 316). From our perspective, this further alienates the client from themselves and others; it promotes distress and dis-ease, rather than contributing to health and a sense of well-being and community. This pernicious process also raises serious ethical questions for the therapist who is then asked to 'intervene' as instructed by the standardized treatment manual. This limits, or renders obsolete, the relationally orientated responses of proven curative value.

While we support the need to demonstrate effectiveness in psychotherapy, we argue that this is best done by broadening the process by which practice is evaluated. We would like effectiveness studies of the future to tap the rich vein of clients' and therapists' perspectives ideally using qualitative research. We believe clients'/therapists' voices need to be heard more. As psychotherapists we honour the client's view of the change process, the co-creation of the therapeutic relationship as the vehicle for change and the context in which therapy takes place. As relational-centred researchers, we similarly want to honour the subjective experience of the research participant(s), the co-created component of the research data and the *context* in which the research is conducted. Central to our work, we believe, is respect: for the client's/research participant's subjective experiences, for their perspective on the issues and problems, and for their views about the credibility of the therapeutic process/research endeavour.

Like many other practitioners, we remain unconvinced about the value of quantitative research as all too often it is unable to touch core issues or shed light on processes which resonate with lived experience. Qualitative, practice-centred research offers one way of ensuring that research focuses on questions of interest to therapists themselves. The scientific 'rigour' that may be lost is more than balanced by the 'relevance' that such research can offer. These themes are followed up in the next chapter on quality in research.

Notes

[i] The guidelines were initially published in 2004 and amended in 2007.

[ii] In RCT experiments, outcomes of treatment with patients/clients who have the same disorder are systematically measured and compared with the outcomes of patients/ clients who receive no treatment. The 'independent variable' (the treatment) is applied to the 'dependent variable' (the client's condition) and the effects are measured. The *random* allocation of patients/clients to treatment groups means that any subsequent difference in outcome can only be attributed to the impact of the treatment.

[iii] These experimental designs use methods other than randomization. For example, a 'matched pairs' experimental strategy could be used which sorts participants into pairs similar to each other on particular criteria such as age, duration of disorder and so on. These kinds of controlled experiments are generally considered to produce a slightly lower quality of evidence but a well-controlled experiment is also seen as potentially offering better evidence than a poorly conducted RCT.

[iv] National Occupational Standards for counselling and psychotherapy are being produced through *Skills for Health*, the Sector Skills Council (SSC) for the UK health sector. This organization, in turn, has commissioned a review of the effectiveness of a range of modalities practiced in the UK.

[v] UKCP Research Committee has recently come out in support of the use of non-controlled studies, case studies and qualitative methods. "Whilst recognising the central importance of naturalistic enquiry for integrative and humanistic psychotherapies, this study has indicated that where controlled studies have been carried out, these have found in support of integrative and humanistic psychotherapies." The Research Committee identified some 78 meta-analyses or controlled research investigations that overwhelmingly reinforced the findings of 58 non-controlled or case study research studies the committee reviewed (UKCP, June 2008).

[vi] The Diagnostic and Statistical Manual of Mental Disorders (DSM) is published by the American Psychiatric Association and provides diagnostic criteria for different mental health problems.

Chapter 5

Quality in Qualitative Relational-centred Research

What makes for good qualitative and relational-centred research? Clarity and accessibility are certainly two important criteria. Academic presentations of research can all too easily appear confusing, daunting, boring and of little relevance to our actual practice. Perhaps you yourself have picked up a research article with good intentions, only to toss it aside after battling to make sense of impenetrable language and jargon.

Beyond clear expression and the ability to be readily understood, in this chapter we suggest that good qualitative and relational research is trustworthy and transparent in its process and impactful in its outcomes. In terms of process, the research needs to evidence that it has been systematically and conscientiously conducted. In terms of outcome, good research challenges or deepens our understanding; it helps us grow and enriches our work as practitioners.

We start by discussing some established criteria which qualitative researchers commonly use and then move on to offer our own criteria. In our view the best relational research shows evidence of *rigour*, *relevance*, *resonance* and *reflexivity* (the 4 R's!). Depending on the type of research, one or other of these criteria might be specifically fore-grounded and valued. By way of illustration, we present three extended extracts from research projects that we believe fall into the category of good qualitative research. While all three pieces of research show evidence of the '4 Rs', the

Relational-centred Research for Psychotherapists: Exploring Meanings and Experience
Edited by Linda Finlay and Ken Evans

first one highlights the importance of rigour, the second is full of resonance and the third demonstrates reflexivity in action. (As all three projects seem particularly relevant to psychotherapy practice, we have not offered a separate extract embodying relevance.)

Qualitative Evaluation Criteria

It would be nice if knowledge claims stemming from psychotherapy research were 'so powerful and convincing that they ... carry the validation with them, like a strong piece of art' (Kvale, 1996, p. 252). Unfortunately, this rarely happens. More commonly the value of qualitative research needs to be demonstrated, argued for and justified. Without this, researchers lay themselves open to the criticism from quantitatively orientated colleagues who regard qualitative research as 'merely subjective assertion supported by unscientific method'! (Ballinger & Wiles, 2006, p. 235).

Qualitative researchers require evaluation criteria quite distinct from those of quantitative investigators: criteria that are responsive to our particular values and goals. (For instance, quantitative researchers value consistent, reliable use of measures to allow for studies to be replicated. By definition, qualitative researchers do not believe situations can be replicated and that what emerges as 'data' is the product of that specific interpersonal and social context.) Our criteria need to acknowledge that 'trust and truths are fragile' and that good research is that which engages 'with the messiness and complexity of data interpretation in ways that ... reflect the lives of ... participants' (Savin-Baden & Fisher, 2002, p. 191).

Lincoln and Guba (1985) propose the four criteria of credibility, transferability, dependability and confirmability, as a way of formalizing the rigour and trustworthiness of qualitative research.[i] *Credibility* replaces the conventional quantitative criterion of 'internal validity' by focusing on the degree to which findings make sense. *Transferability* replaces the concepts of 'external validity' and 'generalizability' by seeking to give readers enough information to judge the applicability of the findings to other settings. *Dependability* and *confirmability* replace 'reliability' and 'objectivity'. They encourage researchers to provide a transparent and self-critical reflexive analysis to act as an audit trail about their research processes which can be laid open to external scrutiny.

Other researchers have challenged what they see as Lincoln and Guba's preoccupation with scientific rigour by arguing for a greater focus on artistic and ethical dimensions. Bochner (2000, 2001), for instance, encourages sociological and narrative researchers to engage an:

[E]thical, political, and personal sociology that listens to the voices of ill, disabled, and other silenced persons ... to ... empower ... engage emotionality ... and give ... sociology a moral and ethical centre. (Bochner, 2001, p. 152)

His criteria for judging this ethically engaged social science include:

- Detail, of the commonplace, of feelings as well as facts;
- Narratives that are structurally complex and take account of time as it is experienced;
- A sense of the author, their subjectivity and 'emotional credibility';
- Stories that tell about believable journeys through the life course;
- Ethical self-consciousness: respect for others in the field, and for the moral dimensions of the story;
- A story that moves the reader at an emotional as well as rational level. (Bochner 2000, cited in Green & Thorogood 2004, p. 244)

How to choose between the positions set out by Lincoln and Guba on the one hand and Bochner on the other? As relational-centred researchers who find value in both approaches, we (Linda and Ken) offer a set of criteria which blend scientific rigour with ethical integrity and artistry. Qualitative research in general, and relational research in particular, we suggest, should be evaluated in terms of its *rigour, relevance, resonance* and the extent that *reflexivity* is demonstrated.[ii] Researchers using different methodologies value these criteria to different degrees.

Rigour asks the following questions: Has the research been competently managed and systematically worked through? Is the research based on methodical critical reflection? Is the research coherent and does the report clearly describe it? Is the evidence marshalled well and is it open to external audit? Are the researcher's interpretations both plausible and justified? To what extent do the findings match the evidence and are they convincing? For example, have quotations taken from an interview been offered to illustrate a theme? Have the knowledge claims been 'tested', validated and argued in dialogue with others (including co-researchers, supervisors or colleagues)?

Relevance concerns the value of the research in terms of its applicability and contribution. Does the research add to the body of knowledge relating to an issue or aspect of social life? Does it enrich our understanding of the human condition or of the psychotherapy process? Is it empowering and/or growth-enhancing for either the co-researchers involved and/or the readers? Have, for example, the co-researchers gained some comfort from being listened to and heard? Alternatively, does it offer psychotherapists any guidance and will it help to improve their practice in some way? To an extent, of course, relevance is a subjective area. What you find relevant may not work for others. However, research that is not useful in some way and cannot be applied more widely to practice is probably going to be of less interest to practitioners.

Resonance taps into emotional, artistic and/or spiritual dimensions which can probably only be judged in the eye of the beholder. To what extent are *you* 'touched' by the findings? Are they sufficiently vivid or powerful to draw readers in? Can readers enter the research account emotionally? Do the findings resonate with readers' own experiences and understandings? Or do they disturb, unsettle, and push the boundaries of the taken-for-granted? Are the findings presented in a particularly power-ful, graceful or poignant way? Polkinghorne (1983) alludes to this idea of resonance in his recommended criteria of 'vividness', 'accuracy', 'richness' and 'elegance' as ways of judging the trustworthiness of phenomenological research.

Finally, **reflexivity** is a broad category which refers to the researcher's self-awareness and openness about the research process. To what extent has the researcher taken into account their own subjectivity and positioning and the possible impact of these on the research? Have they explored how meanings were elicited in an interpersonal, intersubjective context? Has the researcher shown awareness of the possibility of transference/counter-transference processes? Has the researcher monitored the potential for the abuse of power in the research relationship? Have they shown respect for, and sensitivity to, co-researchers' safety/needs? Does the researcher dem-onstrate ethical integrity and concern for the wider impact of the research? At the same time, does the researcher display an appropriate level of humil-ity in acknowledging the limitations of any findings and in the knowledge claimed?

Figure 5.1 presents these four criteria in the shape of a pie whose pieces are a moveable feast. Each of the quadrants can be enlarged or reduced depending on the researcher's aims and values. For example, while some methodologies would emphasize 'rigour', others might showcase 'reso-nance'. The quadrant sizes may also shift according to the stage of research. For instance, more attention might be paid to rigour during data collection and analysis, while resonance might come to the fore at the writing-up stage.

The sections which follow present extracts from three separate pieces of research, all of them good examples of *relevant* relational research. All three have been peer-reviewed and accepted for publication. They are offered here to exemplify what a rigorous, resonant and reflexive piece of research might look like. We have chosen these extracts to highlight the particular

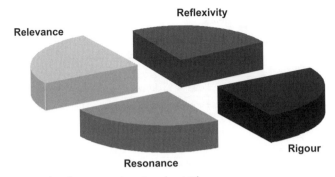

Figure 5.1   Evaluating research using the 4 R's

aspects being discussed. You would need to go to the published source to appreciate the research more fully. Our intention is to open up discussion. Feel free to disagree with our evaluations!

A Grounded Theory Example: The Case for Rigour?[iii]

In this research example, the authors, Anne Thériault and Nicola Gazzola (2008), interviewed 12 experienced therapists to investigate therapists' feelings of incompetence. They note that although such feelings are commonly experienced, there has been little research into the subjective judgment of oneself as inadequate in the role of therapist. Using grounded theory methodology (Strauss & Corbin, 1990), the authors develop a theory describing a relationship between four main categories: intensity of self-doubt; sources of feelings of incompetence; mediating factors; and consequences. The theory is summarized in Figure 5.2 (Thériault & Gazzola, 2008, p. 22).

Discussing their emerging model, Thériault and Gazzola (2008) suggest their study demonstrates that most therapists continue to have doubts at level one or two, where they routinely question whether they are 'right' or whether they are being 'effective'. However, these low-level doubts tend not to contaminate their self-judgment and the doubts are more easily contained with experience. However, experience was not always found to be a helpful buffer. Self-doubt stemming from personal historical wounds seemed to continue to have potency despite experience and therapists noted that they could be regressed to previous levels of vulnerability under certain circumstances. Also, therapists' self-expectations were raised with experience, making them somewhat vulnerable to feelings of incompetence.

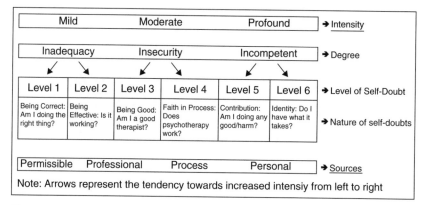

Figure 5.2   Axial representation of relational trends between major categories, sources and intensity. Reproduced from Thériault and Gazzola (2008) with the kind permission of the authors and the Editor of the *European Journal of Qualitative Research in Psychotherapy*.

In our view, this research is a good example of what can be achieved using grounded theory methodology. In the fuller article, the authors work hard to systematically and conscientiously unpack their themes and categories towards building their broader theory. The logic of each category is carefully and clearly spelt out. The addition of quotes from the participants (offered in their fuller paper) provides some transparency about how the researchers reached their conclusion. In these ways, the authors demonstrate the *rigour* of their work.

By referring to psychotherapists' experience and practice, the authors also demonstrate the wider *relevance* of their work. The content of the article, with its emphasis on the poignancy of the experiences being described, should also *resonate* with readers. In common with many grounded theory studies, *reflexivity* is not particularly emphasized. However, the authors provide a transparent account as well as a methodological audit of how they obtained their results.

A Phenomenological Example: The Case for Resonance?

While the subject matter of feelings of inadequacy potentially resonates at an emotional level, some might argue that the presentation of such a subject in terms of a detailed theoretical hierarchy of concepts is somewhat dry. A different approach is taken below by Rameshera Rao on self-cutting.[iv] Striving for powerful description as well as empathy for the self-cutter, she elicits a direct emotional response in the reader.

In the following extract, she offers a phenomenological description of the self-cutter's experience of cutting as 'wounding to heal'. This passage has been taken from a broader study in which Rao demonstrates the care and rigour taken with her phenomenology. In this passage, Rao summarizes her research findings on the basis of a composite account of several cutters' descriptions. Her intent is as much literary as it is scientific.

> Self-cutting occurs in the context of a painful interpersonal event which calls into question the individual's already tenuous competence and worthiness. These concerns and her corresponding self-blame interrupt her daily activities and interactions with others. During previous moments of healthy living, she focused on her relationships and endeavours, while her body disappeared from her awareness. However, when she experiences the pain of rejection, disappointment, or distrust, her body is ... attended to in terms of its limitations ...
>
> Pain always interrupts living and relatedness. When in pain, one takes action to be pain-free. However, for the cutter, conventional expressions of pain are difficult to articulate and/or remain unheard. Prior to cutting, she may have tried other actions to gain a handle on herself, but these do not diminish her pain. Unable to take effective action against the painful and unexpected event, she falls helplessly into despair. She feels trapped, unable to free herself from the intolerable situation and accompanying bodily discomfort. It is in this context – when she struggles to take hold of herself and her spiraling emotions – that self-cutting emerges as an appealing way to "get a grip."
>
> You will understand that she is wounding to heal if you remember the wound beneath the wound, the emotional pain of sadness and anger from which her physical cuts emerge. Cutting is experienced as healing for several reasons: The cutter opens lacerations and feels "a high." The act of cutting diminishes the rising pressure, racing thoughts, and overwhelming emotions. She is assured by the ability to create, localize, and regulate cutting. This is the one action she can take in a time of helpless desperation. Cutting is always a comforting movement that momentarily frees her from the "stuckness" of suffering. It is healing to recover a sense of calm, mastery, and agency when she feels helpless, out of control, and stuck in despair. It is healing to reveal and release hidden emotional pain. Wounding herself makes the invisible, palpably visible and tangible. Hers is a language of pain; her lacerations, efforts to make sense of that pain.
>
> Cutting brings the cutter back to herself. Amid her overwhelm, she is relieved to focus and "get it together." It is healing to experience herself as cohesive, real, substantial, and alive. Without cutting, she may feel nothingness and tortured identity diffusion. Through self-cutting, she can recover a sense of herself. The symptom is an attempt at self-location. Finding "the here" is healing, especially in a world in which she feels invisible, insubstantial, or at the very least unheard. Like pinching the fleshy part of the hand,

self-cutting is a gesture of reassurance. Following cutting, she has a reason to engage in nurturing self-care. Physical healing may parallel emotional healing. She may cut for attention to the deeper wound, namely her distress … The act of self-cutting pulls her together only to tear her apart with its self-destructive, shaming, and addictive consequences. Nevertheless, "wounding to heal" is the cutter's way of coping … and surviving. (Rao, 2006, p. 56)

In her more extended published research account, Rao (2006) offers detailed quotations from her women participants to substantiate her composite description establishing rigour and ensuring resonance. What she does not do is to reveal herself and to discuss her own role within the research: in other words, show evidence of *reflexivity*. This style is in keeping with her empirical phenomenological methodology following Giorgi (1985) which aims to remain focused on participants' descriptions and reflexivity is downplayed (or even ignored) in pursuit of rigour (for instance, in systematically applying imaginative variation). However, in this version of phenomenology, reflexivity is enacted in other ways, such as by showing evidence of careful bracketing and sensitive reflection.

A Discursive Example: Reflexivity to the Fore?

In contrast to the previous example, the following extract foregrounds reflexivity more explicitly. Drawn from a social constructionist study of 'Men, masculinities and discourse', Gough (1999) examines heterosexual men's talk in a group with a view to exploring how discourses around masculinity may be used to subordinate others. In the following passage Gough (called Bren) discusses the use of humour to breach his otherwise potentially 'detached researcher stance' in two reflexive 'registers'.

Jack: … people look to label because it makes them feel safer … they think they know where they stand and they can control, but it's a lot more complex …
Bren: Psychologists are the worst offenders! [group laughter]
Jack: Yeah …
Glen: The media, the Guardian and psychologists on Channel 4! [group laughter]

I suppose the use of humour helps to suggest the illusion of "normal" conversation, with the researcher temporarily colluding as one of the "lads", albeit in this case one limited to one-line questions and interjections. This particular example could indicate a degree of self-deprecation, perhaps in an effort to reduce power differentials, or perhaps more likely, to create distance between myself and (the maligned) psychologists, hence appearing liberal or sophisticated (either way attempting to endear myself to the participants). Perhaps such occasional contributions give the impression of participation, thus rendering temporarily the otherwise peculiar position of polite interrogator less salient.

RV [Reflexive Voice]: *It is also possible that humour is attempted as a defence in the light of anxiety or discomfort around my "difference" (as researcher, tutor, outsider) and "using" participants for data. Humour enables a temporary alliance to be forged so that difference is momentarily erased. By contributing to and encouraging this "banter" within the group, am I perhaps seeking to assuage guilt, to reassure myself that, if nothing else, the participants at least derive some enjoyment from their participation? ...*

Andy: What would you say about a person who wants anal sex with their
      partner?
Bren: I don't know, what do you think?
Andy: Well, I was asking you! [group laughter]

... RV: I opted for the safety of my researcher role. Is it another example too of me seeking to learn about (my) masculinity from the discourse of others?
                                         (Gough, 2003, pp. 151–152, 156)

This passage offers a sound example of researcher reflexivity in action. The author reflects at different levels on his own behaviour and unconscious processes while showing awareness of the potential impact of his responses on the participants and of wider cultural discourses. The rigour of Gough's research is shown by his preparedness to offer up his data and research process for external scrutiny while resonance is indicated by the way he indicates some of his insecurities.

Rigour, resonance, relevance or reflexivity ... Which are the most important dimensions for you? Thinking about the pie quadrants, what sizes would the four pieces be?

Reflections

We consider the special contribution and strength of qualitative research in general, and relational-centred research specifically, is precisely the way it can capture the ambiguity, ambivalence and richness of lived experience while touching the diversity and complexity of the social world. We also value the communicative power of research (and research writing) that challenges, unsettles and disturbs normal taken-for-granted complacency.

Above all, we suggest that qualitative research should draw the reader into the researcher's discoveries and allow the reader to see the worlds of others in new and deeper ways.

Behar once said, 'Call it sentimental … but I say that anthropology that doesn't break your heart just isn't worth doing anymore' (1966, cited in Bochner, 2001, p. 143). We feel much the same about relational-centred research. We both personally believe that the best articles wield emotional power. We especially value the poetry and resonance of research findings. For us, research that sets itself up mainly to establish its scientific credentials is less appealing and shows a loss of faith in the richness of what relational-centred research can offer.

On the other hand, we do recognize there is a place for different sorts of research and writing depending on the audience/readership. Of course both science and art are important. A research article destined for a medically orientated journal would need to engage a lot more with scientific credibility than with artistic flair. A presentation to a user group would probably need to have more emotional and practical credibility.

In the future when you read the examples of research (be they relational-centred or otherwise) ask yourself: Is this research that psychotherapists want to do and read about? Does this research demonstrate something of the value, interest and integrity of our psychotherapy practice? Would this kind of research build a case that will convince sceptical audiences, funding bodies and ethical panels that the research is worthwhile? If the answer to any of these questions is 'yes', then you can be confident you have found some good quality research.

Notes

[i] Guba and Lincoln later reworked their ideas to incorporate a fifth criterion of 'authenticity' (Guba & Lincoln, 1989) which tapped into themes related to ethics and empowering action.

[ii] These criteria have been developed from ones presented in a previous article in the *British Journal of Occupational Therapy* with the kind permission of the Editor, Upma Barnett. See Finlay (2006f) 'Rigour', 'ethical integrity' or 'artistry'? Reflexively reviewing criteria for evaluating qualitative research, *British Journal of Occupational Therapy*, 69(7), 319–326.

[iii] This passage has been reproduced from 'Feelings of incompetence among experienced therapists: A substantive theory' in the *European Journal of Qualitative Research in Psychotherapy*, with the kind permission of the authors and the Editor, Ken Evans.

[iv] This passage has been reproduced from 'Wounding to heal: The role of the body in self-cutting', by R. Rao in *Qualitative Research in Psychology*, 2006, with the kind permission of the publisher, Taylor & Francis (http://www.informaworld.com).

Part II

Relational-centred Research: Being and Doing

Introduction

Relational-centred research foregrounds the co-created relationship between researcher and co-researcher while recognizing this relationship is set within a wider social/relational field. In our version of relational-centred research, the researcher also:

- **reflexively attends to their own embodied presence**, aiming to be open, empathic self-aware, authentic and intuitive of the Other. The challenge for the research is being present and really listening without losing oneself or the Other.
- **yields to the process** in terms of allowing oneself to be unknowing and to respond in the moment to whatever emerges in the here and now. The researcher needs to have the courage to stay in the process and trust that something of value will emerge.
- engages a **dialogical approach** where the researcher is in relation with, and responding to and through the research relationship. The focus is on the mutuality of the 'between'. The reality of the Other – and thus ourselves – is to be found in the fullness of our open relations where we engage in mutual participation (Buber, 1937/1958).

In this middle section of the book, we focus on the *being and doing* of relational-centred research. *Chapter 6* offers basic practical guidelines on how to start research with sections on choosing a topic, locating existing knowledge, deciding methods, gaining ethical approval, engaging co-researchers and setting up support systems.

Chapter 7 examines the process of gathering data. Using examples from practice, we focus on 'interviewing' and 'participant observation' – two common methods used to collect data. However, the special nature of relational-centred research means there are no set recipes or procedures to follow. The process is best seen as co-creating data within a research encounter.

In *Chapter 8*, we build on the theory outlined in *Chapter 3* and illustrate some of the complex relational processes occurring in that ambiguous multi-layered space *between* researcher and co-researcher. Four defining features of relational-centred research are highlighted: Presence, Inclusion, Intersubjectivity and Reflexivity. We show how research processes mirror those arising in therapy.

A significant challenge the relational-centred researcher faces is finding a way to become aware of the layers of relational processes present and then to work with and manage them. The extent that the researcher is able to engage positively with 'process' depends on the needs of the research and the researcher's own experience. *Chapter 9* illustrates this process providing a radical example of research practice. Here, a researcher (Ken Evans) engages an evocative exercise of *reflexive introspection* employing gestalt two-chair work exploring the interface between psychotherapy, religion and spirituality. The process and value of supervision as offering impact and challenge is also shown.

In *Chapter 10*, Linda Finlay writes with Anna Madill, to describe and explain some different ways to analyse data. Four contrasting types of analysis are outlined with practical exemplars: narrative, thematic, discursive and creative. Each type of analysis highlights different aspects and so enables different insights. As such, qualitative analysis is always tentative, partial and emergent.

Chapter 11 focuses on 'relational ethics'. The ethical challenges researchers face when doing relational-centred research include the way we are called upon to be reflexive about our role as researchers at every stage of the research and to critically examine the impact of any imbalances of power that may arise. We are also called upon to acknowledge that researchers and co-researchers alike can be profoundly touched by the research we do.

Chapter 12 concludes Part II spotlighting some questions and answers about how to become and develop as a relational-centred researcher.

Chapter 6

Setting up Research

In *Chapter 1* we likened qualitative research to a 'voyage of discovery'. Pursuing this metaphor, the process of setting up research is akin to preparing for a journey by going to a travel agent, packing and generally getting organized! First of all, the prospective traveller must decide where they are going (in the case of research, they must choose a topic/research question). Next they find out more about their destination by getting hold of a travel guide book or searching the Internet (the equivalent, in research, of doing a review of the literature). After that, comes the planning stage when the practicalities of the journey are investigated and sorted out (a process akin to deciding methods of data collection and analysis). For certain destinations, visa applications may have to be made (just as gaining ethical approval is essential for certain fields of research). Then the traveller may organize relevant tour guides or local people to contact if in need (setting up research supervision and support).

Like an impatient traveller eager to enjoy their holiday, the researcher can find this planning stage tedious and be tempted to rush through it. But it is important to get organized, if only to ensure that the researcher packs the right gear. Engaging this planning process systematically, and early on, saves time and inconvenience in the long run.

This chapter offers you, the relational-centred or qualitative researcher, practical guidance on how to plan your voyage of discovery. We take you

Relational-centred Research for Psychotherapists: Exploring Meanings and Experience
Edited by Linda Finlay and Ken Evans
Copyright © 2009 John Wiley & Sons, Ltd.

step by step through some of the key challenges and decisions you will need to make en route when:

- choosing a topic and research question
- locating existing knowledge
- deciding methods of data collection and analysis
- gaining ethical approval
- recruiting and engaging co-researchers
- setting up appropriate support systems.

Choosing a Topic and Research Question

The process of deciding what to research can often prove more challenging and time-consuming than you might at first think. The challenge is to find a topic and a research question(s) that is *relevant* and *interesting* and that is *do-able* given the time constraints and other practicalities you may face.

The following five tips may help you choose an appropriate topic and question:

1) **Tap into a 'passion'** – Find a topic/research question which excites, or at the very least interests, you. Ideally you need to tap into some passion – it should capture your imagination (Steward, 2006). It is this passion that will sustain you through some of the more intense or tedious stages of doing research. You need to believe in your project and value it.

2) **Keep grounded and modest in your aims** – Pragmatism needs to balance enthusiasm. Novice researchers (and sometimes the more experienced) can fall into the trap of wanting to make a significant or revolutionary contribution. But grand plans are more suited to life projects rather than single research studies and are hard to put into practice (Fischer, 2006). You need to remain focused on what you can actually achieve (given your time frame and the resources available to you) and what you can realistically expect your research to produce. Your research should aim to say 'a lot about a little problem' (Silverman, 1993, p. 3), rather than a little about a big one. If you are relatively new to research you may be tempted to seek out a topic/ question which has never been done before. In fact, your research is likely to be more fruitful if you opt for a topic or area that has already generated literature with which you can critically engage. For example,

you might run a focus group with psychotherapists mirroring research already done with nurses and compare responses. For PhD level research you may be required to make an 'original contribution'. But this does not mean finding a topic that no one has touched before.

3) **Be specific and precise** – As you work towards defining your research question, try to be as focused, specific and concrete as possible. The precise question you are asking is important. In moving from a broad topic to formulating the specific research question, think in terms of 'what' or 'how' questions rather than 'why' or 'whether'. For example, if you are interested in the broad topic such as 'self-harm', you might re-formulate the research question as '*what* does the act of self-harming mean?' If you are interested in researching phobias, pick a particular angle such as '*what* is the lived experience of confronting a phobia?' Or, instead of wanting to investigate the value of thera-peutic interventions in general, it might be more practical to focus more specifically on one aspect such as therapist self-disclosure: for example, by asking '*how* is a therapist's self-disclosure experienced by the client?'

4) **Let your research question evolve** – Sometimes researchers refine – or even change – their question after they get started on the research. A complete change of tack may occasionally be necessary: consider the case of a researcher who sets out to evaluate the effectiveness of a particular psychotherapy group only to discover that the group has folded after two sessions. To give another example, one student started to do a grounded theory study about 'getting lost' as part of the griev-ing process. When she realized she was really trying to explore her own experience of grieving, she switched to a heuristic design. It is not uncommon for researchers to modify their methodology en route which, in turn, means the research question needs tweaking.

5) **Take time to reflect on the nature of your task** – The choice of research topic and question will be driven by personal, professional or academic goals. What is driving you? Are you being required to conduct this research? What expectations have been laid on you and are you laying on yourself? What are the assumptions and presuppositions you already hold about the research topic? Searching questions like these will form the foundation of the *reflexivity* which should be a part of any qualitative project since it enables you to understand your own impact (as a researcher) on the research.

One way to clarify your research and its focus is to explore the existing literature – the topic to which you now turn.

Locating Existing Knowledge

At some point in your research you will need to search the literature and explore the status of what is currently known about your topic. Partly this is an orientating exercise as it helps you to recognize how your topic is currently being framed and to identify key issues and debates. Partly it offers you the opportunity to identify gaps in the literature and thus provide a rationale for your own research. Being thoroughly conversant with the literature will also enable critical evaluation when you come to look at the contribution of your own research. When writing up your research you will need to discuss your findings in the light of existing research, stating whether your research supports, refutes or extends current evidence (Steward, 2006).

Some qualitative researchers argue against engaging in a detailed literature review in the early stages of a project. Their point is that your ideas might be shaped too much by others before you even get started. However, some preliminary reading may help to avoid duplication of effort and a formal literature search may be a required part of gaining ethical approval for the project.

You can access to the literature in a number of ways:

1) Specialist online databases (such as Psych-lit, MEDLINE, CINAHL, BIDS) offer lists and descriptions of relevant theoretical and empirical articles. Often the literature cited here involves quantitative studies and may not tap into the qualitative dimensions you are interesting in.
2) Articles can also be accessed directly from journals which can be searched either online or by hand. Relevant journals include: *Counselling and Psychotherapy Research*; *Psychology and Psychotherapy: Theory, Research and Practice*; *The International Journal of Existential Psychology and Psychotherapy*; *European Journal for Qualitative Research in Psychotherapy*; *Indo-Pacific Journal of Phenomenology*; and *Existential Analysis*.
3) Professional websites, such as the one for the British Association of Counselling and Psychotherapy (www.bacp.co.uk/research/index.html), usually offer information about research and may include databases on systematic reviews, publications and dissertations.
4) Google or other Internet search engines can also be useful for accessing references to relevant books and research articles related to particular topics.

Conducting a literature review to explore existing knowledge takes time and effort. It cannot be done quickly. But it is not all hard slog. Playing 'detective' as you track down elusive articles or unfamiliar research projects can be fun and the process of gaining new knowledge is satisfying.

When you have collected your resources together, your next task will be to synthesize and evaluate the knowledge they contain and write this up. For a research proposal a brief summary of relevant research is usually all that is required. You will want to be similarly selective if you are writing a journal article and limited to around 1,000 words for your review. When writing an article reviewing the literature (approximately 5,000–6,000 words) or a chapter in a thesis, you will need to undertake a more substantial review: one which seeks to be both analytical and critical.

The word 'critical' here does not mean to imply you have to be negative. A good critical evaluation of the literature aims to draw attention to strengths and limitations of what is out there. Rather than just describing the research, you need to grapple with its value or relevance (*see Chapter 5: Quality in Qualitative Relational-centred Research*). To give an example, Granek (2006) carried out some qualitative research on how depression is experienced. In her literature review, she criticized 'objective' measures of depression as embracing medical models which pathologize and do not sufficiently attend to relational dimensions. This point then became her rationale for undertaking a more subjective approach to people's stories of depression.

One of the benefits of carrying out a literature review is that it allows you to explore how others have researched your topic area. This should help guide your own choices of methodology and method.

Deciding Methods of Data Collection and Analysis

Before you jump into deciding your 'tactics' for data collection and analysis, you need to be clear about your research 'strategy' in terms of your aim and research methodology (*see Chapter 2: Competing Qualitative Research Traditions* which spells this out in more detail). If you want to explore individuals' life experiences, then your options would orientate towards phenomenological, psychodynamic, (auto)biographical or narrative research. Here your data collection method is likely to favour interviews or descriptive protocols (where co-researchers write a few paragraphs on their lived experience) which you would analyse narratively or thematically. If you are aiming to examine talk or text, then discourse or conversation analysis would be the better choice and you would tend to focus on naturally occurring talk or documentary evidence for data which you would analyse discursively. If you seek to understand cultural practices, then you will probably opt to do an ethnography or case study research on organizations and use participant-observation methods which you would analyse either thematically or narratively. For heuristic, autoethnographical or autobiographical research, you would concentrate on personal reflection (perhaps through writing a diary) towards producing a narrative or creative presentation.

To help you decide your strategy and tactics you might ask yourself: What sources of data are potentially available and appropriate? Would combining methods offer something more? What can the chosen methods feasibly reveal? You might also ask which methods would be the most practical given the inevitable constraints of time and competing demands. That said methods should not be adopted simply because they seem to be the easiest way forward. Instead, you need to be sure that your choice of methods and procedures are consistent with your methodology and appropriate to the research question you are pursuing.

Having decided your general path, you then need to decide on the specific approach and procedures you will use to collect, and then analyse, data. If you have decided to interview participants, for example, you must next choose between semi-structured or more open approaches. If you are opting to do a participant-observation, will you join in as a full participant or will you remain something of an outside observer? You will also need to work out what kind of relationship you are seeking to have with the people you are researching. For instance, are you going to share the research process with them, in essence co-opting them as co-researchers, throughout the analysis phase? (*See Chapter 7: The Research Encounter: Co-creating Your Data* for further ideas on gathering data.)

Example 6.1   Choosing interviews within a grounded theory study

In the following extract, Mandy Stanley (2006) offers an account of her data collection choices for researching older people's meanings of well-being, using grounded theory methodology. She conducted semi-structured in-depth interviews with 15 co-researchers who were all 75 years or older and living in the community. Her co-researchers were recruited through 'opportunistic' and 'snowball sampling' where the co-researchers suggested future participants from among their acquaintances.

> I chose to use in-depth interviews in my study as it was not feasible to observe older people to gain insight into their perception of well-being. I sought an exemplar to guide my question development, as I needed to make sure that my interview questions fitted with the grounded theory focus on process and social actors ... as follows:

1. In order to understand you a bit better, tell me about how you spend your day.
2. As you know, I am interested in finding out about the perceptions and understanding of well-being of older people. So if I said to you 'what does well-being mean to you?' what would you say?
3. Tell me, how do you achieve well-being?
4. What difficulties do you encounter in achieving/ maintaining well-being?
5. What advice would you give to a person who is not experiencing well-being?
6. What would you like to tell health care professionals about well-being for older people?
7. What would you like to tell your family and friends about well-being?
8. What would you like to tell politicians and governments that would improve the lives of older people?
9. Is there anything else you would like to comment on about well-being?

(Stanley, 2006, p. 66)

When it comes to selecting your analysis method, you have a general choice between engaging in thematic, narrative, discursive or creative forms of analysis (*see Chapter 10: Analysis of Data*). Usually researchers tend to favour a particular method but they might also combine approaches: for instance, presenting individual narratives which are then synthesized into more general existential themes (Fitzpatrick and Finlay, 2008, provide an example of this – *see* p. 145 in *Chapter 10: Analysis of Data*).

Ultimately, the data collection and analysis options chosen need to fit the research aims and methodology. As Holloway and Todres note (2003, p. 345), the researcher needs to be 'considerate of the inner consistency and coherence' of the research as a whole. Procedures need to be consistent with the overall approach taken. It would not make sense, for example, to analyse a psychotherapy session discursively if the aim is to explore the client's inner world or lived experience, since the discursive approach tends to deny that kind of subjectivity.

Too much emphasis can be placed on following methods as 'recipes', however. We would stress the importance of not being too attached to method for method's sake – of avoiding what Janesick (1994) calls 'methodolatry'. Methods chosen are only tools to be used judiciously by the researchers. As counsellors and psychotherapists, we are familiar with this path. While therapy techniques have their place, it is the therapist-client relationship and what happens in the therapy which is of greater importance. Similarly, when conducting relational-centred research, it is important for researchers to avoid becoming excessively preoccupied with method and focus instead on *process*.

Gaining Ethical Approval

Having planned the basic strategy and tactics of the research, the next step is usually to construct a formal *Research Proposal* and/or gain formal approval to go ahead with the research. Different institutions offer their own specific guidelines for information that needs to be supplied in the proposal. If you are doing your research to fulfil course requirements, this proposal may involve a relatively straightforward process ending in your supervisor's formal approval. If your research involves clients or work in NHS and Social Services organizations, you will be required to submit your proposal to a formal Research Ethics Committee.[i]

Whatever the required format of the proposal, you will need to address six main areas:

* Aims/objectives – What is the purpose of the research and the research question?
* Literature review – What is the theoretical, empirical and/or methodological rationale for the study?
* Research design – What data collection and analysis methods/procedures are being proposed and who will be the participants/co-researchers?
* Ethical issues – What is being done to ensure no harm comes to the participants and to protect their interests?
* Planning – What is the envisaged timetable for the research and what resources are required?
* Support mechanisms – What arrangements for supervision, support and research training are in place?

In this section, we home in on the ethical aspects specifically (and these are developed in *Chapter 11: Relational Ethics*).

Many professional groups, including those for psychotherapists, have developed their own codes of conduct for research and research ethics (see for instance, the various professional guidelines laid down such as the BACP ethical framework at <http://www.bacp.co.uk/ethical_framework/> and the guidelines from the British Psychological Society at <http://

www.bps.org.uk/the-society/code-of-conduct/ethical-principles-for-conducting-research-with-human-participants.cfm>.[ii] All of these codes attend to core principles of minimizing risk, doing no harm, being competent and treating people fairly and with respect. These principles find expression through practices that ensure informed consent and confidentiality.

Informed consent – Informed consent means ensuring that co-researchers understand the nature of the project, what the research will involve, the limits to their participation, and the risks they may incur (Social Research Association, 2003). If the research is to involve clients, professional bodies add their voice. For instance, the UKCP (2009) Code of Ethics states that:

> 2.6 Psychotherapists are required to clarify with clients the nature, purpose and conditions of any research in which the clients are to be involved and to ensure that informed and verifiable consent is given before commencement.
> 2.7 Publication – Psychotherapists are required to safeguard the welfare and anonymity of clients when any form of publication of clinical material is being considered and to obtain their consent whenever possible.

Three particular challenges arise for practitioners when trying to obtain informed consent. First, as qualitative researchers, we often do not know in advance where the research is going to lead. While a co-researcher may agree to be interviewed, it is difficult to predict what is going to happen in the interview. It is likely that the interview is going to touch on sensitive issues. The individual needs to know this and understand that personal revelations, and the understandings research can bring, can be unsettling. At the same time the researcher needs to ensure that any such risks are minimized. In this context, Grafanaki (1996) has highlighted the significance of *process consent* as a way of ensuring against unanticipated effects. Instead of simply seeking consent at the start of a study, the researcher needs to build in a series of negotiation points. For example, the researcher could plan to review an interview transcript with the participant before finalizing it to make sure the participant agrees with the wording.

Second, the person being invited into the research needs to be given the right to choose whether or not to participate and they need to be given this information in a non-coercive manner. This can pose particular difficulties in practitioner research where clients are being invited to take part in research. Will they feel obliged to say 'yes' to their therapist and do they feel able to refuse? Will they feel used and exploited? If they agree to take part in the research, they also need to be allowed to change their mind and to feel completely free (and within their rights) to withdraw at any time.

Third, it can be tricky for the practitioner researcher to separate their therapist and researcher roles. For example, for research ends we might want to simply hear an individual's story. Wearing our therapist hat, however, we might be tempted to probe in more challenging ways. The co-researcher needs to know what they are signing up for. This process is made even more difficult when you are acting in both capacities when your co-researcher is a client. Here, both the therapeutic and research contracts become muddied and it is possible both will suffer. For these reasons, it is advisable to avoid research involving your own clients. Working with a colleague's clients is a useful way round this problem.

Confidentiality – In therapy practice, we are well used to ensuring any personal information and records which could identify clients are sensitively managed and carefully restricted. The same process needs to apply in the research situation. Where personal details about co-researchers are open to the public, anonymity should be guaranteed. This is reinforced by the Data Protection Act which requires that 'information obtained about a participant during an investigation is confidential unless otherwise agreed *in advance.*' (Banister et al., 1994, p. 155)

It is often hard to guarantee this anonymity in qualitative research. It is quite possible that the level of personal details offered in narratives and case studies will mean individuals can be identified. The anonymity of participants can also be compromised by the fact that others (your colleagues, for example) know that you are doing research with certain people. Extra care needs to be taken here and possible consequences fully discussed. Researchers have even argued the case for including 'misinformation' (such as changing the number, ages and sex of children) and excluding publicly known information which could identify them in order to maintain anonymity (Christians, 2005; Lipson, 1997).

The process of negotiating informed consent and confidentiality provides an essential foundation for recruiting your co-researchers and engaging them in your research.

Recruiting and Engaging Co-researchers

Not every qualitative research project requires co-researchers. You may decide to draw on other sources of data such as documents or personal reflection and experience. But if your project does involve other people – and relational-centred research by its nature does – at some point in your planning you will need to make decisions about whom to recruit and how.

For qualitative researchers in general and relational-centred researchers in particular, more is not necessarily better because when it comes to sample size the aim is not to get a representative range. This is in contrast to quantitative research where samples are supposedly selected in sufficient numbers to act as a microcosm of a particular population (allowing statistical calculations to be made about probabilities that patterns observed in the sample will exist in the wider population). In qualitative research, the aim is rather to obtain either a 'strategic' or an 'illustrative' sample (Mason, 2002)[iii] designed to offer data relevant to the research question. In a strategic sample, a range of participants are usually chosen to provide a broad picture of the phenomenon being studied. A researcher may seek to recruit participants who share an experience (such as having a gambling problem) but who differ on demographic variables such as age, sex and ethnicity. One version of this is *snowball sampling* as described in Example 6.1. Another version is *theoretical sampling* which aims to construct a meaningful sample which builds in certain characteristics or criteria towards developing a theory. An illustrative sample, in contrast, seeks to illuminate or be particularly evocative, and tends to be *idiographic* in approach (that is to say, the focus is on individual experience and there is little attempt to generalize beyond this particular sample). Case study research often comes into this category. Here a co-researcher may be chosen because their story is particularly interesting and/or powerful.

Who should be recruited, and how many? The answers here depend largely on the aims of the research and what is appropriate given the methodology adopted. There are no hard and fast rules for qualitative research. Each researcher needs to justify their strategy in terms of its specific context. Sue Morrow describes her approach of using a strategic sample in her research with sexually abused women in Example 6.2 (*see also Chapter 16: A Journey into Survival and Coping* where the research in discussed in more depth).

Example 6.2   Strategic sampling for research with sexually abused women

Eleven women in a large ... metropolitan area were recruited through therapists who specialized in working with adult survivors of child sexual abuse ... I sent therapists letters explaining the project in detail, along with accompanying letters to be given to appropriate potential participants. Prospective participants called me if they were interested. A particular attraction for participants to participate was a nine-week research support (focus) group that they would attend at no cost.

> Because I was also a therapist working in the community with survivors of sexual abuse, both therapists and potential participants expressed confidence that the group, although not designed to provide therapy, would be a supportive and potentially therapeutic experience …
>
> The women ranged in age from 25 to 72 years. One was African-American; one, West Indian; and the remainder, European-American. Two identified as lesbian … One was mobility impaired, another experienced multiple physical illnesses, … a third was hard of hearing, and the remainder were able bodied. Participants came from a variety of socioeconomic classes, educational backgrounds, and religious … orientations. All had been in formal healing or recovery processes from one meeting to several years …
>
> Prior to the interviews, I attempted to establish an egalitarian relationship and a context of mutuality with each participant. In my recruitment letter, I informed participants I was an abuse survivor as well as a therapist … From the beginning of the interviews, participants revealed that my survivor status as well as my experience as a therapist helped them to feel safe and facilitated their belief that I would understand them. (Morrow, 2006, pp. 151–152)

From Example 6.2, it can be seen that the process of engaging people in the research involves much more than simply deciding sample numbers, characteristics and inclusion/exclusion criteria. Individuals need to feel positively involved, and this means that a relationship has to be developed with them. To some extent the process of negotiating a person's involvement mirrors what happens in therapy. The individual – potentially vulnerable, distressed or damaged – has to take the challenging step of deciding to work with the therapist/researcher. The therapist/researcher, in turn, has to gain the person's trust and inspire confidence; they also need to deserve this trust. Together the therapist/researcher and client/co-researcher need to evolve and agree the terms of the therapy/research contract. The watch words in relational-centred qualitative research are negotiation, mutual agreement and cooperation at every stage (*see Chapter 11: Relational Ethics* which develops these points).

Setting up Appropriate Support Systems

Alongside developing relationships with participants, researchers also need to set up appropriate support systems and build relationships with supervisors, mentors and/or other researchers involved. Practical support systems are also important in relation to IT back-up, library access and peer support.

If you are a student, it is likely that you will be allocated an official supervisor who will help you manage the research process. At the same time you might seek out various advisors to help guide particular aspects of your research. Independent researchers, working alone or in a team of researchers, will similarly want to set up various support networks, be it in the form of peer support or calling on the services of other consultants or mentors. One particular source of support might even be your therapist. It could prove beneficial to bring your personal issues about the research into your therapy (see Chapter 9: *Engaging 'Process'* for an illustration of two-chair work in action). For example, the empty chair technique can be used in evocative ways to represent, say, the research or a co-researcher: *Engaging 'Process'*.

We cannot help being affected ourselves when we engage empathically with others, particularly if a co-researcher shares painful or traumatic experiences. Sometimes we can even become traumatized ourselves as a result of our engagement with survivors and their traumatic stories. Greenall and Marselle (2007) discuss this experience of vicarious traumatization in relation to the research they did with 9/11 survivors:

> Some interviews were so traumatic ... that afterwards we experienced feelings of detachment and estrangement ... [and] dissociation from the normal world. The trauma we were exposed to made us feel different from others; consequently, one of our team withdrew from social interaction and distanced herself from her partner. (Greenall & Marselle, 2007, p. 545)

Gilbert (2006) similarly recognizes the surprising and profound impact her research (on the effects of a death of a child on Social Services personnel) had on her personally. Despite never having met the child herself, she was overwhelmed with emotions. She describes feeling like she was the 'conduit for all the disowned emotional material floating in the organisation' (2006, p. 7):

> I felt overwhelmed, despondent, despairing, deflated, tearful, agitated and immensely moved. Several times I felt mute ... I was also suffused by intensely vivid images of C, a large head of blond hair, both very alive and playful, and also lying dead in the mortuary looking very little and alone. (2006, p. 7)

How can we cope with such cases of vicarious traumatization? Saakvitne and Pearlman (1996) outline three coping mechanisms: awareness, balance and connection. Awareness involves recognizing signs of vicarious traumatization and employing self-nurturing activities. Balance highlights the need to maintain healthy work/life boundaries. Connection with others is then used as an antidote to the isolation and alienation experienced. Both formal supervision (with supervisor or peers) and therapy can be a helpful support to facilitate this awareness, balance and connection. (*See Chapter 9: Engaging 'Process'* which gives an example of using a supervisor, with their outsider perspective, to provide support and challenge, nudging the researcher towards deeper levels of awareness.)

It is not uncommon these days for research to involve different supervisors, for example, if you are doing research with a client you might have a research supervisor and therapy supervisor. As another example, PhD research may involve two co-supervisors: one perhaps an expert in the methodology or the research area and the other providing institutional or pastoral support. For these arrangements to work, it is essential that roles are clarified and that there are clear lines of communication between the parties involved. Some boundary setting is usually advisable to decide what is appropriate for each of the supervisors to deal with and how. Equally, if you are taking your research into therapy, it would probably be most helpful if your therapist concentrated on how the research is impacting on you personally, and what is figural for you in the field, rather than getting caught up in the research itself.

If you are taking your research process to therapy, you might usefully ask yourself how you are experiencing the meeting with your co-researcher(s). Are you finding the meeting engaging and are you managing to explore in depth? If not, then what or who is getting in the way? You might consider what unconscious forces may be operating and if the poverty of contact is down to your failure of empathy or the co-researcher not fully engaging. You could also consider what more you could do. Might you be willing, for instance, to experiment with self-disclosure and risk what may appear the 'unspeakable' in the grip of projective identification? (Evans, 2007).

Principles of good supervision apply equally across therapy and research. In therapy, supervision is seen as a learning process in which a therapist engages with a more experienced practitioner as part of ongoing professional development. This process, in turn, promotes and safeguards clients' well-being. Similarly, in the research context good supervision enhances the researcher's learning and ensures ethical research. In both contexts, supervision provides a:

> Reflective space where the supervisee can unfold his [sic] own narrative of his Work, … reflect on this story with the supervisor as witness and arrive at possible new meanings and insights. (Gilbert & Evans, 2000, p. 100)

Your experience of receiving/giving therapy supervision will stand you in good stead and help you make the most of your research supervision.

The qualitative research journey, like the therapy journey, is always challenging. While it can be stimulating and enjoyable, it can also prove painful, stressful and, at times, tedious. Ensuring that you have enough support – whether educational, practical or emotional – is essential.

Reflections

This chapter has discussed a range of decisions and issues which need to be engaged when planning research. Decisions taken, from clarifying the research question to determining methods and procedures, should hang together coherently. Some processes involved when setting up research (such as engaging co-researchers and enabling informed consent) are invariably challenging and require careful thought.

While the planning process needs to be engaged systematically and thoughtfully, it cannot be approached with a recipe-following attitude. Every piece of research – like every therapy relationship – is unique and involves different demands which need to be negotiated at different stages of the research. Relational tensions can resonate throughout the research and may need creative handling while ethical dilemmas are not something which can be packaged and tidied neatly away at the planning stage.

We would argue that with careful, reflective planning at the beginning of research, you stand a better chance of producing sound results. But your plans, just like your research expectations, should remain modest. Research findings can only ever be partial and provisional. They may intrigue, resonate and surprise but they are not going to 'change the world'. Instead of setting out to discover 'new territory', plan to just 'go exploring' and see what emerges. Instead of setting up the research with the aim of scaling Himalayan peaks or unveiling new continents, trust that through its respect for individual human stories and experience your research will allow something of real value to emerge.

Notes

[i] Within the UK, the Research Governance Framework (Department of Health, 2001) has attempted to bring together various statutes and guidelines for research. A key component of this system is the development of Local Research Ethics Committees

(LRECs), originally set up in 1968. These committees (comprising relevant people with a broad range of experience and expertise) were set up to review research proposals to ensure ethical research practice. Currently, NHS bodies cannot permit research to go ahead within their organizations unless projects have received formal approval from a local research ethics committee (Ballinger & Wiles, 2006).

[ii] If you are a student, do check whether or not your own training organization has published a Code of Ethics.

[iii] Qualitative researchers might also occasionally opt for a 'convenience' (sometimes called 'opportunistic') sample. However, care still needs to be taken to think through the purpose and desirability of recruiting those particular participants.

Chapter 7

The Research Encounter: Co-creating your Data

When two people meet a new reality emerges. (Symington, 1986, p. 30)

We have titled this chapter 'the research encounter' to capture something of the spirit of relational research where data is seen to blossom out of the research context. In traditional qualitative research approaches, the onus is on the participant to produce what is to be eventually analysed. Relational-centred research is different. As researchers, we explicitly recognize we are part of the world being studied. Any 'data' comes from participant and researcher in relationship with one another. Each such relationship is seen as unique and coloured by its own dynamics. The research relationship is therefore viewed as a dialogical process to which both researcher and co-researcher contribute.

What we can know about another emerges out of the specific embodied, intersubjective space between researcher and co-researcher and within the broader research context. (We further expand and develop this in *Chapter 8: Embracing Relational Research*; see also Evans, 2007; Finlay, 2009 *Forthcoming*). In this *between*, the embodied presences of researcher and co-researcher(s) co-mingle and interact in dialogue. Just as it does in psychotherapy, the relationship is central and provides the all-important context through which co-researchers share aspects of themselves in

Relational-centred Research for Psychotherapists: Exploring Meanings and Experience
Edited by Linda Finlay and Ken Evans

interaction with the researcher. As we see it, the process of gathering data is primarily a co-creation of researcher and co-researcher.

In the first section of this chapter we offer an extended example of an actual dialogue between a researcher and co-researcher. This example is not meant to be a 'model' for how to interview. Rather, it serves as an illustration – a means to sensitize you to underlying processes and dynamics. The second section explores the importance of researchers' embodied presence in terms of two key processes involved in data collection: empathy and openness. The final section focuses on 'how to do' data collection. Pointers are offered about managing two of the most commonly used data collection methods: interview and participant-observation.[i] However, the special nature of relational research means there are no set recipes to follow or procedures ready for easy application.

An 'Encounter' ...

The example below comes from some narrative case study research Linda undertook on the lived experience of having mental health problems. (See Finlay, 2004; also see the section on narrative analysis in *Chapter 10: Analysis of Data* which presents a narrative created out of this dialogue.) Kenny was her co-researcher and agreed to be interviewed about his experience. He was a middle-aged man suffering from anxiety and depression – something he had struggled with for over three years. He told his story over a cup of coffee in Linda's kitchen. They spoke for approximately an hour and a half.

In the Example 7.1 extract below, Kenny tries to describe what it was like living through the early days of his breakdown. Linda, in turn, tries to reflect back his experience. Linda started off the interview by asking Kenny if he could say what it was like to have mental health problems. Beyond that question, Linda had not pre-prepared any further questions. The dialogue that emerged was co-constituted; it developed and took shape in that specific context.

The extract draws upon two sources: the actual interview transcript[ii] *and* the reflexive notes (in italics) Linda wrote after the interview. In relational research, reflexive analysis occurs both during the encounter and after. This process can itself be used as 'data'. We see this in action through Linda's reflexive notes. Here she retrospectively monitored what was said in the interview and highlighted how she explicitly used her own bodily and emotional responses as cues. As you read, note how her reflexivity sheds light on Kenny's experience and so forms part of what can be seen as 'data'.

Example 7.1   An interview dialogue

Linda: When did you first realize something was wrong and you were having difficulties?

Kenny: It started about three years ago. It had been building up in me although I didn't fully realize it.

Linda: What was building up in you – your feelings?

Kenny: The worst thing was the fear factor. Literally being terrified to go out. I virtually locked myself in the bedroom and didn't come out for days, until I went to the doctor. That was quite a daunting experience in itself 'cos I was absolutely terrified. I was jumping at me own shadow. I was frightened to be in a room with people. I was frightened of people – which is amazing because most of me adult working life was with people, I'd worked with people.

Linda: What work did you do?

I recall feeling irritated with myself for my question as it changed the tone. Kenny was doing a nice job of talking about his emotions and then I jumped in with this directive factual question! Yet I also was aware of my impulse to contain Kenny's disclosures. He had jumped so quickly into intense emotional disclosure that I felt somehow concerned to provide some boundaries. In retrospect I suppose I may have been gently reminding him that this was research and not therapy.

Kenny: [nods] In the hotel and retail trade all me life. I was a hotel manager in my last job.

Linda: So lots of working with people. It must have been weird for you to not feel able to be with people(?)

Kenny: It was just shaking, panic attacks. Looking back on it, I think it actually started years before at the hotel … where I walked out. I had had enough. There was a lot of extra pressure. I found it hard to cope. I moved, and never had the confidence, never happy, never content, it was always a struggle.

Linda: So, as you say, it was possibly building up in you for a lot of years?

Kenny: I was just too busy working and coping and pushing the stress away. It was not in me to say 'I can't cope'.

Linda: Was it like you were the man in the family; the breadwinner, so you … [Kenny interrupts]

I'm not surprised Kenny interrupted here. Now reading this transcript at a distance I can see my comment about him being the breadwinner seems to jar. Yet at the time I had this intuition that his masculinity was at stake. I felt 'sure' that this working-class man had not grown up displaying and enacting his feelings so evidently. I somehow sense voices in his head telling him to 'be a man'. And if that was so, his pain and sense of failure would be all the stronger. It is perhaps relevant that Kenny chose not to follow me down the 'man' theme but with his next statement he does acknowledge the pressures on him.

Kenny: There was no question of me not coping. The realization that something was wrong was I was waking up in the morning, praying that there was something wrong with us – anything, just so I didn't have to go to work. I carried on and then suddenly one morning I said 'That's it, I've had enough'. I walked out and never went back. I locked myself in the bedroom. It took weeks and weeks before I would go out. I would read, submerge myself in books, escaped. I wasn't interested in anything. I just wanted to be in my bed. I suppose in some ways it was my little nest. I was safe in my bedroom and nobody could get to us. And I wasn't bothered about anything. The worst part of it was if I was thinking. It seemed to get worse. What's happening? What am I doing? I was scaring myself. It was a dreadful experience that I wouldn't wish on anyone. To be scared is one of the worst things. It is a method of torture.

Linda: It sounds incredibly scary – all the more so because it's being like, that was so different from the way you normally are(?)

Kenny: Yeah, I definitely wasn't me-self.

Linda: Was that the scariest bit, facing someone, facing yourself as someone you didn't know?

Kenny: I was just very fearful – I kept jumping at me own shadow. I wondered 'what am I doing?' But I wouldn't say it was self-inflicted 'cos had I known what was happening I would have done something about it.

Linda: Yes, I guess you wouldn't have got ill in the first place. So what did you do after that initial period?

Kenny: From there we went to see the doctor. He agreed that I should have two weeks off and try to relax. I think in some ways it was a huge relief that I didn't have to go back to work. Fortunately the doctor I had was sympathetic. The state I was in – I was shaking, it was visible, the terror in my eyes. I just wanted to get out of the doctor's surgery. I remember trying to relax a bit then, thinking I've got two weeks, I can sort myself out. But it was never going to happen. I had this desperation of what was happening.

As I was listening to Kenny speak, I suddenly realized that I was reacting quite strongly to him and became aware of my own bodily responses. I remember noticing how my arms were folded tightly across my stomach. I was protecting myself, but also 'holding myself in' and somehow 'holding myself together'. I then saw that Kenny had adopted the same posture as he recalled his trauma (had I mirrored his posture or had he followed mine?).

[The word 're-member' is significant here. Remembering is not just a cognitive function: it's about reiterating responses in the body: we re-member.]

With us both holding ourselves, it seemed an important moment, one that called for me to tune into what we were both doing. I was a little surprised at the sensations and my reactions. Usually, I would interpret this non-verbal gesture as representing a symbolic wish to protect oneself from others or a way of giving oneself some nurturing/comforting. But here in this situation I was somehow sensing an additional, even different, interpretation. I checked it out with Kenny:

Linda: As you're speaking and remembering, Kenny, I can see you're holding yourself tightly. And I'm doing the same as I'm listening to you. [shared laughter] It's like you're trying to hold yourself together. Is it like, kinda to stop yourself falling apart. Is that what it was like for you?

Kenny: Yeah, I would go off to bed and just hold myself like that. Sometimes it seemed like for hours. One minute I was alright and the next I could just go into a rage about the simplest thing. And again, it could be a trivial thing and I'd lose it completely. Again I sought the sanctuary of the bedroom. I knew there I wouldn't hurt people. The worse thing was because I was feeling guilty I was getting more angry about it.

I felt his confusion: his rage against himself and this crazy 'alien' it seemed he had become. I felt his fear of losing himself, of losing it in general, and his concern that he might hurt others in his anger and craziness. I felt his guilt about this anger and understood why he might want to lock himself away. It was the only place he could be safe. Perhaps it was the only place he could recover himself to reassure himself that he was still there.

Later, when I was analysing the transcript, I replayed this dialogue over and over as a way of helping me to focus on what it would be like to be Kenny. I adopted that holding posture and 're-membered' the (my? his?) emotions. Again I got that strong sense of 'holding together' that which was falling apart and holding in the craziness and rage so they didn't break out and destroy others.

Linda: From the way you're describing it I can hear how you were just a bundle of different emotions: fear, anger, desperation, frustration, distress. It must have just felt overwhelming(?)

> **Kenny:** Yeah, totally. And then after two weeks, I went back to the doctor and he recommended I see a counsellor. But I didn't think it would help at this stage. It was two months later that he insisted.
>
> **Linda:** So you went?
>
> **Kenny:** I did go and see this young lady at first. She was very good. She listened.
>
> **Linda:** That was a comfort?
>
> **Kenny:** She was nice and got me to start talking.
>
> **Linda:** Instead of pushing things down and away?
>
> **Kenny:** Yeah. Saying things out loud is different. I thought suicide might be a way out but I never seriously contemplated it. For all that you were really down there was still something at the back of my mind, clinging on by the fingertips, it was still there – 'We can go on from this' …

Processes Involved in Co-creating Data

The Kenny–Linda example above illustrates the process of co-creating data in dialogue. Kenny shares his personal experience in response to Linda's prompts, questions and reflecting back. In turn, Linda responds intuitively, if clumsily, in line with her own subjective history and experience. Another researcher would undoubtedly have gone in different directions, leading to different data and potentially different findings.

It seems that Kenny felt comfortable enough to share his personal experiences with Linda. In fact, he had a specific purpose for the story he was telling: he wanted Linda not only to understand the nightmare of his experience but also to 'spread the word' that it is possible to claw one's way back to mental health. He was giving, at some level, a 'performance'.

> Individuals negotiate how they want to be known in the stories they develop collaboratively with their audiences … Social actors shape their lives retrospectively for particular audiences. (Reissman, 2003, p. 8)

Here Reissman is drawing on Goffman's (1959) drama metaphor: the idea that people 'perform' desirable selves to preserve 'face' in difficult situations (such as when giving an account of the traumatic nature of mental health problems). If the world is like a stage, our narratives are part of the show (Finlay, 2004).

The dialogue set out in the Kenny–Linda extract probably parallels inter-actions you have had with clients in therapy sessions. You may well have asked your client to 'tell their story', then reflected back to check your understanding or asked questions to get them to expand on certain points, as Linda did. This demonstrates that you already have many of the skills and the experience needed to handle such research encounters. Even if you are embarking on research for the very first time, remember that your ability to engage with others means you are far from being a novice. Try to avoid falling into the trap of playacting the role of researcher – perhaps by taking a formal, more distanced approach replete with pre-prepared research-type questions. We believe the most productive research encoun-ter is one where the researcher seeks to relate to the co-researcher in a natural, empathic and genuinely human way.[iii]

In fact, the most challenging thing for you will be to ensure you stay focused on the research project and hold back from making therapeutic interpretations or interventions. This is easier said than done. Not only will your own impulses get in the way but also your co-researcher, knowing you are a psychotherapist, may attempt to elicit that therapist self. Remember that your contract with your co-researcher is to do research, not therapy. Use your research aims to guide your focus and the context to define the lines of enquiry you want to pursue.

In the example above, the focus of the dialogue was on Kenny's mental health struggles. By mutual consent, neither Kenny nor Linda talked about other personal issues such as Kenny's relationship with his wife and family. His domestic circumstances could well have been a source of tension and problems but Linda respected these boundaries. Kenny had not consented to talk at that level and Linda tried to stay with what Kenny was bringing to their encounter. Linda wanted to show her empathy while also trying to make it easy and comfortable for him to tell his story.

Empathic Openness

As we have noted above, you have a number of advantages as a psycho-therapist when it comes to collecting data. You already have the necessary skills to interview and observe. You know how to use yourself in relation to others, how to enable the other to feel safe and to speak, and how to share your warmth and empathy. You have the ability to be a presence which is authentic, energized, active and direct. You already know how to be self-aware and how to respond intuitively in the emerging relational context. You realize the importance of being patient when another tells their halting story and you can tolerate that initial sense of chaos without jumping in to clarify too soon. These are the qualities to draw upon (and perhaps nurture further) in research. Just as therapists use themselves as tools in therapy, researchers use themselves as research tools in relational research.

Linda's reflections offered in the excerpt above give us a glimpse into a researcher's embodied, empathic use of self as a research tool. Her reflexive voice shows something of the complex, subtle and delicate processes involved in a research encounter.

Two particular processes – empathy and openness – characterize the qualities researchers need to successfully engage relational-centred research. We elaborate on these qualities in *Chapter 8* when discussing the concepts of presence, inclusion and intersubjectivity.

Empathy as Felt Embodied Experience

Perhaps the most important ingredient in successfully engaging co-researchers in data collection is the researcher's embodied empathic presence. Here the researcher is 'present as a person meeting the person of the other' (Yontef, 1993, p. 24). This awareness of meeting the Other in the present moment lies at the heart of any authentic encounter – be it therapy or research. It is this authentic meeting which provides the Other with an experience of being seen and acknowledged (Evans & Gilbert, 2005).

As a therapist, you will not need reminding of the value of empathy and creating for the client a sense of being understood is core to relational therapy.[iv] Theorists such as Rogers (1951), from the humanistic tradition, and Kohut (1984), from the tradition of self-psychology, underline how essential it is for the therapist to be able to enter into the subjective world of the Other in a concerned and empathic manner (Evans & Gilbert, 2005). You also already know, from your work as a therapist, that empathy is a relational process, unique to each encounter. Empathy cannot be reduced to mere technique (Myers, 2000).

The value of empathy applies equally to research where it can be understood as a process of seeking ways to allow co-researchers to present themselves to and through oneself as the researcher. It involves an 'intersubjective process of imaginal self-transposition and mutual identification where self-understanding and Other-understanding is intertwined' (Finlay, 2005, p. 290). Here, empathy is not just about emotional knowing; it is a *felt, embodied*, intersubjective experience. We therefore need to talk about 'a research process which involves engaging, reflexively, with the participant's lived body, our own body and our embodied intersubjective relation-ship with the participant' (Finlay, 2005, p. 272).

By her manner (verbal and non-verbal), Linda helped Kenny to feel safe enough to share. She followed her intuitions and drew on her bodily felt sense in the 'here and now' to possibly shed light on Kenny's 'then and there'. She also attempted to empathically reflect back. She played a part in negotiating the intimacy-distance of the moment – at times, encouraging more disclosure; at other times gently protecting Kenny and containing his disclosures.

As researchers we need to be aware that co-researchers can become stressed and distressed when being observed or talking about difficult sub-jects and their personal experience. Compassionate, empathic care is needed to support them positively. While unduly stressing/distressing a co-researcher is to be avoided, sometimes a level of upset may be unavoid-able. However, if such a situation arises it is important to check that the co-researcher is happy to continue. This is one area in which research differs from therapy. It is not within the researcher's remit to push or chal-lenge as a therapist might.

Openness as Unknowing

In relational research, our aim is to discover some new awareness, to find out more about another individual or a specific phenomenon. We hope to be touched, surprised and to have our horizons expanded. This can only happen if we are *open to* our co-researchers and if we start from a relatively 'unknowing' position characterized by curiosity and compassion. We need to be prepared to allow things to spontaneously emerge in the inter-subjective space between researcher and co-researcher and to have faith that it will. If we are closed to new possibilities and understandings then we will only be able confirm what we knew already and the value of any research outcomes will be diminished.

Openness is emphasized in phenomenological research through the practice of 'bracketing': the attempt to suspend presuppositions. This process is often misunderstood as an attempt to be more objective. In fact, what is being called for is a special, attentive attitude of openness and receptivity. Max van Manen (2002) describes this process as 'the unwilled willingness to meet what is utterly strange in what is most familiar'. The aim is 'to see through fresh eyes, to understand through embracing new modes of being' (Finlay, 2008, p. 29). With this openness comes fleeting moments of awe and wonder:

> When we are struck with wonder, our minds are suddenly cleared of the clutter of everyday concerns that otherwise constantly occupy us. We are confronted by the thing, the phenomenon in all of its strangeness and uniqueness. The wonder of that thing takes us in, and renders us momentarily speechless. (van Manen, 2002)

Such moments of openness and wonder can be powerfully transformational, if elusive (Finlay, 2008).

Two Methods of Data Collection

Reading the previous sections you will appreciate that 'data collection' in relational research is more about relational *doing* and *being* and less about carrying out protocols, procedures and techniques. It is about letting go of fixed agendas; being receptive to whatever is emerging in the field and responsive to the Other.

However, it is still useful to consider some practical issues arising from the different procedures available to us. Two of the methods of data collection most commonly used in relational research are briefly explored here: *interview* and *participant observation*. (Of course there are other ways to collect data, such as through groupwork, creative media or documentary sources, but space does not permit a broader exploration here.)

Interview

> A qualitative research interview is not a situation where a person is passively reporting facts or opinions, but is better seen as an 'encounter' where the person is actively engaged in exploring the meaning of events or experiences that have been significant for them. (McLeod, 1999, p. 125)

Interviews can either be unstructured conversations (as in the Kenny–Linda example) or semi-structured with questions loosely prepared in advance to act as an aide-memoire (as in Example 6.1 in the previous chapter). Interviews can take the form of informal conversations or involve a more formal approach. Usually a combination of guiding questions, reflecting back, and prompts are used. Haumann's approach to researching psychotherapists' experience of having personal therapy, for instance, was based around asking a few trigger questions like:

Could you describe as fully as possible how your own therapy or analysis influences your work as a therapist? Please try to describe this in terms of your own experience rather than just giving a theoretical explanation of what happens. (Haumann, 2005, p. 23)

She then asked further questions about the participant's own therapy experiences offering prompts or probes if she sensed the participant needed encouragement to expand.

Whatever the approach, it is often more productive when doing relational research to allow the interview to progress with some fluidity. As the researcher, for example, you might suddenly choose to probe an area based on your intuition. Alternatively, your co-researcher could take the interview in unexpected directions. Providing you stay reasonably focused on the research topic being investigated these diversions should probably be followed. Follow your intuition and allow yourself to yield to whatever comes up in the moment (providing the co-researcher is also content to proceed).

As a psychotherapist you have the advantage of being trained to listen and help others express themselves. The downside of this is that you may too easily lead a person to emotional disclosures beyond the terms of the research. Alternatively, you may be so worried about 'not being a therapist' that you become curiously flat, stiff, distanced or disengaged (McLeod, 1999). For this reason, it might help you to conduct one or two pilot interviews before you begin your actual project.

Here are 10 tips we would offer to you for carrying out research interviews if you are inexperienced in this area:

1) Do not underestimate the importance of preparing your co-researcher in advance. While you do not want your co-researchers to be overly prepared (in the sense of giving you previously rehearsed answers), they need to know what is going to be expected of them. Before the interview you need to explain to them: what you need them to focus on; the likely length of the interview; and the extent to which they can refuse to answer particular questions. They also need to be clear about the degree of confidentiality you are promising them. All this should form part of the process of gaining informed consent – a process which should be ongoing throughout the research.

2) Prepare your environment carefully, thinking in terms of your co-researcher's comfort, ease and emotional safety. Often co-researchers will prefer to be interviewed in their own home or work space. If so, you may need to make extra arrangements to ensure interruptions are kept to a minimum.

3) Think about how you are going to record the interview. Increasingly, digital equipment is popular and less unwieldy and unobtrusive than traditional tape or video recorders. While being recorded can be initially inhibiting, most people relax after a few minutes. It is worth checking your equipment is working throughout the interview. Most researchers have at least one story to tell about equipment malfunctioning, causing much disappointment and costs in terms of wasted time and energy!

4) If you are going to take notes, think about how to put this idea to your co-researcher. Some people feel that you are taking them more seriously when you write notes; others can react negatively – perhaps because note-taking can seem like a distancing move. If you do not want to interfere with your co-researcher's flow by taking notes throughout the interview, it is still helpful to have a pad of paper handy to jot down stray thoughts or questions to remember later.

5) Allow a few minutes at the beginning of the interview for your co-researcher to settle down. It can help to remind the person about the topic being discussed and the terms of your agreement (for example, saying that it is in their control what they say and how deeply they go).

6) Asking open, non-directive, singular questions usually bears more fruit than asking ones that are closed, directive or multiple. Sometimes the co-researcher just needs a place to start. You might, for instance, ask them to describe in quite concrete terms a typical day or an actual situation in which they had experienced the topic being investigated. Returning the co-researcher to actual lived events may also steer them away from any tendency to talk in overly intellectual or abstract terms.

7) Try to listen carefully. It is all too easy when interviewing to lose focus by thinking about what you are going to ask or say next. As you will know from your therapy experience, the skill of listening actively involves tuning into – really trying to hear with both curiosity and compassion – what the person is saying. It requires you to have a genuine interest in what your participant has to say. It is also about giving the person time to try and find a way to express what they want to say. As a therapist, you will have more of these enabling skills/qualities than most researchers, so that should give you some confidence.

8) Be mindful of what a privilege it is to have someone share personal experiences with you. You have an ethical responsibility to respect their privacy and dignity and ensure they are not harmed in any way by your interview. For this reason you will need to monitor and

take cognizance of the impact the interview may be having on your co-researcher.

9) Give some time at the end of the interview to debrief your co-researcher. They may value the opportunity to reflect on what doing the interview was like. They may also want to add points they may have missed, or emphasize elements they feel they had not stressed enough. This opportunity for feedback further reinforces the all important aspects of mutuality and co-creation.

10) Try to leave your co-researcher the richer for the experience. As McLeod (1999, p. 125) notes, following Kvale (1996): 'One of the hallmarks of a good qualitative interview lies in the extent to which the informant learns or gains from the experience.'

If you are an experienced therapist, you are likely to feel quite comfortable with these 10 tips for carrying out research interviews. You probably routinely navigate these issues in your practice. The bigger uncertainty or dilemma you will have is to know where the differences lies between the kind of dialogical encounter you would have in therapy practice in contrast with that in research. The lines here are blurry. Much depends on the type and number of research interviews involved (influencing the depth of your research relationship) and your own 'style' (*see* the discussion on researcher presence in *Chapter 8: Embracing Relational Research*).

In a one-off research interview, for example, you are less likely to probe and challenge and to engage with co-researchers' unconscious issues, to any significant extent. (In the Linda–Kenny example above, Linda had a strong intuition that Kenny's masculinity was at stake. While it is likely that Kenny's issues around masculinity play out in his marital relationship, Linda respected Kenny's boundaries and detoured around these personal questions.) However, where deeper research relationships are involved, the researcher's task may well be akin to that of the therapist's in terms of aiming to facilitate awareness – of both conscious and unconscious aspects – and thus explore shifts in understanding and meaning that can emerge from increased awareness (*Chapter 9: Engaging 'Process'* offers some examples of this in action).

If a co-researcher, in coming into deep relational contact with a researcher, becomes aware of previously unconscious material, some anxiety is likely to be generated. With this anxiety comes a natural self-protective desire to defend against new and potentially disturbing awareness. Some 'resistance' may ensue (Perls, Hefferline & Goodman, 1951/1994).[v] This process of resistance is usually out of awareness and, if challenged, creates ambivalence such as feeling confused and torn between conflicting desires to hide or to let repressed material into consciousness. This ambivalence about whether to maintain the status quo versus thinking/behaving differently affects the relationship with oneself (for example, denial and depression shown possibly as unexpressed anger) and with others (for example, gaps in memory or displacement of anger onto someone else).

In some research encounters, then, it may be important for the researcher to sense when a co-researcher is resisting going deeper into some aspect being explored. Here the researcher needs to reflect on *if* and *how* s/he might nudge the co-researcher to further exploration (as opposed to being intimidated by the resistance and backing off prematurely – possibly due to the researcher's own issues). One way for you to do this, as a researcher, for example, might be to model the process by disclosing your own uncertainty about pushing further.

There is a critical balance or decision to be made about respecting the co-researcher's direction and boundaries. If you, as the researcher, sense your co-researcher might go deeper (and has the capacity to do so) then you need to find a way to support and challenge by gently pulling (not pushing or forcing) the co-researcher outside his or her comfort zone and by backing off if it seems too much. Rescuing the co-researcher by stepping back from doing any challenging may sometimes show a failure of 'presence' (*see Chapter 8: Embracing Relational Research*) and may actually infantilize the co researcher.[vi]

Participant observation

Participant observation involves a researcher going into the 'field' and doing naturalistic research in situ. For example, a researcher might go into a school and observe a personal development group in action. If you were to do such research, you would need to determine beforehand the extent to which you would participate in the group's activities. For example, you might decide to join in as the teacher's assistant. Alternatively you might opt to observe from a distance. In broad terms you are choosing between taking an insider versus an outsider perspective.

Often this decision between participation and observation depends more on the practicalities of the context. It can prove especially challenging in covert field studies where you may have to put yourself in potentially risky situations. For example, one researcher, who wishes to remain anonymous, was studying drug use in the British clubbing culture and admits taking drugs in order to be accepted by the group he was researching. While most qualitative research does not involve such extreme decisions, the degree and manner of participation/observation always involves choices with practical and ethical implications attached.

Participant-observation also poses three other challenges: how to negotiate access to the research field; how to comply with the need to observe naturalistically; and how to approach the difficult task of managing one's emotions in the field.

Negotiating access to the research 'field' can prove problematic as often there are 'gate-keepers' (i.e. people who control access to resources and participants) who need to be satisfied. Studies attempting to explore service users' views and experiences of their treatment, for example, could be derailed by a gatekeeper manager reluctant to have user 'complaints' researched by a stranger. To give another example, Abrahams (2007) discusses the challenges of gaining access to women's groups working in the field of domestic violence. Some of these women had experience of being insensitively used and exploited by researchers in the past and Abrahams needed to do a fair amount of damage reparation before she could engage in her own research.

Once the researcher has gained access, the next question is how to observe without unduly changing what is being studied. Care needs to be taken to minimize any intrusions and ensure that observations are naturalistic. For instance, the use of video is gaining popularity as a means of recording details of interactions such as during a counselling session. Here, having the camera in place before recording starts can help co-researchers get used to its presence.

Example 7.2 below illustrates the kinds of pragmatic considerations which arise in participant observation research. As part of her research project exploring the life world of the occupational therapist, Linda shadowed and observed three occupational therapists over the course of their working weeks in a hospital (Finlay, 1998). She took detailed notes, including both observations and reflections. Linda then developed her observations into a preliminary analysis of the therapist's lifeworld, while her reflections entered her reflexive analysis.

Example 7.2   Example of a participant observation

Negotiating access – I started the participant observations by gaining official permission to observe the therapists concerned … My public role as far as all the managers and therapists were concerned was to act as an 'observation student'. This ensured that access to all areas was relatively easy as the system was accustomed to accommodating student observers. Also, my professional qualification acted like a passport; I was accepted as a professional who could be trusted to behave appropriately and keep information confidential …

Once inside the field, my professional qualification also eased my passage. I was, by definition, a stranger, an outsider. Yet in a subtle way I was accepted as an insider by the occupational therapists concerned and their occupational therapy colleagues (who knew me or knew of me). I, too, felt on familiar ground … The health care issues, the jargon, the practical problems, the home visits, the 'caring' staff interactions and tensions within the wider team, were all familiar to me. Despite this commonality of experience, I was also in alien territory. The focus on diagnosis, physical problems and bits of equipment was all unfamiliar …

The participant observer role – I adopted different sorts of observer roles (Junker, 1960) depending on the context. When in the presence of patients/clients (for example, on the wards or in their homes), I tended to adopt a 'complete observer' role where I was not expected to participate actively. Sometimes the patients/clients would include me non-verbally through their eye contact, and although I would respond warmly when required, I tried to remain unobtrusive (for instance, placing my chair a little to one side).

With staff, I was accepted as a 'participating student/colleague'. This role allowed me to ask questions, write notes and check out impressions generally. In formal meetings I did not wish to interfere with their normal working so I remained quiet. I believe the non-occupational therapy staff accepted me as a ('complete participant') student – a perception which afforded me legitimacy and a right to be there but limited perceptions of my status: I was judged to be not worth talking to.

Data collection – My means of data collection included unstructured observation, reflection and note writing. In an effort to appear relatively unobtrusive when the therapists worked with patients/clients, I took my lead from the therapists. For example, while observing Jane, I made it a point when we visited clients' homes never to accept a coffee until she did first. I only wrote notes when she did; I spoke only when asked a direct question; I would wait for her to choose her seat and sit down with the client before I sat. With all these behaviours I aimed to have minimum impact on Jane, her work and her clients, I wanted to emphasize her relationship with the clients and maintain my marginal observer status.

Being relatively unobtrusive allowed me plenty of space to sit back, observe and reflect. My observations were unstructured in that I was alert to picking up a range of verbal and non-verbal behaviours. However, I was particularly interested to observe any personal reactions and relationship dynamics between the therapist and his or her patients/clients.

Once back in the office ... , I would 'interview' (informally) the therapists about their clinical reasoning and responses. In this way I was able to compare my observations and reflections with theirs.

As all three therapists had to write notes themselves fairly frequently, I had plenty of opportunity to write and reflect throughout the day. On returning home after each day, I made notes and expanded them. I then audio-taped my observations and reflections, including my personal responses and some analysis, transcribing the tape in my own time. This daily exercise was time consuming, absorbing around two hours a day, but it enabled me to capture considerable depth of data. (Finlay, 1998, pp. 124–127)

Example 7.3   Example of reflexive analysis during participant observation

One aspect of working in the hospital context that Linda found disturbing was that she was required to wear a uniform. Glancing in the mirror on her first morning of work she caught sight of herself in a uniform and panicked. She was aware of her resistance here and used her reflexive notes to shed light on how her participants felt wearing their uniforms every day. An extract is offered here:

1) The uniform is quite nice in that it offers me a sense of being an insider; being accepted and legitimate somehow. This particularly hit me when a doctor entered into a fairly deep personal/professional conversation with Peter and had automatically included me. Clearly the uniform acts as a sort of passport – and I quite like the inclusion.

2) The negative side of my experience ... is that I dislike the restraints, the anonymity, the lack of individuality. I find myself wanting to have the staff I am working with (particularly Peter) see me in my usual wear and thus how I 'normally' am ...

3) Then there is the feeling of power which I find myself feeling both negative and positive about. People are passing me in the corridor and giving me what I interpret as 'respectful nods'. This uniform clearly has some power and I am feeling it too. I have always known I feel negative about this kind of thing – but my positive response to the feeling of power comes as a horrible surprise ...

4) I notice in the changing rooms at the beginning and end of each day how naturally staff wear and take on/off their uniforms in front

> of each other. It is part of the routine. It has a practical purpose. But I also sense that they too like the identity/status/belonging that it affords them. Their uniforms are always so clean, white and crisply pressed. It is part of how they 'present' themselves.
>
> (Finlay,1998, p. 236)

Perhaps the most challenging aspect of participant observation is finding a way to manage your emotions and allegiances which inevitably build up as you become immersed in the field. For example, Scott (Johnson & Scott, 1997) carried out some research on child protection practices by intensively shadowing 10 families with 17 allegedly abused children as they moved through the child protection system. She also interviewed and observed the professionals involved. She was shocked by the unexpectedly strong emotional reactions the experience triggered in her. As a social worker with extensive clinical experience in the child protection field, she had not anticipated the intensity of her feelings. It seems the most anguish was caused, not by the abuse, but seeing children and parents suffering at the hands of professionals she herself had taught. She describes how the suffering of the parents and children seemed more visible to her as a researcher than when she was a more desensitized practitioner exposed daily to such distress:

> I felt a sense of helplessness ... which I had no way of alleviating and an unease with the voyeurism inherent in the act of observation ... Most painful ... of all was listening to the intense anguish of a father who had been falsely suspected of sexually abusing his four year old daughter. (Johnson & Scott, 1997, pp. 35–366)

Reflections

In the field of relational research, data emerges from the relationship between researcher and co-researcher rather than through the pursuit of protocols and procedures. The process of gathering qualitative data is much more of an art or craft than science. Potter (1997, pp. 147–148) emphasizes this point that it is not like following a recipe when tongue in cheek he explains that doing discourse analysis is 'more like bike riding or sexing a chicken than following the recipe for a mild ... rogan josh'! As Potter acknowledges, this makes it hard to describe and learn.

We (Linda and Ken) both celebrate the emphasis on human qualities and relational values. However, it is not always easy when gathering data to be a presence that is empathic, intuitive, compassionate, curious and non-judgmental. It is always testing to leave ourselves in an unknowing position and open to being touched by the Other. The researcher needs a strong element of faith, a basic optimism that something of value will emerge in the course of an encounter. The researcher also needs some patience to stay with any initial chaos or vagueness when 'answers' to research questions are distant and elusive.

When you set out on your research journey, we can only recommend that you try to enjoy the uncertainty and unpredictability of that space *between* – that opening where anything can, and often does, emerge. In our research, we embrace those special moments when we are surprised, touched and awed; when we find ourselves truly in the moment of a relational encounter. For an instant or two, the researcher shares something profound with the co-researcher. Out of their intersubjectivity may come 'something elemental, unexpected and almost beyond the possibility of being put into words' (Finlay, 2009 *Forthcoming*).

Notes

[i] For more detailed information on how to conduct a research interview, we recommend Steiner Kvale's (1996) comprehensive textbook: *InterViews: an introduction to qualitative research interviewing*, London: Sage. Two recommended references which detail the practice and issues of fieldwork are: (i) Hammersley & Atkinson, (1983), *Ethnography: principles in practice*, London: Routledge, and (ii) DeWalt & DeWalt (2002), *Participant observation: a guide for fieldworkers*, New York: Altamira.

[ii] The interview questions and answers have been transcribed largely word for word, except for some grammatical confusions, 'ums', 'ers' and hesitations which have been edited out to aid clarity. Similarly we have not included the kinds of pauses and notes on intonation here which other transcription methods highlight.

[iii] Students often ask us 'what questions should I ask?' The answer, of course, depends on the type of study. For some studies you may not need to ask any at all! Even when you are interviewing, you might take the slightly radical step and consider simply having a conversation rather than explicitly asking questions.

[iv] Empathy, in some quarters, means to leave oneself and go over to the others' experience; to walk in their shoes, so to speak. We prefer to understand empathy more in Buber's terms when he speaks of 'inclusion'. This process involves a kind of bifurcated experiencing of the other's experience while not leaving one's own ground.

[v] The word 'resistance' implies negative connotations and judgment so we prefer to use instead the gestalt term 'creative adjustment' emphasizing the survival component in the process of resistance. For example, it would be an unconscious threat to survival to recall a deeply repressed memory or to express anger directly to the person concerned. The fantasized or real loss of connection to the other may be too devastating to contemplate in awareness. We respect a person's creative adjustment while also recognizing it can have a cost of staying 'stuck' or remaining in ignorance.

[vi] In gestalt therapy, individuals who block or avoid something are usually viewed as making positive choices because something else is needed or because there is a need to go slower to assimilate new ideas or because there is a wish to avoid something which feels truly overwhelming at that moment. The therapist's role in response needs to be to support the individual's choice while providing opportunities for the individual to become aware of the options at stake.

Chapter 8

Embracing Relational Research: Learning from Therapy

In this chapter we expand upon and further develop important aspects of the co-created nature of relational research introduced in *Chapters 3 and 7*. As we have said, our approach to relational-centred research is inspired and shaped by our understanding that research data does not 'speak for itself' but largely through the author/researcher and what is born in the *between* of the embodied dialogical research encounter (Evans, 2007). We believe that much of what we can learn and know about an Other is co-created and arises within the intersubjective space between researcher and co-researcher (Finlay, 2009 *Forthcoming*). Here we ally ourselves with the philosopher Martin Buber who maintained, the reality of the Other – and thus our self – is to be found in the fullness of our open relation when we engage in our mutual participation (Buber, 1937/1958). Each person in the relationship touches and impacts on the other and that affects how any research unfolds. 'In this "opening between" lurk ambiguity, uncertainty and unpredictability; anything can, and does, appear' (Finlay, 2009 *Forthcoming*).

Building on the theory discussed in *Chapter 3*, this chapter aims to describe and explain four defining features of relational research, what we are calling: presence, inclusion, intersubjectivity and reflexivity. *Presence* is the capacity to be open and both emotionally and bodily present. *Inclusion* is the capacity to put oneself into the experience of the Other (and thereby

Relational-centred Research for Psychotherapists: Exploring Meanings and Experience
Edited by Linda Finlay and Ken Evans
Copyright © 2009 John Wiley & Sons, Ltd.

confirm the Other's existence and potential). Presence and inclusion are, in fact, twinned processes as each requires the other in relational-centred research. With presence researchers are focused on themselves; with inclusion the focus is on the Other.

Put together, the challenge is how to be inside the research (practising inclusion) but sufficiently outside (maintaining a grounded presence and not lost in the Other) simultaneously. This capacity of holding both grows and develops with experience. (In *Chapter 9* we suggest the wisdom of using a second 'outsider' – a supervisor – as an essential resource for the researcher.)

Although researcher and co-researchers are separate, the concept of *intersubjectivity* highlights their intertwining. Any relational encounter between two people potentially involves multiple entangled subjectivities – both conscious and unconscious – such as how past and current aspects of the self of one person can be elicited and interact with those of an Other in the present. Given the complexity of this intersubjective space, a radical research approach is called for requiring the researcher to engage in *reflexivity* – a self-aware thoughtfulness about the research dynamics and process. Here again we suggest the wisdom of having a supervisor to support and challenge the researcher in critical reflection.

We share with a range of relational approaches to psychotherapy (*see Chapter 3: Embodied Co-creation*) an emphasis on viewing the research encounter, like the therapeutic relationship, as a co-creation to which researcher and participant(s) contribute from their own subjective experience, both in and out of awareness. There is an obvious need for the researcher, like the psychotherapist, to be adaptable and versatile when engaging in therapy or in research. There is no easy rule book of techniques laid down to conduct a particular research project or to explore a particular client issue. Researchers will not always succeed in engaging or sustaining these four features. That said, these four features of relational-centred research will be present to a greater or lesser degree in all relational research projects though with varying emphases.[i]

Presence

> The essence of work with another person is to be present as a living being.
> (Gendlin, 1996, p. 297)

We see the researcher's presence and way of being as critical to engaging the all-important research relationship. The researcher's presence involves them endeavouring to be: (i) bodily and emotionally engaged; (ii) receptive; and (iii) transparent.

Taking these three ideas in turn, firstly, presence involves the capacity for being emotionally and bodily *engaged* – for 'being there'. Here the researcher is in contact holistically, i.e. with the whole of themselves (own bodily sensations, emotions, thoughts and fantasies) in order to respond to the emotions arising in both researcher and co-researcher. Explaining this concept, Zinker and Nevis make the important distinction between presence and charisma describing the latter as calling for attention and admiration. 'Charisma', they say, 'calls to itself, whereas presence calls to the other' (Zinker & Nevis, 1994, p. 386).

Relational-centred research is a holistic and embodied research process that invites the researcher to first contact and ground themselves in their breathing and physicality. From a holistic perspective the body is more than a vehicle that transports our head around the world. It has wisdom in its felt-sense (Gendlin, 1997) that we can draw on. Todres (2007, pp. 25–26) describes the process:

> I attend to a definitely felt but conceptually vague experiencing. This is done after I bring my awareness into the body and wait for some felt relationships to what I am engaged in to form … A "felt sense" comes that is recognized as pregnant with some meaning that is not yet articulate, for example, "something about my unfinished paper that needs attention" … There is a subtle kind of dipping back and forth between the "felt sense" and a way of "languaging" this.

Secondly, presence involves *receptiveness* to the Other. In being receptive, the researcher is ready to respond to whatever emerges and is prepared to tolerate and cope with not-knowing, uncertainty and ambiguity (Evans & Gilbert, 2005).

Dahlberg et al. (2008) develop the idea of receptiveness in their version of Reflective Lifeworld Research. They call for the researcher to adopt an 'open discovering way of being' and develop a 'capacity to be surprised and sensitive to the unpredicted and unexpected' (2008, p. 98). In this version, 'vulnerable engagement' and 'disinterested attentiveness' are simultaneously present. There is a 'true willingness to listen, see, and understand. It involves respect, and certain humility toward the phenomenon, as well as sensitivity and flexibility' (Dahlberg et al., 2008, p. 98).

Being receptive involves the researcher clearing a space for the Other and making an ongoing effort to put aside previously held understandings in order to see the Other afresh (*see* the discussion on openness in *Chapter 7: The Research Encounter*). It is about being prepared to be surprised, perhaps even expecting to be surprised. Wertz (2005) applies these ideas to the process to bracketing (epoché) in phenomenological research where he suggests that the researcher needs to attempt to enter fully into the participant's situations and adopt a special attitude involving an extreme form of care that:

> Savors the situations described in a slow, meditative way and attends to, even magnifies, all the details. This attitude is free of value judgments from an external frame of reference and instead focuses on the meaning of the situation purely as it is given in the participant's experience. (Wertz, 2005, p. 172)

Thirdly, the concept of *transparency* refers to the way a researcher is honest, authentic, and open about his or her method of work, beliefs/values, personal experiences and responses. This process can help co-researchers to feel safe in the presence of the researcher and it can strengthen the integrity of the research. In Example 8.2 below, Ken demonstrates transparency when he acknowledges that Joe's capacity for forgiveness feels more developed than his own. In Example 8.4, Linda displays transparency when she checks out her own bodily experience with Kath.

Transparency may include some researcher self-disclosure (selectively and judiciously applied) where the researcher shares personal experience, uncertainties and acknowledges fallibilities.[ii] Such disclosure – seen most commonly in feminist research – involving reciprocity and mutual sharing can be enormously effective and impactful. However, decisions to self-disclose or not need to be made in the context of what best serves the research and the co-researcher's interests. To give an example, a researcher studying the 'lived experience of being a carer', might share the fact that she, too, is a carer. The fact that this researcher is also a lesbian might not be shared. However, if this same researcher went on to do some research on sexuality it may well be valuable to disclose her sexuality.

Being present in these engaged, receptive, transparent ways, ultimately allows the researcher to *be with* the co-researcher. Presence allows the possibility of mutuality in the 'between'; neither person controls the other. They stand – both together and apart – in their vulnerability and difference. Presence, in this sense, is *not* a technique or tool to be used to manipulate the other. It is rather 'a way of being with, without doing to' (Zinker & Nevis, 1994, pp. 385–386) which requires 'authenticity, transparency and humility' (Yontef, 2002, p. 15). The researcher needs to have the courage to stay in 'the process', to be emotionally present, even transparent, while being prepared to take some risks in the co-creation of experience, understanding and knowledge.

In practice, this engaged, receptive presence can be hard for the researcher to maintain. Two examples from our research practice follow that illustrate this challenge and show how (inevitable) 'failures' in presence can be used constructively.

Example 8.1   'Ann'

One example of when Linda struggled with presence occurred during an interview she carried out with a co-researcher (Ann) about her lived experience of multiple sclerosis (Finlay, 2003b). She remembered the moment during the interview when she caught herself thinking, 'I've heard this story before' but then realized she had not. Linda understood then that she had, for a moment, stopped being properly present to Ann; she had stopped listening to Ann's story as an individual one. It was Ann who prompted Linda to bracket previous scientific/medical pre-understandings and return to being open to Ann's own world as she was living it:

> In my research on exploring the lived experience of early stage multiple sclerosis, I interviewed Ann. She talked powerfully of how her relations with others were under threat from her multiple sclerosis – specifically, from the loss of sensation in her hands. Poignantly, this impacted most on her relationships with her children.
>
> Ann talked quite a bit about how the loss of sensation in her hand interfered with her daily functioning, but it took me a while to tune in. Initially, I fell into the trap of thinking about her experience and her loss of sensation in almost medical terms – I'd been looking at her body as an object. I even found myself thinking, 'well her disability is not that severe – its only partial loss of sensation and she still has some motor function'. Then she did something that yanked me into her lifeworld ...
>
> She described the sense of almost panic which hit her when she suddenly realized she may not ever again be able to reach out to feel the 'softness of her baby's skin properly'. She gently caressed her own cheek and then reached out to caress the child imagined in front of her. She described this as doing the 'mummy thing'.
>
> Those fleeting, imaginary, subtle caresses disclosed a profound understanding. Suddenly, I understood that I needed to tune into her bodily experience – specifically her feeling of being unable to connect with – being unable to love – her children. Without sensation, she loses her ability to caress and hold and to express her love to her children. Intimate relations are disrupted as her ability to embody her loving presence is thwarted. A dynamic relation between body–world is revealed when Ann reaches out to touch – and be touched by – her children but discovers she cannot feel them (Finlay, 2006e, p. 23)[iii]

Although Linda had been striving to be open and receptive to Ann's story, she had been only partially successful. She fell into the trap of regarding Ann's neurological problems as being relatively mild (from a medical perspective). It took Ann's subtle gesture to yank her back to thinking about Ann's lived experience. Only then could she grasp what Ann's symptoms meant to *her*: a major disruption disconnecting her from her world. Linda had to bracket those objectifying medical understandings of multiple sclerosis and simultaneously be open to Ann's experience of being a therapist and a mother. She needed to be open to Ann's *being* in a more holistic way.

Example 8.2   'Joe'

Another example of presence (and partial failure of presence) comes from research engaged in by Ken who was researching Joe's experience of shame and forgiveness. Joe's mother was Jewish and she had lost some members of her family in the holocaust. Halfway through their interview Joe said he had had a dream, about a week ago, wherein he felt sadness for a concentration camp guard and this sense of sadness had remained with him all week and he could not shake it off. He was now questioning his former universal indignation of all oppressors.

Ken found himself questioning Joe's statements in a manner that Joe felt were discounting of him and there emerged a kind of low-level power struggle in the research interview. Ken found it very difficult to contain his profound disagreement with Joe's new-found forgiveness of the oppressor.

In a subsequent supervision session, Ken described Joe as a man 'stuck in denial' and he admitted that he was not looking forward to the follow-up interview. Ken's supervisor called his attention to her experience of him as behaving in an uncharacteristically oppressive manner toward Joe – feedback which shook Ken. With the support of supervision Ken uncomfortably reflected on aspects of his own life and was able to take responsibility for what the participant had awoken in him as unfinished business from his past.

Subsequently the follow-up interview was experienced as humbling as Ken acknowledged to Joe that he considered Joe's humanity and capacity for forgiveness further developed than his own. This led to a more mutual and constructive dialogue, unlike the previous interview.

Both Ann and Joe in the examples above solicited a shift in Linda's and Ken's presence and responses which resulted in a deepening of their learning and understanding. Researcher presence enables the participant to identify and contact 'his own powers of listening, perceiving and being, in his own style and as all of his own person' (Shepherd, 1992, p. 240). Presence is the 'ground against which the figure of another self or selves can flourish ... and stand out fully' (Zinker & Nevis, 1994, p. 385). The presence of the researcher calls forth, and perhaps even gives permission, for the presence of the participant to come forth, and then there is usually a mutually reciprocal dynamic where each impacts further upon the other. 'A genuine relationship can't be established if there aren't shared meanings' (Hycner, 1991, p. 135). Crucially we believe that the presence of the researcher (and practitioner) models the process for the participant and thereby creates the frame that will hold and contain unfolding and emerging awareness. The researcher listens holistically (with the whole of themselves – physical sensations, feelings, thoughts, fantasies) and equally to self and other, with curiosity and not judgment. This attitude of curiosity to whatever emerges into awareness in turn supports the researcher to remain transparent.

Both research examples show how the researcher can be challenged to learn and grow from the participant (just as therapists can learn and grow from clients). 'The presence of the other solicits a responsiveness and openness from the self ...' says Halling drawing on Buber's ideas, 'It renders inaccessible, irrelevant, or at least significantly incomplete previously taken-for-granted or habitual ways of interacting with and perceiving this person' (Halling, 2008, p. 25). Halling goes on to note that one of the most profound aspects of becoming present to another is how the Other, 'through their very existence, bring a world into being' (2008, p. 30). In this way, the relational approach involves recognizing the profound and dynamic interaction which can occur between researcher and co-researcher.

These concepts concerned with the interactive impact of the Other are discussed further in the next two sections.

Inclusion

Inclusion is the ability to perceive and comprehend the wholeness and uniqueness of the Other; it is being able to imagine and empathize with the reality of the Other. It involves the capacity to put 'oneself into the experience of the patient as much as possible, feeling it as if in one's own body – without losing a separate sense of self' (Yontef, 2002, p. 24). While presence supports us to be as fully available to the Other as possible, we also need to have a sense of where the other is and to include the other without losing oneself or the other, or losing oneself in the other.

Taking a relational approach, we aim to be in a space where researcher and participant alike can recognize the Other as a separate person in his/her own right while remaining in dialogue with the other. Inclusion refers to a developing process where a person is able to stay in his or her own world of experience, empathize with the world of the other *and* hold a meta perspective on this relational mutuality.

The importance of inclusion is generally accepted as essential to the establishment of a firm working alliance. Both Rogers' emphasis on empathy (Rogers, 1951) from the humanistic tradition and Kohut's emphasis on empathic immersion from the tradition of self psychology (Kohut, 1984) underline how essential it is for the therapist/researcher to be able to enter into the subjective world of the client/co-researcher in a concerned and empathic manner. This process of empathy or empathic immersion is very much part of any relational way of working to create for a client or research participant a sense of being understood (*see also Chapter 7: The Research Encounter*). As Rogers defines it, empathy involves engaging the other's private world and becoming:

> Thoroughly at home in it. It involves being sensitive, moment to moment, to the changing felt meanings which flow in this other person … It means temporarily living in his/her life, moving about in it delicately without making judgements … as you look with fresh and unfrightened eyes. (1975, p. 3)

The Jewish philosopher and educator Martin Buber, from whom the concept of inclusion is derived, is a significant influence in contemporary relational-oriented psychotherapy and research. Students grow, he maintained, through the direct encounter with the person of the educator (Buber, 1923/2004). The educator needs to enter the phenomenological world of the student, to experience it and feel it (Buber, 1967). Such a relational approach, whether applied to education, psychotherapy or research aims to reach a place where educator and student, client and psychotherapist, researcher and participant alike recognize the other as a separate person in their own right while remaining in relationship with them, respecting and celebrating difference (Evans and Gilbert, 2005).

Yontef (1993), writing of relational gestalt therapy, considers inclusion to be the essence of true dialogue. In therapy the process of including the client and confirming the person's existence is seen to provide the client with a reparative experience of a positive relationship in the present. The client gains an experience of being seen and acknowledged which may have been largely absent in their prior experience. By meeting the client in the way they are at the moment – and not aiming to make them different – the client is supported to identify with their own experience. These ideas can also be applied to research: the co-researcher may feel seen, heard and understood at the deepest level of their being. If the co-researcher says, 'you don't understand', then the researcher needs to accept the co-researcher's authority as they are the ones with direct access to their experience (Yontef, 1993).

Alongside being able to put oneself into the experience of, and 'take in', the co-researcher, the relational researcher lets him- or herself be affected by the experience. Here, the researcher may well change as he or she feels a range of emotions in response to the co-researcher and is impacted by the experience of the other. In most relationships (including client–therapist, participant–researcher) there is a greater or lesser degree of mutuality,[iv] a greater or lesser degree of influence of self on other and other on self.

Together, presence and inclusion lie at the heart of the concept of co-creation in relationship, making possible this sense of mutual influence, of both persons changing in response to the other. To be present without inclusion is to be cut off or alienated from the other. To be immersed in the other but lose one's sense of being present is to be overly merged with the other. In either case there can be no real meeting or engagement since one is either isolated from the other or fused together with the other. Presence and inclusion are two sides of the same coin. Practising inclusion, while remaining fully present, is probably the most challenging skill for both therapist and relational researcher alike.

In the next example, Ken shows that by tuning into his co-researcher's (Maggie's) experience, he was paradoxically enabled to go deeper into his own presence. Then by being able to tolerate his own deeper sense of presence, he was in turn supported in his capacity to more deeply attune to Maggie (i.e. he practised inclusion).

Example 8.3   'Maggie'

During an interview with Maggie, Ken was exploring her experiences as a result of the recent death of a much loved parent. Maggie began in a very animated way to speak warmly of her relations with her deceased parent but after some 10 minutes abruptly stopped speaking and appeared to withdraw. After some moments she quietly and seemingly fearfully related a recent dream subsequent to her parent's death. In the dream Maggie was in a space suit outside a spacecraft, miles above the earth. The rope/wire that attached her to the spacecraft had broken free and she was drifting away into the blackness of space. Hearing this account, Ken felt stuck and strangely distant from Maggie and not at all impacted by her dream. He made several empathic attempts to elicit her experience but was met with a mute response. Maggie looked terrified. Seemingly unable to elicit any information from her Ken turned his attention inward to himself:

> *How might I be missing Maggie? I realize I am not feeling anything and I am immediately impressed by the incongruence of my emotional response. I realize that, out of my awareness, I am not allowing myself to experience her dream, to really feel it. In all likelihood this is my counter-transference. But what am I avoiding? What may Maggie be wanting me to avoid?*

Rarely, if ever, is a counter-transference experience a simple one-way or unilateral phenomenon but rather a reciprocal or bilateral process, where each person is co-creating the field. With this in mind, Ken shared with Maggie that he was going to take some time to recall what she had said about her dream. He then actively imagined himself inside a space suit, cut off from the spacecraft and drifting far away into the blackness of the universe. Consequently he hit upon a personal experience of loneliness and isolation in his life which Maggie's dream was now evoking in him, out of his awareness. Ken decided to share with Maggie the sense of bleakness and coldness her dream was having upon him. However, even before Ken actually spoke he noticed that Maggie already seemed to be more present; her demeanour transformed, she once again began to speak acknowledging her fear of feeling lonely and bereft. Significantly, Maggie went on to say she no longer felt alone and went on to share in depth her experience of the death of her parent.

   This was a research interview related to bereavement but it bears a striking resemblance to therapy. Ken's initial lack of empathy threatened to seriously curtail the quality of the engagement but his subsequent commitment to deepening his contact with himself (presence) renewed and deepened his empathic understanding toward Maggie (inclusion). Curiously Ken's deepened sense of presence and empathy was intuited by Maggie even before he spoke to confirm it. Gerson refers to this phenomenon as the 'relational unconscious'; describing it as 'the unrecognized bond that wraps each relationship, infusing the expression and constriction of each partner's subjectivity and individual unconscious within that particular relationship' (Gerson, 2004, pp. 72–73). The concept of the relational unconscious high-lights the interconnection between self and other which forms 'an unseen bridge' between them.

Alongside this practice of inclusion is something of a surrender, a yield-ing, to what might be emerging between two people in relation and a recognition of mutual intersubjective interconnection. As Halling (2008, p. 31) notes, 'We cannot have genuine conversations with ourselves; instead, the call of relationship is precisely a call for us to move beyond ourselves.' The beyond being referred to here is a focus on the wider context including the intersubjective space between self and other.

Intersubjectivity

In therapy, research and life there is a reciprocally interacting world of experience, interconnection and interdependence between ourselves and our environment. It is precisely our capacity for intersubjectivity which creates the possibility of real empathy and understanding of another. It is our 'intersubjective horizon of experience that allows access to the experi-ences of others' (Wertz, 2005, p. 168).

In this intersubjective context there is a 'reciprocal insertion and intertwining' of others in ourselves and of us in them (Merleau-Ponty, 1964/1968, p. 138). This intertwining occurs in all sorts of seen and hidden ways, as different parts of ourselves interact with and merge with parts of the other. In the extract below, for instance, Linda discusses how in her research with therapists about their lifeworlds she simultaneously inhabited intertwined roles of researcher, participant, therapist and client (Finlay, 1998).

It's like seeing simultaneous reflections in multiple mirrors. As I dwell with the transcripts of conversations between participants and myself, the images become blurred and identities converge. The therapist I am interviewing becomes my client. The 'I' who is both researcher and therapist divides and I slide inadvert-ently into my therapist body. As therapist I feel a familiar sensation in my belly – a stirring of excitement as emotional empathy expands. I experience a sense of 'humble-power'. I feel honoured as the participant opens herself, discloses secrets, shares her tears. I know something of the power I have used to 'facilitate' this. Yet, simultaneously, I feel powerless and helpless. What can I do in the face of this distress? I am not her therapist. Then, as I witness her strength, wisdom, caring, I am reminded that she is a therapist herself with a capacity and her own ways to cope. Then images converge again and a new relationship comes into focus. Suddenly, I am the client, feeling tears, needing solace, wanting this caring, listening therapist to nurture and reassure me. Then a point of interest captures my professional attention. The axis spins, and I find myself being the researcher. I can stand back now and draw a cloak of power around me once more as I select what to hear, what to report. I decide how to represent my participants and which stories I tell.

One way of understanding these complicated entanglements where we find ourselves responding to another at multiple levels, is to recognize the multiple, interacting subjectivities present.[v] The 'here and now' contains something of the 'there and then' where subjectivities of one person elicit those of another. As the selves set each other off, they trigger responses that are habitual to the persons involved. De Young (2003) describes these relational entanglements as 'thickly populated' encounters. She calls our attention to the need to take a layered relational perspective illustrating this point well with an example from therapy which considers just one person's thickly populated existence:

> So when a client tells you a story as if there were no other people in it – last night he was desperately trying to finish a project without falling into his private pitfalls of perfectionism and procrastination – you know how thickly populated that scene really is. You know that just out of his awareness, there's how hard it is to please his father, and how his mother is on another planet, no help at all, and how his older sister can do whatever she sets her mind to. You keep the relational story in mind. It's as true from him today as it was 20 years ago, though different actors (a boss, a wife, a colleague) may be playing the main characters … But as far as he knows, working hard to finish his project, this is just his internal, individual struggle to dodge inevitable failure. As a relational therapist, you swim against this stream of 'isolated self'. (2003, p. 2)

The following example of research illustrates how entangled, and even merged, subjectivities can become. The example comes from a group phenomenological study engaged in by Linda and some of her colleagues (King et al., 2008) where they explored the phenomenon of mistrust. Linda conducted an in-depth interview with one participant, Kath. The group of researchers then analysed the transcript of the interview, producing a layered analysis which contained both consensual and individual components. The following extract is taken from Linda's reflexive account:[vi]

Example 8.4   'Kath'

Kath likened her lived experience of mistrust to being 'attacked' by others and then finding herself becoming a different person – a 'ghost' of herself. 'I became a different kind of me, a lesser me.'

As I heard Kath say this I felt it had profound significance. I was struck by the way she lost the embodied way of being she had previously relied upon. Having once been vivacious, bright, open, dynamic and humorous, she was describing the experience of 'pulling herself in' and becoming quiet and wary. Where once she had felt herself to be a 'big' person – in terms of both her presence and her personality – she was now made to feel 'reduced'. In the process of being forced to reduce, she had become a different person. This is how she describes the process:

Kath: It was this kind of shift and change and the pulling in and the unsafeness of that environment which before had felt secure, clearly wasn't. I was shaky. Lots of the sort of firm things that you believed in were now shaky. Does that make sense?

Linda: Yes, so, when you say 'pulling in' you pulled yourself into yourself.

Kath: Yes, I withdrew …

Linda: It seems like your very way of being is kind of quite open (mmm, mmm) and direct. And here you've lost even your way of being.

Kath: … that really sums it up actually. I felt the person who left that college was not me. Or was a paler shade of me … I had to kind of slow down in a sense, not in speed sense but in a kinda closure sense … in a protective sense.

As Kath was speaking I was very aware of her 'big presence'. I had previously known Kath as a 'big personality' and as someone who physically embodied a big, attractive presence. Yet, in the course of our interview, she somehow started to 'fade' in front of my very eyes. I could feel a strange sensation within myself, a sense closing down, closing in, shrinking, trying to become smaller, trying to become a 'paler' version of myself. *Slowly I was disappearing. Then I realized that, strangely enough, this new reality actually felt safer. If I couldn't be seen, I wouldn't be hurt* … I dwelt there some more … I could understand and accept Kath's need to 'reduce' and close down. At the same time, I began to feel something else. *Losing myself, also felt slightly scary. Who would I be and who would I become if I was to disappear to be replaced by a paler-shade of me? I became aware that I felt somehow sad at the loss of my customary embodied way of being.* I looked at Kath and she too, seemed to me to be sad and a little lost – indeed, vulnerable in her loss. (King et al., 2008, pp. 95–96).

As this excerpt shows, Kath was impacting on Linda emotionally, bodily and empathically but, at the same time, Linda was impacting on Kath. The illustration shows the way that Linda checked out her bodily perceptions with Kath in dialogue and her response of 'that sums it up' suggested it was possible Linda had mirrored something of Kath's experience and in that mirroring there was an intersubjective merging.

However, other group members who analysed the transcript had a different perspective and alternative understandings. Two members of the group, for instance, pointed out that through her form of questioning, Linda might have fostered an explicit concern with emotionality and engaged a dialogue akin to that found in a therapeutic relationship. They suggested that Kath's narrative initially had a neutral tone but through Linda's therapeutic reflecting back took on the tone of a brave battling 'victim'.

Linda subsequently reflected on this:

> *I may have introduced into the mix something from my own history as a 'caring therapist'. This, in turn, may have triggered something in Kath, encouraging her to edge towards the stance of 'victim'. However, this process is probably even more complicated. While I had several roles which I was inevitably juggling (chief among them in this instance, the roles of therapist and researcher), questions can also be raised about my habitual interactional roles and pattern of operating ... If I reflexively probe my motivations, I understand that I have an emotional need to give care to others, perhaps as a result of significant gaps in the care I received as a child. I know that I tend to thrive on the empathy I once longed to receive; my providing of care can be seen as an effective way to deny my own need to be cared for. My child self can be seen as entwined with my adult therapist and researcher selves ... What selves were activated in Kath?*

Relational researchers assume that both researcher and co-researcher bring to the encounter the 'sum total of who they are in all their complexity and with their own individual histories and ways of organizing their experience [and] their unconscious processes.' Both are then 'faced with the challenge of meeting the other in all his/her complexity' (Evans & Gilbert, 2005, pp. 74–75). The co-researcher's life experiences and ways of interacting with another will impact both consciously and unconsciously on the researcher, and vice versa. These intersubjective dynamics deserve attention and need to be probed reflexively.

Reflexivity

In our study and practice of contemporary relational approaches to psychotherapy and research, we are increasingly aware of the need to recognize the individuality and person of the researcher, as a well as the dynamics around the research relationship. The researcher, like the relationally oriented therapist, is no longer viewed as a neutral presence but as a person in his/her own right. Each of us brings to the research encounter our unique ways of being in the world[vii] stemming from our own personal histories (including our age, gender, ethnicity, and personality). These shape perceptions of events and so influence the relational encounter (Stolorow & Atwood, 1992).

The previous four examples offered in this chapter are all good illustrations of reflexivity in practice. They show the researcher as being thoughtfully and critically self-aware and aware of broader dynamics and processes of the relational field. The issue at stake is the need to appreciate how the researcher *and* the research relationship may impact on both the research process and findings (Finlay & Gough, 2003). Researchers' subjectivity and intersubjectivity needs to be fore-grounded through reflexivity so as to begin the process of separating out what belongs to the researcher rather than the researched.

It is important, however, to not over-emphasize the researcher's perspective. The researcher needs to avoid undue navel gazing and preoccupation with their own experience or the research will be pulled in unfortunate directions which privilege the researcher over the participant (Finlay, 2002a, 2002b). The research focus always needs to stay on the participant, the evolving relationship and the phenomena being researched.

If you are a psychotherapist reading this chapter you will undoubtedly appreciate the value and significance of being reflexive, that is reflecting critically on self and process. In your own therapy work, you will be very familiar with the need to explore relational processes, including the possibility of transferences, counter-transferences and parallel processes occurring. For instance, you would recognize the probability of an unconscious process emerging if you suddenly found yourself feeling critical or sleepy in response to a client and you might question whether or not this signalled a 'counter-transference' related perhaps to the client's own critical or disinterested parent.[viii] You will equally appreciate the need to gently interrogate yourself if you sensed some 'resistance'. (See how Ken explicitly handles this reflexive analysis in *Chapter 9*.)

You will also recognize how valuable supervision can be to untangle some of the complicated subjective and intersubjective issues which could impact significantly on therapy. (*See also p. 71 in Chapter 6: Setting up Research*.) The same applies to the research process. We would suggest that relational-centred research ideally requires both academic supervision and supervision of the research process (Evans, 2007). The latter is perhaps best offered by person(s) competent to support the therapist-researcher in his or her exploration of personal conscious and unconscious experience.

The following example from research conducted by Ken and Linda shows the value of exploring relational dynamics – in this instance, parallel process – in supervision. (We consider the process of supervision so central to relational research that its impact, challenge and efficacy are further demonstrated in *Chapter 9*.)

Example 8.5   'Ken'

In this example, Ken and Linda conducted some focus group research in 2008 on the proposed statutory regulation of the psychotherapy field in the United Kingdom (Evans & Finlay, 2009). In view of the profound impact that impending state registration was expected to have on the profession, we sought to explore the views, thoughts, expectations, hopes and fears of 10 psychotherapists who were taking part in a professional development group. When Ken presented the idea of this research to the group, he was uncharacteristically hesitant, even timid, in that he suggested that (if everyone agreed) the research group could be 'squeezed into' the lunch hour. The group, in response, challenged Ken about why he was marginalizing the research when it was so relevant to the personal and professional development remit of the group.

At the time, Ken was deeply immersed in concluding his doctoral dissertation about the professionalization of psychotherapy in Europe and such a hesitant request about a subject which had preoccupied him for over 25 years was puzzling (Evans, 2009). With the hindsight of supervision, it was apparent that the request was put in such a way as to invite the group to decline the invitation. While at a conscious level, this would have been deeply disappointing to Ken, he became aware that there may be some advantages at an unconscious level.

Exploring this reflexively in the group and in subsequent supervision, Ken expressed shock, amazement and anger when he made the link between two historical experiences of feeling marginalized (1985 and 2001) and with marginalizing his own research interests. He had internalized the oppression of these historical experiences and, trapped within a parallel process, he had mirrored his own sense of marginalization by unwittingly marginalizing the focus group (Evans & Finlay, 2009).

This incident was a clear and dramatic example of the influence of unconscious forces on the research endeavour. Uncomfortable experiences from the past had interfered with Ken's availability to be fully present. In turn, Ken 'missed' (failure of inclusion) the other members of the focus group who nevertheless were sufficiently self-possessed to challenge his suggestion to marginalize them. This example, flags up how crucial it is for the researcher to acknowledge the inevitability of unconscious processes at work. We should expect – and *welcome* – these even when they are uncomfortable as they are almost always significant data. Developing an attitude of curiosity (rather than judgment) will support the researcher towards greater degrees of transparency, hence presence.

The example above also supports our view of the wisdom of process supervision when engaging with relational-centred research, especially as we cannot always count on the research participant(s) to be as emotionally literate and challenging as our focus group of experienced therapists! Working with parallel processes, in particular, can be a powerful tool for a supervisor to use (Jacobsen, 2007).

Relational therapists and researchers face the challenge of bringing themselves fully into the room and dealing directly with the relational impasses that occur between therapist–client and/or researcher–participant. This calls for the ongoing monitoring of our responses in relation to the unfolding process. A decision needs to be made about what is useful to share in the interests of deepening and widening the exploration. There are no easy rules in this regard: it depends more on the ongoing awareness on the part of the therapist/researcher of his/her own counter-transference and what may be learned from this, combined with a careful and respectful attention to the needs of the other (Maroda, 1991). At times, a researcher may use counter-transference awareness indirectly to understand the other's struggle/stuckness more clearly. At other times the researcher may choose self-disclosure, as above, as a more powerful and appropriate option. What all relational approaches share, however, is attention to the researcher's/therapist's personal process as a valuable resource to deepen the focus on the co-researcher.

We reiterate here our belief that relational-centred researchers need to consider the need for supervision from a researcher who is also a therapist. This will develop and grow awareness in the researcher of their own unconscious processes (perhaps co-created with an Other) to hinder, restrict, limit, or in some way curtail the work. This work needs to be conducted with curiosity and not judgment, since the latter promotes shame while the former supports a deeper level of reflexive practice where 'mistakes' are viewed as a path to growth and learning.

Reflections

At the centre of our understanding of relational psychotherapy and research is a focus on the co-creation of the relationship as an interactional event, a constantly evolving co-constructed relational process to which client and therapist, participant and researcher contribute alike and impact on each other in an ongoing way. The therapeutic relationship and the research encounter are thus both viewed by us as *dynamic processes* between people in mutual interaction and always *unique*, because of the separate individualities of the persons involved.

Whether engaging in research or psychotherapy, a sensitive, 'relationally tuned' attitude needs to be adopted in relational research which means letting go of control and committing to whatever arises between researcher and participant. It means not predicting, shaping or moulding the course or direction of the meeting by, for example, rigidly sticking to the six questions that have been devised for the semi-structured interview or by getting so overly enmeshed and anxious about outcomes that we are not fully present. Committing to relational-centred research requires the practitioner–researcher to surrender both to the between and to whatever emerges into moment by moment awareness.[ix] Herein lies both challenge and possibility in the research endeavour. What does it mean for us as researchers when we are extolled to be 'fully present' in the research encounter? How do we recognize and deal with a failure of inclusion? What may be the potential impact on our capacity to commit to the 'between' of powerful unconscious processes and how can we bring this meaningfully into a thoughtful research approach? These are questions worth continuing to reflect on.

Practising presence and inclusion, committing to the between and engaging reflexivity can all be immensely meaningful and rewarding but they may also be challenging and uncomfortable. In this chapter we have provided a number of examples of relational research processes which have involved varying degrees of researcher 'discomfort' or 'failure' in their capacity to engage relationally. Such failures are common, indeed inevitable in the relational approach – be it in therapy or research. We would expect momentary lapses in the researcher's concentration or ability to stay present in a lengthy interview, for instance. We see these failures as often emerging from unconscious processes as well as being co-created in the engagement with the participant(s). However, once mis-attunements in the research endeavour emerge into awareness they may be used constructively both to deepen the research encounter (Zvelc, 2008) and as a path towards growth and learning.

Tuning in to the Other and to me, I also tune in to the between. It is as if I am listening intently and with all of me for a tune that is all of us (me, other and us). I listen to the tune being sung by the Other. I try and connect with the deeper song – the song of contact, meeting, connectedness, longing. Even when hidden beneath the negative or closed and cut off, I strain gently to listen to the quiet hum of faith buried beneath the weight of the life of the Other. The weight that I also know and have known – that we all know – of joy and sorrow and hope and despair ... It feels like being grounded in a repose of lightness that is yet full and deep and open and present with myself and the Other in a spirit of acceptance and compassion to myself and other ...

Notes

[i] To give some examples, phenomenological research approaches especially highlight the need for researchers to maintain an open presence as part of the bracketing process. Integrative and Dialogical gestalt psychotherapy researchers will foreground inclusion and the nature of intersubjective intertwining of conscious and unconscious aspects. Feminist versions of relational research are likely to highlight, reflexively, gender and power issues.

[ii] If you are interested in exploring the issue of self-disclosure further, we can recommend Baker & Benton (1994), The ethics of feminist self-disclosure, in K. Carter and M. Presnell (Eds), *Interpretive approaches to interpersonal communication*, New York: SUNY; see also Zahm (Fall 1995), Self-disclosure in Gestalt therapy, *The Gestalt Journal*, New York: The Gestalt Journal Press.

[iii] This extract has been reproduced from Finlay (2006e), The body's disclosure in phenomenological research, *Qualitative Research in Psychology*, 3, 19–30, with the kind permission of the publisher, Taylor & Francis (http://www.informaworld.com).

[iv] Although the research relationship is mutual, it is not symmetrical. 'A mutually constructed relationship does not necessarily mean equality or equality of influence or similarity of contribution' (Aron, 1996, p. 248). Mutuality does not imply an abrogation of the researcher's role, rather it is an acknowledgement that two people cannot be in an encounter with one another without impacting on, or being impacted by, the other. Put another way, there can be mutuality of contact/trust/concern but not 'mutuality of inclusion' (Friedman, 1985). The researcher's role and purpose regarding the need to empathize with the other is different from the co-researcher's role and purpose.

[v] The idea of multiple subjectivities or selves is a challenging and contested one; understood differently across different theoretical perspectives. While traditional modernist humanistic theory championed the idea of a self-contained, private, unique, core or 'real' self, postmodern versions now recognize the plurality of self concept and the idea of 'subpersonalities'. In other fields, more explicitly relational and social theories about multiple subjectivities have also evolved: Psychoanalytic theory considers each person as being psychologically made up of introjected or unconsciously internalized parts of others. Social constructionism argues for the concept of 'selves' which emerge relationally in different contexts. A particularly useful book unpacking these debates is: Rowan, J. and Cooper, M. (1999). *The Plural Self: Multiplicity in everyday life*. London: Sage.

[vi] This extract has been taken from King et al. (2008), "Can't really trust that, so what can I trust?": A polyvocal, qualitative analysis of the psychology of mistrust, *Qualitative Research in Psychology*, 5, 80–102, and reprinted with the kind permission of the publisher, Taylor & Francis (http://www.informaworld.com).

[vii] This 'way of being in the world' is, for example, variously known as a person's 'organizing principles', 'creative adjustment' or 'life script', in psychoanalysis, gestalt psychotherapy and transactional analysis respectively.

[viii] The emphasis in relational-oriented psychotherapies is often focused on the power of the counter-transference as an essential resource. We refer you to Karen Maroda's excellent short book on this subject: *The Power of the Counter-transference* (1991) in which she makes a case for the carefully considered use of the self-disclosure of counter-transference responses, particularly when exploration, in therapy or research, appears to have reached an impasse.

[ix] This practice is akin to the notion of 'creative indifference' in gestalt psychotherapy and the practice of 'mindfulness' in Buddhism. The process involves stepping back from your and the Other's habitual responses where the open non-judgmental clearing of the *between* space is claimed.

Chapter 9

Engaging 'Process'

The process of engaging in relational research is complex and hard to pin down, not least because innumerable processes are involved. Relational-centred researchers assume that both researcher and co-researcher bring to the encounter multiple subjectivities. We are creatures of our family, social and cultural context and we have been formed by our interactions with others throughout our lives. We bring a host of our past relational experiences (intra-psychic and interpersonal; conscious and unconscious) into any one encounter. Inevitably the psyche of one person becomes entangled with the psyche of the other.

As a psychotherapist, you will be familiar with the idea of engaging unconscious, emotional and relational processes. These processes can be equally relevant in research as shown in Examples 8.4 and 8.5 from in the previous chapter, referring to multiple selves and parallel processes respectively.

The challenge a relational-centred researcher faces is finding a way to first become aware of the possibility that layers of relational processes may be present and then to work with and manage them. The extent that the researcher is able to engage positively with 'process' depends largely on their experience as well as their degree of reflexivity and self-awareness, and their preparedness to probe challenging, ambivalent, uncomfortable unconscious aspects.

Relational-centred Research for Psychotherapists: Exploring Meanings and Experience
Edited by Linda Finlay and Ken Evans
Copyright © 2009 John Wiley & Sons, Ltd.

In this chapter we wanted to find a way of foregrounding and illustrating some of the complexities of the research process and how valuable – indeed essential – supervision can be. We decided to offer an example of research process in action, in the 'here and now' specifically highlighting ways data may be gathered in dialogue.

In the following example, Ken engages heuristically *with himself* as the research participant using gestalt two-chair work[i] to explore the interface between religion, spirituality and psychotherapy. We offer this (somewhat radical) illustration of reflexive introspection to demonstrate 'presence' and 'inclusion' in action (the 'what' and 'how' of relational research) as well as showing how ambiguous layers of conscious–unconscious meanings can be teased out in the 'between' of research and supervision relationships.

In this example, **Ken 1** is 'the researcher' and **Ken 2** 'the participant'. The supervisor is an experienced relational-orientated psychotherapist and trainer enlisted specifically for this project. The two-chair work, coupled with supervision, helped Ken become aware of unfinished business from the past that he had hitherto kept out of his conscious awareness and that consequently had a significant impact on his understanding arising in the research exploration.

While some people might question whether or not this exercise constitutes 'research', we argue strongly that it does. We put forward this use of heuristic reflexive introspection (or it could be called autoethnography) as an entirely legitimate approach – one which can potentially explicate powerful relational and unconscious dimensions. The material can thus be considered both 'process' and 'outcome'.

We invite you to participate in this research as you read, noting your own embodied reactions to this 'data' as it unfolds. Then think about how you might begin to analyse this material by monitoring any emerging understandings. (The following *Chapter 10* focuses more specifically on approaches to 'analysis'.)

Exploring the Interface between Religion, Spirituality and Psychotherapy: The Process of Relational-centred Research under the Microscope via Two-chair Dialogue[ii]

Ken 1:

So we are going to explore together the interface between religion, spirituality and psychotherapy via two-chair work and in an unstructured way to allow the exploration to freely go where it will. My role as **Ken 1** is to practice inclusion, presence and raise issues and questions that will seek to challenge you, **Ken 2**, to deeper levels of awareness. In turn, you will take blocks or confusion in our exploration to supervision. The supervisor will, in turn, seek to support and challenge you to deeper levels of awareness, through her presence and inclusion.

Ken 2:

Yes, I will commit to being as open and honest as I can and seek to hold nothing back – on a conscious level anyway! I welcome your commitment to being present and to support me to explore, in supervision, issues I can then bring back to our exploration.

Ken 1:

So where would you like to start?

Ken 2:

Mmm . . . with religion I think. I want to get it *out* of the way.

Ken 1:

Why?

Ken 2: Because it gets *in* the way. In my experience religion contaminates spirituality and interferes unhelpfully in the practice of psychotherapy.

Ken 1:

OK Ken, it seems you have found your starting place.

Ken 1:

Yeah . . . . . . David Boedella once wrote that there were two kinds of religion, formative and deformative. Formative religion is basically simple and connected to the original message of equality and the practice of compassion. Deformative religion is when this original message is lost or contaminated by dogma, enshrined in doctrine such as the Apostles' Creed, whereby believers regularly declare what the Church considers the 'true' doctrine and 'correct' behaviour. Whenever you have 'true' doctrine you inevitably have heretics and the history of all religions demonstrates an often ruthless and cruel intolerance of difference.

Ken 1: (*Practising inclusion, invites **Ken 2** to commit to what is happening in 'the between'*)

What's going on Ken I'm noticing you are hardly breathing?

Ken 2:

Mmm..yeah....I am getting upset.....phew..... It really gets to me..the intolerance, arrogance, brutality and betrayal at the core of deformative religion.

Ken 1:

Say some more.

Ken 2:

Well, where do I begin?

Ken 1:

With your own experience?

Ken 2:

It's easier to reflect 'out there' you know........ the crusades... religious wars..uh...witch hunts in Europe. The ruthless attempts to exterminate native beliefs...inquisition...enforced conversion..all in the name of God. And...uh...this is not confined to Christianity. Islamic fundamentalism, suicide bombers, the twin towers.....and maybe it goes beyond religion.. something about the human condition?

Ken 1:

(*Offering challenge to be more present*) And your *own* experience Ken? I sense you are finding it difficult to go into this.

Ken 2:

Phew.....yeah...uh... yeah I think I am avoiding that... to make more personal my experience.... I intuit I need to do that to go deeper. Mmmm (*Breathing out heavily like a deep sigh*)

Okay...uh...we, M and I, and our two young children left Cambridge for our first curacy. I had been a senior social worker before studying for the Anglican ministry and so I was not exactly 'wet behind the ears'. But....nothing could have prepared me for this first posting in the C of E. It was ensnared in civic duty and tourism and there was a distinct absence of the numinous. The Church Council was like any other Company Board meeting with the emphasis on issues of business, church fabric, raising the quota.

I joined the local branch of CND and got castigated by the vicar for being 'political'.

I took to going over to the church very early in the mornings to quietly sit and pray. Ironically only at times like this, when the church was empty, was it possible for me to be in touch with my spirituality. Eventually under the weight of a relentless superficiality in the daily life of the parish, these early mornings once so cherished, began to fill with a bleak emptiness. I began to grieve even the loss of longing for a glimpse of holy inspiration. I was 'drying up' somehow, perhaps dissociating? Maybe I was depressed?

Ken 1:

Mmmmm...... maybe(?)

Ken 2:

We moved to rural ministry for three years to recover as a family ... but by slow degrees of attrition I got sucked into the shadow lands, by the acid tongues of gossip from thin and bloodless lips of one neighbour against another. Village intrigue is disproportionately greater than the ageing and dwindling population. The Church Council frequently descended into banality ... for example, the row between the flower arrangers and the cleaner. The cleaner, who the head of flower power triumphantly declared didn't even go to church, had committed what appeared to be the ultimate sin by omitting to replace an old flower pot in the same spot on a window ledge in the nave. I was practically frogmarched to the church where, to my innocent eye, the flower pot had been returned to the exact same spot whence it had been for centuries! In my naivety I remarked such, whereupon the entire flower tribe drew breath as a chorus, and began to lambast me for my lack of understanding and support. This quickly led to an avalanche of criticism about my wife for declining to take up the tradition of chair of the *Young* Wives. I labour the word *young* because no one in this esteemed and revered party was less than 70 years old. M had the good sense to get a job as a teacher to avoid being hijacked by these women. They all now appeared as cracked and ancient as the flower pot and I, perhaps foolishly, told them so, ending with a resounding and somewhat dramatic flourish about my wife needing to work to compensate for the pittance of a salary paid to the parish priest. I stormed off into the blessed relief of a cold and crisp winter evening. I walked alone along a country lane, stopping to look up to the night sky. The glittering majesty of a trillion stars along the Milky Way transported me from where I had just been – hell perhaps? – and my spirit began to lift.

Subsequently we removed to the Midlands where I spent three constructive and – by comparison – reasonably sane, years as a Mental Hospital Chaplain. Ironically some years later, I gathered I had been greatly 'missed' by the dwindling congregation! And to be fair there were some genuine people, 'true' saints, who remain faithfully committed long after a succession of priests have come and gone.

Ken 1:

Mmm.....

Ken 2:

In the Midlands chaplaincy I could begin to integrate my former profession as a social worker and therapist with my office as a priest.

The Manager of the Mental Hospital agreed my request to use NHS funds set aside for a full-time assistant to recruit several part-time chaplains from different denominations, including a multi-faith worker. I was aware that community-based chaplaincy was a radical departure from tradition and that the appointment of a Moslem multi-faith worker might not go down well with the bishop. However, to my utter astonishment what really upset and angered him was that I had included an Anglican lay person as one of the chaplains. She was a woman ... a vicar's *wife*! Back then the ordination of women was a controversial issue and one that threatened to split the Church.

Ken 1:

I can see your astonishment even now all these years later.

Ken 2:

Well, I was paid by the NHS, not the diocese. Frankly I had now had all I could stomach of religiosity and I turned on the bishop. To be fair I think he copped for all my pent-up frustration, disappointment and disillusionment. To his utter astonishment I chastised him for his patriarchal and bigoted opinions. I still recall the look of open-mouth incredulity on his face. I decided shortly after to become a full-time psychotherapist.

Ken 1:

You look animated, kinda sad and angry(?)

Ken 2:

Actually I am bloody angry with him, the Church and its arrogant abuse of power and ....yes I am sad also (tears welling up)

....

Ken 1: (*Allowing time for silent reflection and to experience the immediacy of the affective level of the exploration. This is a commitment to* **inclusion** *whereby the researcher does not 'fill the silence' with his/her need to comfort/rescue. This would be empathic failure – an unwillingness to stay with the Other's uncomfortable experience and thus an abandonment of the Other.*)

What's happening?

Ken 2:

I'm not sure...uh.. I think I have dissociated..... maybe from feeling... well alone I think, profoundly alone...... I'm distancing myself, I can feel me doing it...... I want to focus on spirituality and move on to something positive.

Ken 1:

(*Drawing on his counter-transference of 'not knowing' and responding with presence via self disclosure*) Mmmm......I am in a place of 'not knowing' but I feel heavy and intuit that something is not being said.......... being avoided perhaps?

Ken 1:

You know me too well (*giving a wry smile*)... Yeah I am more in touch with feeling heavy.... The feeling deepens.

Ken 1:

The feeling.

Ken 2:

OK, yes of course *my* feeling................... Look – I think this is right – I feel....I'm not sure.....ambivalent...I guess... I'm avoiding something and I can't think my way through it. I'm resisting..... not letting myself know what I know.

Ken 1:

What are you feeling? (*Feeling on the edge of frustration*)

Ken 2:

Like I want to talk about spirituality and I guess that's avoidance and I'm beginning to feel..angry with you... yeah just let me get on exploring spirituality, get some light and I'll then get back to this stuff...I feel the need for some air..so I can breathe...um.......

Ken 1:

Well, I'm stuck....um (*Honest self-disclosure reflecting authentic presence*)

Ken 2:

Me too I....(*Reciprocal honesty*)

Ken 1:

Alright let's not fight it but go with exploring spirituality (*going with the resistance for now rather than forcing it*)...... We are both stuck in 'not knowing' at this point..... Come back to it later perhaps?

Ken 2:

Oh well..let's see................Spirituality is difficult to define...perhaps we get close to its essence or meaning only through description. But once you think you have 'got it' you lose it...... It slips through your fingers like water...

Watching the sun rise or set over the fields at La Volée...kinda grabs me here in my guts. I feel a sense of awe at the wonder and beauty of this planet.....sounds a bit naf and twee I guess, but it impacts me at a deep level. Frost on the branches of trees, crisp white snow that squeaks under you warm-booted feet....sun reflecting countless diamonds over a vibrant stream. The wind dancing among the branches.. You can't see it, like the Holy Spirit, but you can see the impact. So the natural world is a source of inspiration to me, getting behind the concrete, steel.... plastic....

Ken 1:

(*Authentic presence in the response*) Mmmmm, I'm not quite connecting with you....I'm aware of feeling some distance even though I appreciate what you are saying..

Ken 2:

(*Resisting the challenge and continuing to try another way to convey something of the essence of spirituality*) I'm remembering the birth of my daughter when I seemed to levitate.... really, truly I felt I floated off the floor for a long second or two.......... It was amazing. I guess spirituality for me is close to the word 'inspiration'. Those moments, experiences, events, people, often unexpected that touch us deeply and lift us up...yes that's what I mean uplifting...spirituality speaks of life-fullness. It touches the soul, to raise up not bring down.

Ken 1:

I am still with my experience of 'not knowing' but also feel hugely ambivalent now. On the one hand your reference to your daughter and the life-fullness of spirituality impresses me, but I am still back there with your heaviness.... my heaviness also. I don't think we can really move on with what seems a big piece of unfinished business hanging around. It is a distraction....whatever you talk about will not have a sense of real genuineness...for me.

Ken 2: Phew (*deep exhale*) Mmmm.....I'm sure you're right but ... When I hear this I want to protest ....OK I'm stuck.... I'll take it to supervision. (*Only a self-imposed deadline for completing this exercise supports Ken taking it to supervision*)

*   *   *   *   *

Supervisor:
So what are you bringing?

Ken:
I've got to a stuck place....uh... what I want to contract today is to explore my ambivalence about going more deeply into my personal experience of religion. After exploring parish ministry and chaplaincy I felt heavy and (*tears welling up and feeling embarrassed*). Oh hell, I don't believe I'm upset.... I've hardly begun!.... Anyway I was exploring parish ministry and how I felt isolated (*more tears and struggling to get the words out*) .... and then again...

Supervisor:
Perhaps you are isolating your self in this research?

Ken: (*Feeling frustrated and not understood; tense sounding voice*) Well, I am sharing with you... now.... and this complements the two-chair work I am doing.

(*Supervisor nods*)

Ken:
(*Rushing his words and speaking quite fast and in a disconnected kind of way*) So......... in parish ministry I recalled in the research how I had a run in with the flower arrangers' group about the location of a bloody flower pot and their criticism of M for taking a teaching job and not committing to the parish as an unpaid slave.... So in rural ministry I felt as isolated...............

Supervisor:
Can I share my counter-transference with you?

Ken:
Mmm, OK, I... (*Feeling anxious and irritated*)

Supervisor:
(*Being fully present, self-discloses her counter-transference response; Supervisor assumes Ken has sufficient self-support (ego strength) to hear and reflect*

on this, even if it feels uncomfortable) As you are talking I feel like I want to laugh.

Ken:

Ouch.....about what? That touches my shame.....(*struggling to contain anger and hurt*).... In my head I understand this is a part of the process that somehow I'm co-creating...but I don't think you understand what I'm (*slipping into resistance*).....I feel alone..... Oh hell.....(*feeling heavy and sad*). I've just realized something (*new awareness emerging out of the challenging presence of the supervisor*)... Oh this is hard (*tears up*)..... When M took a teaching job I was more alone in the parish. She couldn't commit to the role offered her by the church, which I appreciate and accept, but ultimately she had to create some distance from me... She could only take her support so far....she was critical of me, of my investment in parish ministry which she perceived was sometimes at the expense of our relationship and our children.

Supervisor:

(*Responding with challenge and authenticity*) I feel supportive of M... What about her life?

Ken:

Yes............. I do appreciate what you are saying and I tried really hard to get a parish in xxxx so M would not need to leave her job. I did not resent her working really, but I am now aware of just how lonely and terribly isolated I was. I have never let in that I felt alone within my relationship at times. I found the isolation only just bearable by believing I shared it with M. Actually I now realize... ultimately...we didn't. I could not have borne the truth at that time. It might have broken me.

I am appreciating now the weight of isolation. What is a priest supposed to be/do? What is their role? (*Speaking with passion*) To baptise, conduct weddings, preside at funerals? Important rites of passage but hardly relevant to daily life. I struggled to find meaning. The more I tried to translate and apply ministry in a radical and meaningful way, the greater the opposition I experienced from all levels of church life. Compliance with religion means accepting a 2,000 year old dogma, attitudes suited to an agricultural society. The symbols, metaphors and stories of the Bible are rural and enshrined in a romanticism that is largely irrelevant in the modern technological world. Fundamentalist Christians get into amazing rationalizations to evidence the creation story, disprove evolution theory or prove the miracles as recorded in the Bible. This same fundamentalism is current in all religions. Believers are asked to leave their brains at the entrance before entering the church, mosque, temple.

Anyhow...I am deflecting...I think...right now. It's a real shock for me and very upsetting to become aware of the full extent of my isolation, loneliness and struggle to find meaning. It was *truly awful*. I feel very shaken.....vulnerable.......kinda weak at the knees.....anxious.

The retired Bishop of New Jersey, Bishop John Selby Spong...a truly lovely man...concluded after a lifetime in the ministry that the Church would have to die if it is to discover itself anew. I think he's right. And again you see I am oscillating between staying with my affective experience and 'talking about' related matters.

I need to stop and let this in at a heart level. I feel raw.....thank you for being honest with me....it hurts but it helps ....phew (*loud exhale*). I am clearer.................

*   *   *   *   *

TWO DAYS LATER
Ken 2:
Well, that was some supervision session! And it certainly shows its value in uncovering what may be being avoided and in raising levels of awareness.
Ken 1:
And how do you feel?
Ken 2:
I feel vulnerable but open, as far as I can tell..I was really shaken up there.
Ken 1:
Do you have any reflections on your supervision session?
Ken 2:
Uh...yeah.....I am often reminded how in the process of therapy a client will let into their awareness something profound that they did not have the self-support and/or external support to let in at the actual time of the experience or event..... Deeper levels of awareness rarely come from a position of comfort but rather discomfort, when we are pulled just beyond our current level of awareness. Awareness or insight is a challenge to the status quo........a kind of interior journey which is perhaps the authentic nature of prayer?
Ken 1:
Yeah be careful what you pray for you might get it!
Ken 2:
(*Gallows laughter*)
Yeah.
Ken 1:
Before we left off last time you used the word 'soul' in connection with your daughter's birth...well actually you spoke of **the** soul?

Ken 2:

Oh God you're are asking me what I mean by soul?...... Yeah ....
well I guess I'll introduce some theology at this point. Mmmm..why not?

Ken 1:

(*Being present by disclosing excitement*) I feel strangely excited, strange because normally the idea of talking theology would not be experienced by me as exciting.

Ken 2:

Thank you.. Yeah I'm aware that I'm excited too...

Uh....okay,..............uh Wolfhart Pannenberg, a great theologian, in his book *Jesus: God and Man*, thought the most significant message in the scriptures was that human beings were made in the image of God. Now this is most relevant to my understanding of spirituality and is connected with psychotherapy. Christian doctrine has forever *split* body and soul, spirit and matter, human and divine.

In Jesus of Nazareth it is enough for me that he was a truly human being, not some super hero extraterrestrial being that simply assumed the form of a man. Now.....if human beings were made in the image of God uh...
...then in the very *personhood* of Jesus we witness a human being as God intended us all to become, yeah? Uh.....in other words *to become more human is to become more divine.* There's no split and we can fully honour the Imago Dei in us all. This is the crucial theological link between spirituality and psychotherapy.........for me. As a psychotherapist I work to support and challenge people to grow as a human being...... To grow and develop as a human being is to grow more into the divine mage, to become more of whom God intended us to become. So.....there is none of the constraint....uh.....the oppression of dogma here. Becoming more human can be related to the age and culture in which we live and move and breathe; in which we work out and through our becoming...uh....each in their own way. We can draw inspiration from many sources.....
uh...yeah.....even religion! But not be driven by external sources....
instead kind of....evolving the God within and...uh by...manifesting the human without....in our life and through our relationships. This is a personal and community endeavour.

Ken 1:

I am with you on this and feel the passion in the theology.

Ken 2:

(*Telling a meaningful story with authentic presence*) I recall a story about Turgenev. He was sitting in a small country church somewhere in Russia at the turn of the 20th century and found himself next to a farm labourer. He was almost overcome with nausea at the stench of farm animals emanating from the body of the peasant who sat alongside him. He was astonished to be gripped by the overwhelming thought he was sitting next to the Messiah. The thought would not go away. How could this be, such an ordinary, ordinary man? (*Tears welling up*) Then it came to him.... (*Tears still; struggling to get out the words*) as a resounding awareness.... just....just such.... an *ordinary* man...was Jesus of Nazareth.

Ken 1:

(*Tears rolling down face*) I am very moved.

Ken 2:

(*Tears rolling down face*) Yeah......it touches me here in my stomach and all over...a kind of..uh..tingling that breathes life. And that's another thing... spirituality is life-full. So much of religion impresses as life denying, full of rules... regulations, dogma.....punishment. Spirituality is about life...uh...about becoming. Exploring and uh..sometimes making mistakes....but not being overwhelmed with guilt but rather looking with curiosity rather than judgment; growing through, not turning away or turning back or turning inward with shame.

Open-ended living, not an existence fearing the wrath of a God who exists in this or that authoritarian form only to serve our basic insecurities and anxieties. This kind of God serves only the desperate needs of those who seek security over exploration, control over liberty, order over passion, death over life.

I once saw some graffiti on the door of a public toilet which sums it up exactly:

"*Is there life before death?*"

Phew...I feel animated, alive.

Ken 1:

It's contagious! I sense there's more..(?)

Ken 2:

Yeah.....there is .....the 20th Century was a period of individuation, a rapid secularization of society in the West. The human growth movement brought a greater freedom from the prison of religious dogma. The downside is we've lost touch with a sense of community. Individual growth and gross national product has left the planet seriously deficient ecologically. Spirituality for me..is about connection...between people and....creatures and our planet. To survive as a species we need to recognize this connection....uh I've written elsewhere of the possible emergence of a new paradigm for the 21st century:

You Are therefore *I Am* (We-centred)

rather than

God Is therefore *I Am* (God-centred) or *I think* therefore *I AM* (Me-centred)

I discovered a wonderful example of this new paradigm in action in Israel in 2006 in a grass roots movement called the Family Circle, through which Jewish and Arab families dialogue and find a meeting and meaning through their mutual grief, consequence upon loss of loved ones on both sides of the conflict...........

Ken 1:

I am aware of the time, do you want to do more today? I'm feeling a bit bushed.

Ken 2:

Me too....I'm satisfied that I've put out there or out here, what I wanted to share. There's something niggling at me though...at the edge of my awareness....but maybe that's for supervision?

$$* \quad * \quad * \quad * \quad *$$

Ken:

Well, I was pretty shaken in supervision last time but thank you for your challenge which, while very uncomfortable, helped me to a deeper awareness. I trust this process, as difficult as it can be.

Supervisor:

Yes Ken, you were......upset...(*Practising inclusion*)

Ken:

Yeah....today, I am aware that I have identified a very important theological link between spirituality and psychotherapy and the positive aspect of this connection to my work as a psychotherapist.... But I've been quietly processing this a bit and I want to acknowledge the...uh.. shadow side. At the end of the last two-chair dialogue..uh...I felt something nagging at me and it's in this area......I think. (*Committing to whatever emerges in the between*)

Supervisor:

Say some more.

Ken:

For as much as my theology enables me to integrate my professional life with my spiritual life there remains the shadow component. The profession of psychotherapy often behaves in ways that are all too reminiscent of deformative religion. I would like to explore this in supervision and I also recall, after reading through the last two-chair dialogue the question arose 'what is the soul?'..... I never actually tackled this..........and I wonder why(?) (*Committing to Presence*) First I would like to share the theological link(?)

Supervisor:

OK.

Ken:

Well...the idea that human beings are made in the image of God and to become more human is to grow into divinity. I don't think I mean that human beings become God (*feeling anxious*), but rather that human beings may grow more toward the divine. For me Jesus of Nazareth is relevant only because he was *fully* human in the way we are intended to become. As a psychotherapist I guess I am supporting and challenging people to become more human, more accepting of themselves......I recall recently reading something by Elinor Greenberg which speaks to this... I have it here actually.....(*Trembling with excitement and anxiety....fear?*)

> The role of therapy is to help people acknowledge and face old hurts........ find adaptive ways of dealing with their pain.....and explore their real self. In short, to help the client delight in himself.[iii]

It's this last sentence that speaks to me especially...*to delight in oneself...*so different from the guilt and shame-based internalization of deformative religion.

But uh ...now as I am speaking to you..I feel anxious...no ..uh...fear maybe...yeah..something about isolation. I....the exclusion I experienced as priest and yeah.....now as a psychotherapist...um...yeah...I feel heavy ... There's a connection here between religion and psychotherapy ..uh.... Both can marginalize... Mmmm..... Last week I attended a conference in London organized by the IAPT (Improving Access to Psychological Therapies). Actually it came over as the 'gospel' according to CBT. CBT is clearly driving and managing this initiative...and uh speaking about the need for guidelines for applying therapeutic models and how supervision is about the fidelity of the model... So the role of the therapist is marginalized and especially the person of the therapist... It all strikes me as like the 'managed care' programmes in the USA...appealing to the government of course because it promises quick cheap treatments. While they responded to questions of bias toward one model by saying interpersonal approaches would be considered...a sentence or two in two whole days? It felt to me and others in the audience that this was a bit of a sop....giving the mere appearance of inclusivity. A vote on the debate on supervision as best serving the fidelity of the model was actually lost by some two-thirds majority against. A second debate, on the NHS being ready to implement IAPT across the nation, was resoundingly defeated with only 4 in favour out of about 40 attending the debate. But those managing the process appeared completely undeterred by these votes. They seemed to me to have that evangelical zeal that is convinced of the rightness of its cause.... One of the few verbal opponents was admonished for 'being wrong'... We were not told the reasons for this assertion!... They are on a roll and backed by a government, with I think good intentions, but wanting to be convinced, perhaps by the apparent economic benefits. One member of the audience suggested people were voting in one way but too scared to speak out in any other way for fear of their careers(?)

Supervisor:

May I share my thinking at this point?

Ken:

(*Sensing his supervisor is speaking tentatively as though knowing this might be another challenging intervention while feeling touched by his sense of the supervisor's gentleness and concern but nevertheless steadfast authenticity*) Yeah please do..I am drowning in my words..overwhelmed by this...uh link between the oppression I feel from religion and from the profession.

Supervisor:

Well I sense that what connects your sense of isolation and exclusion is..... uh...perhaps.....shame?

Ken:

Mmmm yeah of course............ Shame as a response to a rupture in important relationships....(*'Fear' feelings now translating into 'angry' feelings....*) Why is it that I put myself in situations like this...as a priest..a psychotherapist..... Why do I always steer toward the radical and unconventional and find myself marginalized? Am I addicted to this shit...? (*Potentially becoming 'vicitimy' and retrospective; Instead of feeling the anger toward the oppressive Other, turning it on himself*)

Supervisor:

And in the UK you are kinda isolated....most of your work is in Europe now......

Ken:

Mmmmm..uh ....cannot be a prophet in one's own land? In Europe yeah...but back home.....not so much.... Isolation again (*Feeling sad but puzzled about not feeling hugely sad....something stirring*).

Supervisor:

And of course you straggle two modalities... Integrative as well as gestalt (and more recently also relational psychoanalysis)..so you don't *fit* completely in any one mould... There's a price to pay for that.

Ken:

Yeah....(*deep sigh*) and I'm seeing one important difference though...

Supervisor:

What's that Ken?

Ken:

I'm not on my own...like before....as a priest in ministry...I have some great colleagues with real integrity who I value big time... This is a *major difference* for me now...I didn't know this until now...well I knew it but didn't really truly appreciate it. Ahah this is about *community* the new paradigm...that's it...that's the difference....uh connection.... I *feel connected* with them........... not alone in the oppressive practice.. I experience being alongside enough significant others............................

Supervisor:

So.....?

Ken:

I'm making some more connections....uh... The word heretic comes to me.... In the Church and within the profession the radical and unconventional connects with being seen as a heretic, hum..... Mmmm...and we all know what happened to heretics throughout history... Brrr..(*shaking with a cold chill*).

Supervisor:

What do you mean?... Say some more.

Ken:

Well my theology would be seen as heretical... certainly not mainstream... ...gestalt and integrative psychotherapy – along with many others – are frowned upon by the fundamentalist elements in the longer established modalities. In both religion and in the psychotherapy profession the denominational or tribal tendency in human nature is a frightening force... They burned heretics in the past.....Today they marginalize, exclude, and oppress in more subtle but devastating ways...like trying to wipe out whole sections of the psychotherapy profession...what the sociologists call 'social closure'.

   Well we won't go away or be excluded ...... Mmmmmm

Supervisor:

What?

Ken:

I am talking now more about psychotherapy and how – with others – we will fight against oppression and exclusion... But with the Church...religion... Mmmm I guess I still feel very isolated.

   Mmm...I am remembering the soul...uh... My theology of the soul is very radical and I guess...uh... I fear speaking or writing about it......some primitive fear of the scapegoat perhaps....you know being put outside the community and sent into the desert...uh...a desert of isolation and aloneness. The notion of soul, is long cherished by religion and also by those who are not religious but seek to develop their spirituality.

   Well.........let's cut to the chase...uh............I have come to think of 'soul' as a process not a static entity......not a thing waiting to be found...rather a process waiting to unfold moment by moment. How often in literature do we read of someone 'losing their soul' as if it were a thing you possess in the first place. It's not that I don't believe in soul......but not as something to be found but rather as something that functions as a dynamic process. Soul *is* life or life-fullness and we are called as human beings to step into life. So when we behave and live in the fullness of life................and this does often mean engaging with the fullness of life when it is uncomfortable, disturbing, distressing... It's *how* we engage: in life-enhancing ways or life-denying ways...living with doubts rather than deluding ourselves with false security; opening up to the vulnerability of contact, speaking kindly, living compassionately, connecting with self and ....uh......encouraging others both in joy and in sorrow...phew (*deep exhale and body shaking with excitement and connection*). This puts a response-ability on each human being..a call to step into the process of life and experience your soul which is the stuff of life.... Hold back and the soul doesn't cease to exist but rather remains patiently in the ground of our collective being....well actually in the ground of everything...waiting for us to engage with it...connect with it, whence it then becomes figural once more. I guess I'm talking about soul as the very ebb and flow of life itself. Engage and you experience soul....... disengage or step back from engagement and the soul eludes us.....or rather we elude soul.... Mmmm

I feel in touch with soul right now and I want to shout a resounding YES to life..............all of it..warts and all... YES.... YES....YES (*tears welling up of joy and pain*).

Reflections

In this chapter we have sought to capture and convey to you the lived experience of deep reflexive engagement, as well as showing how ambiguous layers of conscious–unconscious meanings can be teased out in the 'between' of both research and supervision relationships. We trust the example of the research process in action, in the 'here and now' offered by this example of reflexive introspection has succeeded in demonstrating the *art* of 'presence' and 'inclusion' and how these can enable new understandings.

We began this chapter by acknowledging that engaging in relational-centred research is invariably complex and hard to pin down because of innumerable processes involved. As a psychotherapist, the idea of engaging unconscious, emotional and relational processes will not be new to you. The challenge for you, however, is to find a way to engage positively with these processes *in the research context*. Here, contact with co-researchers may well be fleeting (certainly time-limited) and curtailed. Further, your co-researchers may not give permission to you to work with their 'process' or to check out any of your tentative interpretations. All these constraints put the onus much more on your reflections as the researcher and how you might use these to gain deeper understandings.

It is also never easy to engage in deep reflexive analysis. 'The process of engaging in reflexivity is full of muddy ambiguity ... as researchers negotiate the swamp of interminable deconstructions, self-analysis and self-disclosure' (Finlay, 2002b, p. 209). As researchers we risk getting bogged down in overly self-absorbed emoting and may lose sight of the Other or the phenomenon being investigated. Self-reflection needs to be used, not for its own sake, but in order to shed light on the research topic.

Ken is an experienced psychotherapist who has been practising for 30 years and capable of engaging positively with the complex and multi-layered nature of relational-centred exploration. Nevertheless his capacity for, and willingness to probe, challenging, ambivalent and uncomfortable unconscious aspects was stretched and extended through the challenge of an Other, in this case the supervisor.

Maturity in the practice of relational research includes the capacity and wisdom to invite the challenge of an Other; to look outside one's self (*I-It*) in order to deepen awareness and understanding of self (*I-Thou*). This is *I-It* in the service of *I-Thou*.

Notes

[i] Two-chair work is a psychotherapy technique which typically involves two chairs facing one another. The client sits on one chair with an imagined Other in the opposite one. Alternatively, the client moves back and forth between the chairs expressing different aspects of him- or herself (Kellogg, 2007). Two-chair work is about changes in awareness, leading to the emergence of a new gestalt. Awareness impacts not only on emotion but cognition and behaviour as well, leading to new understandings and meanings.

[ii] This dialogue has been transcribed as it emerged in real time. (Subsequent editing was kept to the minimum though some more personal passages have been omitted.) Key: '.....' = pause; more dots suggest lengthier pause; '( )' = significant non-verbal behaviour

[iii] Elinor Greenberg, Unpublished paper, New York, 1998.

Chapter 10

Analysis of Data

Linda Finlay and Anna Madill

There is no one way to do qualitative analysis. Analysis varies according to the methodology adopted, the type of data collected, the researcher's own predilections and what may be required by others. Some approaches to analysis emphasize scientific rigour and a careful, systematic working through of analytical stages while others emphasize fluid, intuitive, evolving, dynamic presentations. Some approaches try to *describe* and stay as close to the data as possible; others prefer to pursue more explicitly *interpretive* versions. And while some aim to develop conceptual categories towards theory building, others will use theory to make sense of the data.

Whatever the approach, however, the researcher must make sense of the data and synthesize it in such a way that the co-researchers' voices (or other data) are adequately re-presented. With qualitative analysis, the focus is on unpacking both explicit and hidden meanings through iteratively examining the data. Engaging in analysis involves researchers 'dwelling' with their data, examining it and then progressively deepening their understandings as meanings come to light. Wertz (2005, p. 174) describes the process well: 'When we stop and linger with something, it secretes its sense and its full significance becomes ... amplified.'

In this chapter, we outline four general types of analysis: Narrative, Thematic, Discursive and Creative.[i] Of course, in practice, analysis is often not so 'clean' and several types of analysis might be usefully combined

Relational-centred Research for Psychotherapists: Exploring Meanings and Experience
Edited by Linda Finlay and Ken Evans
Copyright © 2009 John Wiley & Sons, Ltd.

(provided their epistemological goals are compatible). Phenomenologically orientated research, for example, may well interweave narrative, thematic and creative forms of analysis. Narrative research commonly includes some discursive analysis.

As you study the examples given, you will see that the different types of analysis highlight different aspects of the data and enable different insights. Each method reveals certain aspects or dimensions while concealing or de-emphasizing others. Different interpretations assume *figural* significance against a *ground* of possible meanings; choice of analysis can be seen to shape emergent understandings. Any one analysis, says Churchill (2000, p. 164), can only be presented as a 'tentative statement opening upon a limitless field of possible interpretations'.

Narrative Analysis

Narratives can be presented in different ways. Commonly, the researcher tells their participant's 'story' about particular life events or experiences, following the participant's own chronology. The researcher may then engage in some form of secondary analysis: for instance, examining the narrative genre or type of story (for example, a 'heroic quest story') and identifying relevant themes, scripts and metaphors. Some researchers will also reflexively evaluate the social context (relational and discursive) of the story telling.[ii] (For an example, *see Chapter 15: Relating Through Difference* where Darren Langdridge offers a reflexive critical analysis of one person's narrative.)

The precise tenor and tone of the narrative analysis varies considerably across different methodologies (Reissman, 1993). The example below offers a taste of what a narrative analysis might encompass. This extract has been taken from a fuller published article (Finlay, 2004). It is based on the interview with Kenny conducted by Linda, described in *Chapter 7*. Part of the analysis is offered here to help you get a picture of how researchers might move from the data collection to analysis phases. In this example, we first present Kenny's 'story'. This is then analysed in terms of plot and the context of the storytelling.

Narratives offer a way into individuals' life stories in all their particularity and richness. Through hearing individuals' voices we are reminded to honour their experience – to truly listen. While research narratives are usually grounded in participants' words and may be presented as reflecting the individuals' reality, their constructed and collaborative nature needs to be emphasized. Researchers need to take care to distinguish between living

The story

Rock bottom

Five years ago Kenny was a 'gibbering idiot' – he had hit 'rock bottom':

> 'I was absolutely terrified. I was jumping at me own shadow ... I was frightened of people – which is amazing because most of me adult working life was with people, I'd worked with people.'

He realized something was wrong when he began to wake up in the morning and pray there was something wrong with him. 'Anything, just so I didn't have to go to work.' Suddenly one morning, it was all too much. 'That's it', he said, 'I've had enough'. He walked out of his workplace and never went back ...

> 'I was just shaking the whole time, having panic attacks. I locked myself in the bedroom. It took weeks and weeks before I would go out. I would read, submerge myself in books, escape. I wasn't interested in anything. I just wanted to be in my bed ...'

Doing something

Suddenly one morning, something in his head shifted. He found himself thinking: 'You've got to get out of this! You've got to do something!' The same day, his wife came home with the news that a friend of a friend had some repairs that needed doing to a van and would Kenny like to have a go? ... Previously Kenny had been a senior hotel manager but he had always liked working with his hands, so he decided to give it a try. He recognized how destructive it had been to have 'done nothing' for so long. 'I was beginning to feel useless', he admitted. He made the decision that day that he was going to get back into work somehow. That was the beginning of his recovery ...

Narrative analysis

Kenny's story is a chronological account of his illness and journey back to health and work. This *progressive occupational narrative* (Braverman et al., 2003) is a simple story – not particularly dramatic or unusual. Kenny tells of everyday experiences and ordinary events. He speaks of the value of occupation and a special relationship with an understanding employer. His story can also be understood as a *quest story* (Frank, 1998) in that Kenny seems to have framed his illness as a condition from which something can be learned and passed on to others. His quest was to find meaning and purpose in his mental health problems and to re-emerge stronger with new qualities and insights: in fact, with a new identity. The life Kenny has re-claimed has involved compromise and sacrifice. He shares his victory while recognizing its provisional status ...

An experiential view

Primarily Kenny's story is one of survival and self-discovery (Davies, 2001). In such narratives individuals heroically emerge from difficult experiences to share their story. Emphasis is placed on surviving the illness and perhaps becoming an even stronger, better person in the process. So, we hear something of Kenny's fight to regain control and how he progressed from being a 'gibbering idiot' to becoming an 'iceman' who can master stressful situations without getting ruffled.

We hear first of Kenny's experience of his illness. Locking himself in his bedroom, he hides from a suddenly threatening world in a desperate attempt to be safe, protecting both himself and others. We catch a glimpse of his aloneness and terror as he struggles to understand what is happening to him. As his feelings intensify, he loses control over himself and his life. His relationships with both himself and others are anxiety provoking – a feeling experienced all the more acutely as it is alien to his previously habitual way of being ... Past aims and projects have been derailed while the future becomes profoundly uncertain and bleak.

Then we hear of Kenny's journey of self-discovery and how he confronts and surmounts barriers of increasing challenge. Being able to successfully 'kick down' each new hurdle empowers Kenny and gives him more confidence. He describes some of the self-help strategies which have helped him cope. Through various metaphors he talks of 'climbing up the ladder out of the pit' and 'chipping away at the concrete block to find his confidence'. We gain a sense of how he has motivated himself through his journey out of his mental health problems. In the end he is reconciled to letting his previous occupational identity go. He understands that certain possibilities are now denied to him and compromises need to be made. In order to maintain his sense of being in control, he trades his previous high status job for a less stressful factory job ...

A contextual view

Underpinning Kenny's apparently straightforward story is another: a story involving a complex, and entirely hidden, negotiation which took place between Kenny and myself as 'listener' ... I had invited Kenny to share the story of his experience. While he chose what story to tell, he did so in the context of my responses and the questions I was asking.

His story was, at least in part, created through our dialogue. Our relationship had an impact on the way Kenny spoke to me, particularly in terms of what he felt safe enough to reveal. I had been helpful to him in a friendly professional capacity, offering him some support and advice. Kenny knew I was an occupational therapist and that I was interested in the value of productive activity and doing. He therefore produced a story – one with a positive spin – with work as the focus. He probably would not have felt comfortable talking about his relationship with his wife, domestic matters or financial hardship problems resulting from his long-term unemployment. These were other stories which lurked, unspoken ...

Kenny's performance can also be understood as a way of 'doing' masculinity (Edley, 2002). His struggle to respect himself through finding a work role needs to be seen in the context of the stigma attached by his working-class community to an unemployed man who is not fulfilling his family breadwinner role. Through his narrative performance focused on returning to work and becoming an 'iceman' he reasserts his preferred masculine identity. As Bourdieu and others have noted, 'narratives about the most 'personal' ... articulate the deepest structures of the social world.' (Bourdieu et al., 1993, cited in Reissman, 2003, p. 24).[iii]

a life story, telling and reliving that life story and then retelling that life story (Clandinin & Connelly, 1994). Individuals present what they want to be known about themselves (Reissman, 2003). Then the researcher retells that story. The story heard, interpreted and analysed by one researcher is likely to be different from the one another researcher would hear.

Thematic Analysis

Thematic analysis is a method for analysing and describing important patterns (themes) within data (Braun & Clarke, 2006). Most qualitative methodologies include elements of thematic analysis. For some methods this is just the initial step in finding sequences for in-depth analysis. Other methods specify their own sophisticated procedures for identifying and working with themes. Braun and Clarke (2006) provide a step-by-step guide to typical phases:

- Familiarizing yourself with your data
- Generating initial codes
- Searching for themes
- Reviewing themes
- Defining and naming themes
- Producing the report.

It is often said that themes 'emerge from data'. While it is true that themes need to be grounded in and reflect the data, the idea that they somehow pop out and are self-evident is not true. It does not do to sit waiting passively for themes to arrive. Mostly, meanings have to be searched for and themes shaped up painstakingly in successive iterations. Haumann (2005) makes this point when she describes the way she interrogated her data on psychotherapists' experiences of their personal journey. In the initial phase of textual analysis she used intersubjectivity theory to generate a conceptual framework. This underscored the shifting power distributions and identification processes. The Jungian notion of the wounded healer was used to draw attention to the way therapists relate to patients as objects rather than subjects. The effects of personal therapy were then understood in terms of enhanced abilities to relate person to person and for reflective thinking. The final stage of analysis involved generating an intersubjective model of personal therapy and development.

While the eventual form taken by themes can vary, a good thematic analysis is one which does more than string together extracts from the research. Instead, it will seek to identify and synthesize themes that are coherent, convincing, consistent and grounded in the data (Braun & Clarke, 2006). Ideally, themes should be more than ordinary category headings: they should also be interesting, written in a lively style or they should resonate in some way.

In the following exemplar, Fitzpatrick and Finlay (2008), discuss one theme which emerged in their research on the lived experience of the rehabilitation phase following flexor tendon surgery. In this rehabilitation, participants were required to complete an hourly exercise regime and wear a splint constantly for four to six weeks. Three themes were identified overall: 'denying–accepting', 'battling–retreating' and 'struggling–adapting'. Just the first is offered here as a taster.

Denying–Accepting

As normal life roles and valued projects are relinquished, a new 'disabled' persona begins to emerge. One particular lesson that needs to be learned is to accept bodily limitations or risk further long-term damage. But finding the appropriate level of function and the safe way to move is difficult, not least because mind and body seem to be pushing in different directions.

Somehow individuals need to find a way to enact their disability while still hanging on to the person they once were.

It can feel easier to sometimes deny there is a problem. With that denial the individuals can once more claw back some sort of normality into their life. The risks and long-term costs of not accepting disability are pushed away. It is as if they gain a sense of stability and normality by trying to 'pass' as the person they once were. People with disability often strive to maintain 'normal' functioning by minimising and disguising their problems – a point picked up by several commentators (for example, Charmaz, 2000; French, 1993).

So, Dawn returns to work at her hairdressing salon just one week after surgery despite being advised to take six weeks off. After her initial fear that her 'hand was wrecked', she determines to reclaim her life. Despite the risks involved in pushing herself, she refuses to take more time off work. John feels awkward and tense in public and does not like revealing he is disabled to others. Somehow feelings of shame arise in the gaze of others (Sartre, 1943/1969).

The experience of being cared-for is double-edged (Frank, 2000). When people find themselves injured or disabled, the fact that they need help stirs a cocktail of contrasting emotions within them. In all probability they will feel grateful for the care and support they receive. But such dependence will be realised with varying degrees of resistance. Feelings of guilt, loss of dignity and vulnerability may push an individual to resist others' help.

Although accepting care from others also involves conceding some degree of dependence, care is also experienced positively as a source of strength and support. Each of the participants sought and received help from others – in different ways and to different levels. Adam accepts a large amount of support from his work colleagues and housemates. John, too, relies greatly on support from his new wife, family, colleagues and friends. Even Sally eventually draws on her family's support by returning to live in the parental home.

At different points in their rehabilitation, all five participants begin to accept their current level of disability and to respect the risks involved if they don't comply with the rehabilitation advice. They accept that treatment and recovery will take time – longer than they had originally appreciated. They begin to come to terms with the multiple traumas and losses experienced and they understand that compromises in their lives are necessary. They learn to expect the frustrating inconveniences and work around them, appreciating the love and support offered by others. They accept the uncertainty surrounding the degree of functioning they will eventually attain, recognising that they may never regain the level of arm function they had prior to the trauma. Eventually, they can acknowledge, even celebrate, their progress and achievements.[iv]

Thematic analysis offers the opportunity to highlight important conceptual features or nuances of lived experience. Yet, as themes open up possibilities, other avenues are closed. Researchers need to be cautious about offering an account of 'general themes' which are assumed to fit all participants. The particular voices and experiences of the individuals studied can blur or retreat into the background, with some individuals' experiences being more strongly reflected in the themes than others. The themes can also become somewhat inflexible and may not sufficiently reflect the evolving nature of participants' experiences during the relational research.

Discursive Analysis

Discursive analysis (for example, Potter, 2003; Potter & Wetherell, 1994) starts from the assumption that talk and text (discourse) does not merely represent the world but actively shapes, or constructs, it. In particular, discursive analysis draws attention to how the world – our place in it and experience of it – can be described in many different ways in our communication with others.

When considering subjective or lived experience, discursive approaches are, at best, agnostic about the existence of a psychological interior. Discursive analysis avoids appeal to motivations, thoughts and emotions. Instead it considers how such concepts are used creatively by people to account for themselves and others. Psychological attributes, then, are analysed as discursive or textual; they are not assumed to represent underlying mental processes or predispositions. This view of the person is counter-intuitive and may feel uncomfortable as it seems to deny the existence either of an inner experiential life or of an outer material reality. It does, however, ask us to consider what we might be taking for granted about ourselves and the world: things that may be, to some extent at least, only conventionalized ways of talking.

Discursive analysis can focus on minute detail of dialogue and social interaction (micro-level) or on the content of discourses considered a product of a wider historical and cultural context (macro-level). At a micro-level, analysis highlights the performative qualities of talk. When a person speaks they give an account of themselves. The aim is to understand what is achieved by offering that particular version of the world, given that particular context, and to explicate the 'rhetorical strategies' by which accounts are made persuasive or are challenged.

At a macro-level, discursive analysis highlights how discourse constructs subjects and objects in ways that are constrained by wider social practices. Here the aim is to explore the images, representations and ideologies which circulate through every day discourse and how these impact on the way people position each other: for example, as 'victim' or 'terrorist' or 'mentally ill'.

Below an exemplar analysis considers an extract from psychodynamic-interpersonal psychotherapy during which an adult female client came to describe herself as feeling anger towards her mother despite having rejected this understanding earlier in therapy.[v] The analysis does not attempt to discover what the client's real emotions are, but aims to understand the micro-discursive processes through which an understanding of her feelings was *negotiated in interaction* with the therapist. The analysis also demonstrates how macro-discourses constituting our contemporary understanding of the emotions must be assumed in order for this sequence to 'make sense'. The following exchange occurred in the second session during discussion of the client's relationship with her mother and immediately follows the client's statement that 'anger does not come into her repertoire':

C[vi]: It it really <u>doesn't</u> (T: mm) (.) no.[viii]

T[vii]: So that sounds like there as if you're sort of sort of feeling sort of frustrated (.) frustrated with me for going on about it or something? it really <u>doesn't</u> (*C laughs*) it sort of (tails off).

C: Well it's just not <u>part</u> of me to <u>get</u> angry (.) (T: mm hm) it's just not in my make up (T: mm) I <u>don't</u>.

T: Mm you don't.

C: No (*C laughs followed by T*).

T: I suppose at <u>some</u> is in <u>some</u> way I suppose I don't believe it I suppose that's what's happening (.) it feels like what you're saying that there's a whole bit of you that isn't there (.) and I just don't believe it (2) or something you (.) I mean only that that sounds very I don't know I mean that sounds funny it's not when I said I don't believe it I mean I feel that there must be part of you that you're not expressing and you must you know that must be <u>costing</u> you something (.) that by by writing it out of the script like that you're you're doing yourself some harm I suppose that's what I feel.

At the beginning of this sequence the therapist comments on the way in which the client has expressed herself and hence introduces this as a relevant topic for discussion. An appropriate response is for the client to comment on the therapist's suggestion and she does this by offering an explanation for why she might 'sound frustrated'. She suggests that not getting angry is an established and natural part of her constitution, with the implication that her frustration is due to being challenged about something which, to her, is self-evident.

The client's statement could have been understood as a claim that she is merely not easily roused to anger. However, the therapist's reaction of disbelief suggests that a more extreme interpretation is being taken forward in the conversation: that *she never gets angry*. In contemporary Western culture anger is considered a fundamental human experience (Ekman, 1985). Interpreting the client as challenging this common-sense under-standing of the emotions makes the client's position appear untenable and her laughter may indicate acknowledgement of the unusual nature of the claim being developed in the conversation.

Why might the client collaborate with such a seemingly extreme claim? Throughout this session the client had had her account of her feelings questioned by the therapist. This is an unusual situation as another feature of contemporary understanding of the emotions is that a person is gener-ally considered to have privileged access to their interior states (Lutz, 1988). The client therefore has to defend an account which would not normally be open to question and extreme case formulations (for example, com-monplace exaggerations such as 'never', 'always', 'forever') are often used in interaction when one needs to assert the strongest rebuttal of what has gone before.

Moreover, the client's statement, which allows the interpretation that she never gets angry, was made specifically in response to the therapist's sug-gestion that she might be feeling frustrated with *him*. To avoid appearing ungrateful or disrespectful, one requires particularly good grounds for expressing frustration with an expert to whom one has turned and who is offering help. So, the client's suggestion that she 'doesn't get angry' can also be understood as an exaggeration aimed at legitimizing the irritation awarded to her during the conversation. However, this leaves her vulner-able to challenge and for the development of a 'problem formation' (i.e. type of implicative summary) regarding her emotional inhibition. This particular trajectory is enabled by the client's contextual positioning as 'in therapy' since a pertinent exception to the understanding that one has privileged access to one's own internal states are situations in which an individual is considered troubled and in which accounts of disturbed psy-chological processes may be invoked. And this is what the therapist goes on to do.

This analysis illustrates part of an ongoing process through which a problem formation is co-constructed within the therapy interaction. An account in which the client appears to suffer a particular kind of emotional problem is worked up from her use of an extreme case formation which functioned at a particular juncture in the dialogue to defend herself against unusual challenge and which was oriented to specific and contextual social mores. Moreover, the problem formulation rests on contemporary Western 'common sense' about the emotions – an understanding which is neither fixed nor universal.

It may feel frustrating that no attempt is made to establish the client's 'real' problem, assuming that she has one. The analysis may also appear to undermine therapeutic interventions by offering, at best, mere 'word play'. However, discursive approaches do allow us to see how a different version of ourselves and our experience can evolve through discussion with others – to our benefit when we forge more productive ways of being. Discursive approaches also ask us to reflect critically on the networks of meaning – the discourses – that create us as human subjects and to challenge their effects at a social and individual level where these effects seem damaging or repressive.

Creative Analysis

Discursive analysis challenges certain assumptions about academic work: for example, that accurate description of a pre-existing objective reality is an appropriate goal. Creative forms of analysis challenge the goals and format of academic research in a different way. Creative analysis includes the use of poetry, prose, drama, visual arts and dance to express or represent the voice of researcher/co-researchers. In this sense, creative analysis can be both the way of handling data and presenting research findings. Researchers may set out explicitly to use alternative forms to juxtapose, disrupt or challenge taken-for-granted assumptions. The aim underlying the use of creative media – mirroring the processes used in the arts generally – may be to evoke, unsettle or even shock. At the same time, the creative process may itself inspire new expressions and insights.

> In these texts, concrete action, dialogue, emotion, embodiment, spirituality, and self-consciousness are featured, appearing as relational and institutional stories affected by our history, social structure, and culture. (Ellis & Bochner, 2000, p. 739)

Unsurprisingly with such creative approaches, the lines between 'fiction' and 'fact' may be fuzzy. Similarly, the process of data gathering, analysis and writing up (or publicly sharing one's work) is often blurred. There are no 'rules' in this genre.

Two examples of *autobiographical* work are shown here to illustrate the possibilities opened up by creative analysis. The final *Chapter 16* in this book by Susan Morrow further demonstrates how creative forms might be used both as part of the process of 'gathering data' and as 'analysis'.

Example 10.1   Integrated feminist creativity

Shields (1998) has felt negatively about her appearance all her life. Coming from a long line of beautiful women, she felt she was the 'ugly duckling' who had not met family expectations. She wanted to gain a deeper understanding of what physical attractiveness meant to her and so chose beauty and body image as a topic of inquiry. She followed her intuitions arising in her dreams about how to proceed with the research. She eventually collected 15 hours of dialogue with her mother and grandmother.

When writing up her dissertation, she eschewed standard report formats and, instead, presented the dialogues in their original forms and gave accounts of her dreams using different kinds of fonts. She also included photographs of her female lineage. Looking back, she describes how her relationships with her mother and grandmother have been significantly deepened. For her, the research had been a transformational experience which continues today. She writes, 'It has been gratifying to hear that many women have been moved to tears when reading my dissertation.' (Shields, 1998, p. 198)

Example 10.2   Experience of writing

Milloy (2005) researched the actual lived experience of doing research and writing. In the following passage she offers a phenomenological description of the process describing how words can be generated in the body – what she calls the 'proprioceptive register':

> The whole body is poised in between, and resonates with, movements, spilling toward words that mark out the journey along the markings on the page … Paperthin, the page weighs nothing. The words slowly weigh it down, and page by page, the heaviness transfers and shifts, yet I don't become lighter: there is more. More to breathe, more to feel, more to birth, more to penetrate. The words re-invent themselves after the coitus of momentary truth, pass further into more. And I am inside and outside this language, I merge with it, merge with the world. Writing is the moisture I excrete, the air I breathe. (Milloy, 2005, pp. 546–547)[ix]

Creative analysis – in whatever form – can evoke, resonate and offer new ways of looking at a topic. Potentially powerful art forms they may be but what is their status? What relation do they bear, if at all, to rigorous scientific methods of inquiry? Is there a danger that researchers (and participants) may get caught up in the artistic endeavour, with its soaring flights of the imagination, while in the process losing sight of the research focus? Such questions continue to dog this intriguing – and controversial – approach to analysis.

Reflections

Qualitative analysis is always challenging to do. It is easy to feel overwhelmed by the quantity and complexity of data that needs to be analysed. Given the complex, opaque, ambivalent and ambiguous nature of human experience, it is challenging to make sense of our social world, or of an individual's confused expressions and experiences. In our view, qualitative analysis should be judged not on its ability to present 'solutions' but rather on its capacity to capture something of this 'mess'.

Whichever analytic approach we choose to use as researchers, we need to remember that it will only offer a selective glimpse. However powerful, comprehensive and nuanced our findings, they must remain tentative, partial and emergent. It is always possible to see *more* in data at a different point in time, while another researcher may unfold a different story. Modesty, rather than grand claims to 'truth' or 'self-evident' findings, lies at the heart of qualitative research. As Dahlberg et al. (2008) recognize, analysis can never be complete, further explication is always possible, and our understanding of others stands perpetually open to exciting new possibilities.

Notes

[i] For more detailed guidance on how to do particular types of analysis we recommend going to specific chapters and books which highlight particular methods such as Smith (2003) (Ed.), *Qualitative Psychology: A practical guide to research methods*, London: Sage.
[ii] Narratives thus involve both a person's *story* and a *method* of inquiry where the researcher attempts to reconstruct and write up the story.
[iii] This extract has been taken from Finlay (2004, pp. 476–479) and has been reproduced here with the kind permission of Upma Barnett, Editor of the *British Journal of Occupational Therapy*.
[iv] This extract has been taken from Fitzpatrick and Finlay (2008), 'Frustrating disability': The lived experience of coping with the rehabilitation phase following flexor tendon surgery, *International Journal of Qualitative Studies on Health and Well-being*, 3, 143–154. It has been reproduced here with the kind permission of the publisher, Taylor & Francis.

[v] For a more extended analysis see Madill (2009), Construction of anger in one successful case of psychodynamic-interpersonal psychotherapy: Problem (re)formulation and the negotiation of moral context, *The European Journal for Qualitative Research in Psychotherapy* (www.europeanresearchjournal.com)

[vi] The client was female, in her forties, and in full-time, white-collar employment.

[vii] The therapist was male, of similar age to the client, and had 18 years experience with psychodynamic-interpersonal therapy.

[viii] The transcription conventions are a modified version of those developed by Jefferson (Atkinson & Heritage, 1984):

(0)	Pauses timed in seconds
(.)	An untimed short pause
word	Stress on word by speaker
T: (mm)	Overlapping utterance
.	End of turn
(whispered)	Tonal information

[ix] Permission to reproduce this passage has kindly been given by Dr Brent Robbins, Editor-in-Chief of *Janus Head*, Trivium Publications.

Chapter 11

Relational Ethics

Relational ethics requires researchers to act from our hearts and minds, acknowledge our interpersonal bonds to others, and take responsibility for actions and their consequences. (Ellis, 2007, p. 3)

Professional guidelines for the ethical conduct of research tend to emphasize certain key principles: participants should be respected, protected and never deceived; their informed consent should be gained beforehand; they should be debriefed afterwards; confidentiality should be maintained; and so on.[i] These guidelines sound reasonably straightforward. In practice, however, every research encounter brings up context-specific ethical uncertainties and challenges (Finlay & Molano-Fisher, 2009). No matter how strictly and carefully various ethical procedures and protocols are followed, situations arise in the field that make our heads spin and hearts ache (Ellis, 2007). The process of negotiating an ethical path can be tricky, and compromises usually need to be made.

Relational-centred researchers tend to experience these ethical challenges particularly acutely. In addition to respecting and protecting the dignity of the co-researcher, relational ethics demands that we recognize the interconnection between researcher and researched, and our wider communities. We are called upon to be reflexive about our role as researchers at every stage of the research and to critically examine the impact of

Relational-centred Research for Psychotherapists: Exploring Meanings and Experience
Edited by Linda Finlay and Ken Evans
Copyright © 2009 John Wiley & Sons, Ltd.

any imbalances of power that may arise. We are also called upon to acknowledge that researchers and co-researchers alike can be profoundly touched by the research we do.

This chapter focuses on the relational ethical challenges which arise at different stages of a research project: pre-research, data gathering, analysis and concluding the research. During each stage, as researchers, we confront the tricky task of minimizing the impact of likely (some argue inevitable) power imbalances between ourselves and our co-researcher(s). How do we move towards more collaborative, egalitarian, open relationships as opposed to exploitative, instrumental ones? For us as relational researchers, understandings of the other are found in the fullness of our open relation (Buber, 1937/1958), hence the importance of engaging a mutual participation where 'dialogue, parity and reciprocity' are threaded through all phases of research (Heron, 1996, p. 11).

Pre-research Phase

If you are a practising therapist, you will be familiar with the tensions generated when negotiating an initial therapy contract. Often a delicate balancing act is involved as you seek to set boundaries and establish trust. Similar tensions arise in the research context, except that the research you are proposing is not something that potential co-researchers have asked for and, furthermore, it may not offer them any direct benefits.[ii] Thus a different sort of contract needs to be negotiated.

It also may be necessary, depending on the type of research you are planning to do, to negotiate a broader contract for entering the 'field'. If, for instance, you are intending to do a participant observation study, then you may need to negotiate the contract and boundaries with a number of people including at an organizational level.

All this means that a great deal of ground work needs to be done before any relational research project gets underway – ground work that reaches beyond purely procedural concerns such as obtaining informed consent and ensuring confidentiality/anonymity (*see* the section on gaining ethical approval in *Chapter 6: Setting Up Research*). The research contract as a whole needs to negotiated and a level of trust and/or consent established with all involved. (*See Chapter 15: Relating Through Difference* where Darren Langdridge discusses the care he took to work with his client and time the research encounter.)

In this pre-research stage, the foundations of mutual trust within a dialogical relationship need to be put in place and the research aims and process generally agreed upon. In Buber's terms, we are called on to move beyond a functional '*I-It*' relationship, in which we see the Other in terms of their use to us, towards an '*I-Thou*' relationship – one of openness to their personhood. This process is easier said than done. In a situation where the researcher initiates and controls contact and holds professional knowledge, the relationship is inevitably an uneven one. Fuhr (1992, cited in Krüger, 2007) goes so far as to compare this initial phase of research to the relationship between parents and child: just as the researcher-parent has a clear sense about what the research is going to involve, the co-researcher-child is the one who complies and surrenders.

The significant step demanded of the relational researcher is to release control, or rather take 'control in a new humanistic sense by being clearly conscious of the choice' of ensuring co-researchers have both choice and voice themselves (Krüger, 2007, p. 19). This lays the ground for a true, authentic, mutual interaction. Two examples below show some of these relational ethical issues involved.

Example 11.1   Participative action research

In this first example, Abrahams (2007) conducted a collaborative participative action research project informed by feminist ideals. The research aimed to examine the personal, emotional and practical needs of women who had left an abusive relationship and come to a refuge. In the early stages of her research Abrahams realized that women's groups working with domestic violence tend to be 'extremely sensitive to being "used" or exploited by outsiders, including academics who might not be in sympathy with their ideas and values' (2007, p. 241). As a result, the groups Abrahams approached expressed apprehension and uncertainty about becoming involved and they were wary about giving her access as a researcher. She found her initial interactions crucial to build trust and open communication:

> Each group needed to … talk to me to be sure that they would feel able to work with me and be confident in my personal style, motivation and research abilities … they needed to satisfy themselves that the research would not be exploitative and that it would be of use to them. (2007, p. 241)

Abrahams engaged in many extended visits to ensure she was present in the refuge for long periods enabling the residents and workers to talk to her informally in their own time.

Example 11.2   Feminist collaborative research

Morrow (2006) describes how, in her feminist collaborative research with sexually abused women, the process of gaining consent circumvented her control over data collection. (*See Chapter 16: A Journey Into Survival* for more details of this study.)

> I had originally planned to meet for a short time with each interviewee to explain the project, get acquainted, explain and have participants sign the informed consent form and schedule our longer interview. I had explained this expectation to the first participant, Paula, when we first made telephone contact. However, after we had finished the informed consent process and I pulled out my calendar to schedule our interview appointment, she objected, saying, "I thought we were going to do the interview now. I'm ready to talk!" I consented and, feeling a little panicky, searched for my interview guide. Unable to find it, I finally responded, "Well, uh, er, um. Tell me, as much as you are comfortable sharing with me right now, um, what happened to you when you were sexually abused." This kind of question, both very personal and potentially disturbing for a participant, is not the kind of question with which I would normally begin an interview, but Paula's desire to tell her story and my own personal style (I've been described as an "earth mother" who elicits trust very early in a relationship) converged to make the question both appropriate and effective. (Morrow, 2006, p. 153)

In the collaborative research examples above, both researchers indicate that they place their ethical concerns for co-researchers above any pre-planned instrumental research strategy. Such an impulse fits the recommendations of the phenomenological philosopher Levinas (1969) who puts concern for the Other at the centre of his ethics. He argues that ethical human relating involves an ongoing effort to constrain one's own freedom and spontaneity (or allow oneself to be constrained) as part of a project of being 'open' to the Other.

Data-gathering Phase

During the early stages of research when gathering data researchers face ethical challenges relating to the use (and mis-use) of power to do with their duty of care to keep participants safe.

In relational-centred research, researchers have power which comes from their professional authority and the way they control the research. However, researchers also work hard to relinquish their 'power' yielding to whatever might be emerging in the relational moment.

Inevitably, researchers will find themselves being instrumental at times. Alert to opportunities to obtain data from the other, they may push hungrily ahead. This is exposed at a simple level when, during interviews, we are selective about which questions/answers to follow up. At a more subtle level, the researcher is the one who uses 'expert' knowledge (such as using empathetic responses and reflecting back techniques) to both 'open up' a co-researcher's expressions and close them down again. There are no clear-cut answers here about what level of disclosure or degree of restraint is desirable. The negotiation can only take place within the dialogical relationship, as the next example illustrates.

Example 11.3   Co-researcher distress

In a tape recorded interview, Maria, the informant, becomes excited and emotionally involved with the story of her life as a mother of her handicapped child. Suddenly, and to her own surprise, she bursts into tears – but continues with her story. At this point, the researcher becomes particularly alert and tempted because behind the tears and a sad destiny, he detects that the informant actually reveals something which is right to the point of the theme he wants to explore in his research.

So, how should the researcher in this example handle the dilemma on the one hand, to obtain substantial research result and, on the other, to heed the necessary precautions to protect the personal integrity of Maria? Should, in the name of science, the tape recorder be stopped and the interview cancelled in order to take care of the informant's personal process?

As a matter of fact, the solution lies within the relation itself, provided that the researcher is aware of the obligation to stay in the impasse, and at the same time to situate the problem where it belongs: in the relationship. In this way the theme is lifted to a dialogical level of interaction, and the acutely conscious becomes the guideline for his work (Krüger, 2007, p. 20).[iii]

Example 11.3 above shows how tricky it can be for us to manage our own power as researchers while seeking to protect (and perhaps even empower) our co-researchers. Ideally, the research process is at once strategic *and* respectful. As in therapy, we attempt a balancing act: we seek to use our professional skills to enable and facilitate disclosure while at the same time intervening to protect our co-researcher from too much exposure. Such 'dialectical oppositions' (Ellis, 2007, pp. 20–21) involve moving back and forth between expression and protection, between disclosure and restraint (Bochner, 1984).

As in the therapy situation, the researcher endeavours to enable co-researchers to feel they have control over what they are sharing and they consent to whatever is going to constitute the 'data' to be worked with. At the same time researchers need to be reflexively aware of the power (and lack of power) they wield. Power, of course, comes in different guises, inhabiting structural dimensions such as class, race/ethnicity, gender, and so on. Relational-centred researchers need to be alert to how these different types of power cross-cut each other. It is too simplistic to suggest power is exerted in only one direction. Not only can participants control the agenda, they can claim power by, for instance, acting in a passive aggressive way. As a different example, consider how you would feel if you were a woman interviewing a violent male sex offender; or if you were a relational-centred researcher interviewing a doctor who was hostile to 'unscientific' qualitative research.

Beyond questions of power, researchers have a 'duty of care' to ensure the safety (emotional and physical) of their co-researchers. Relational research often taps sensitive material and can be emotionally intense to experience (possibly for the researcher as well as the co-researcher). Co-researchers may feel exposed and vulnerable while the experience of re-telling their stories has the potential to re-traumatize them. The next example illustrates ways in which the research challenged one participant. In this example, Pat (co-researcher) explains to Linda (researcher) in an email why she had wanted to disengage from their research on exploring Pat's experience of receiving a cochlear implant. (*See* Example 3.1 in *Chapter 3: Embodied Co-creation* for a fuller discussion of this research.)

Example 11.4   Research and emotional intensity

Pat: Hi Linda. I am ready again, sorry about [being out of touch for such a] long time, thanks for the space … couldn't handle the analysis. Felt I wanted to move on, not to dwell in the past …

Linda: It's understandable you want to move on – totally understand-able. Rest assured that you don't need to do any more … if you don't want to. I'm happy to run with it and you can say what level of involvement you want to have … For now, I want to understand more about what is scaring you if you feel able to talk …

> **Pat:**   What scares me is that I don't want to face deafness, disability, implants anymore. I don't like that I cannot follow things like others do even with the implant. It scares me that I really like my silence and miss it … Even if I have progressed, I feel I will never feel 'normal' as I felt before because my bubble has been burst!! I am scared because I feel very angry with the world!!! … I am scared about what else I don't know will come in the analysis and I rather hide it and don't face it! (Finlay & Molano-Fisher, 2009)

In this example, both Pat and Linda needed to balance the potential harm of their focus on Pat's emotional world against the potential benefit of telling her story. They made the decision to carry on. Pat felt she wanted to share her experience as there were lessons to be learned by professionals as well other deaf individuals considering the possibility of implants. As Cutcliffe and Ramcharan (2002) and others acknowledge, emotionally charged research may be distressing for some but it can also often be therapeutic and validating.

The fact that what arises needs to be sensitively handled and then managed is further highlighted in the next example.

Example 11.5   Collaborating with while protecting co-researchers

In the following passage Ellis describes the relational ethical process she engaged in when collaborating with two other researchers on their experience of bulimia nervosa. She was mindful of the personal and emotional nature of the project, and this was intensified by the fact that ethical concerns arose as her co-researchers were her PhD students. They decided to write privately and hold any disclosures as confidential until they all agreed to disclose more publicly. As a group they also had to continually process how they were feeling and whether or not to stay with the project.

> I emphasized that Christine and Lisa not reveal anything to me they might regret later because they might be concerned with how I, their professor, saw them … In each meeting, we created opportunities to change our minds, and to add to or delete from the stories we had told. (2007, pp. 20–21)

As Ellis shows here, a number of steps can be taken by researchers to protect their co-researchers. In the research by Ellis and her students, they agreed to use mild discomfort as a cue to explore further while they were also committed to protecting one another from distress. As she notes: 'We tried to develop trust by openly sharing our lives; however, we also had to respect each other's needs for privacy and restraint' (Ellis, 2007, p. 21).

Relational-centred researchers need to recognize the potential for the research to be intense and painful. Even research that seems apparently straightforward may deeply touch participants. We need to appreciate the gift they are giving us by sharing and to be prepared to handle whatever comes up.

While being supportive of research participants, however, we need to take care to not transgress boundaries between research and psychotherapy and that means trying to stay within the terms of what you have negotiated in your research contract. Also, unlike the therapy context, we might negotiate terms where certain personal or sensitive material is ring-fenced as 'no go areas' or the material may later be deliberately excluded from the research. Towards the end of the research, a separate post-research discussion may prove fruitful to help the co-researcher integrate their experience. It may also be necessary to arrange for some external counselling or psychotherapy to be offered if extra support is needed.

The above discussion and examples highlight how the data-gathering phase of research involves so much more than simply collecting data. Ethical and relational negotiations, concerned with power, protection, respect and the safety of the co-researcher are similarly intertwined when it comes to analysing the data.

Data Analysis Phase

In this phase, qualitative researchers confront the question of the extent to which they can, or should, involve participants in the analytical process. The outcome depends, in part, on the type of research involved.

In discursive forms of research, for instance, participants are unlikely to get involved in analysis given its highly technical and/or ironic nature. Discursive methods tend to 'utilise counter-intuitive, and possibly impenetrable, understanding of subjectivity which participants may reject, not least because it appears to undermine the felt immediacy of their lived experience' (Madill, 2009, p. 20). While these researchers usually carry out their analysis on their own, the process of identifying and naming discourses still involves ethical as well as moral and political choices on the part of the analyst (Parker, 1992). For this reason, discursive researchers are encouraged to be reflexive about how they position themselves and their participants within the social world.

In contrast, collaborative and participatory action forms of research rely on the process of iteratively taking evolving understandings back to participants. Arvay (2003), for instance, advocates her Collaborative Narrative Method which thoroughly involves co-researchers in each of seven stages of research, from pre-interview negotiation, through transcription and interpretation to eventually sharing the stories. Halling and Leifer (1991) suggest another kind of collaborative approach where research is conducted entirely through group members' dialogue. They work together comparing personal experiences and interviews with each other which allows them to come to a collective understanding of the phenomena being studied. Halling's dialogical phenomenological study of forgiveness saw him collaborate with a group of Masters' students, with positive results. Witnessing the group members' ability to be imaginative and playful with their interpretations, he notes that:

> Freedom infused the process with a spirit of exploration and discovery ... Trust provides the capacity to be genuinely receptive to what is new and different in the others' experiences. (Halling & Leifer, 1991, p. 11)

While Halling is committed to the fullest possible collaboration with his co-researchers, other relational researchers involve their co-researchers only to the extent that the latter *wish* to be involved. The reflexive account in the next example is a case in point. Here, Linda discusses the ethics of her collaboration with Ann in a phenomenological study on Ann's lived experience of multiple sclerosis. (*See* Example 8.1 in *Chapter 8: Embracing Relational Research* which discusses this research further.) In the extended extract below, Linda shares something of the relational ethical process involved in negotiating their collaboration.[iv]

Example 11.6   Participant validation?

Ann and I collaborated in this research in a number of ways. First of all she agreed to share her experience with me as she was keen that I 'spread the word' to therapists about what it was 'really like to have MS'. Together, we embarked on a project whose findings, we both understood, would eventually be made public. Ann was content for me to share the findings with therapists. That the interviews were conducted in a natural conversation style helped foster that sense of collaboration. As I moved on to analyse the interviews I consulted Ann several times, discussing with her my perceptions and analysis. In these ways Ann can be said to have played a part in co-constituting the findings.

As Ann was a physiotherapist she had a reasonable understanding of the aims, process and intended outcomes of my case study research. This was important as it meant that her consent to take part in the research was properly informed. It also meant that Ann could take on a more collaborative role in the research *to the extent that she wanted to.* In a spirit of openness, I left this decision to her. While she wanted an opportunity for discussion, she seemed content to hand authorial control to me, understanding that this would be *my* research. As a health professional, Ann was interested to discuss both the findings of my broader study and my analysis of her particular interview. I was pleased to share my findings with her. In return, she offered me her reactions.

Ann was particularly active on hearing my preliminary analysis of the interviews with her. She affirmed certain themes, suggesting I had captured her experience 'nicely'. At other points she suggested my analysis (particularly my metaphorical flourishes) needed to be 'toned down' as she didn't feel they adequately represented her ordinary, everyday experience. One notable example here was my initial use of an analogy: that of Ann's situation being akin to 'living with an alien monster'. I rather liked this metaphor, regarding it as both punchy and poetic, and was reluctant to let it go. However, it was not something Ann could relate to. I therefore deleted all references to the monster while retaining (I ruefully acknowledge) some sense of the notion of alien infiltration.

In retrospect, I can see that it was useful to get Ann's feedback. For one thing, it helped me to better appreciate how Ann had, in fact, managed to reconnect with her 'disconnected' arm. I remain uncomfortably aware that our collaboration was partial and not entirely mutual. While Ann gave me some feedback, I retained control of my analysis and writing. In the end it is I who was choosing where, when, what and how to publish the findings. And, in the end, these are my findings, my interpretations. I could have involved Ann much more collaboratively, but chose not to. (Finlay, 2006c, pp. 194–195)

Many qualitative researchers embrace the idea of participant validation or member checking as a way to 'prove' the validity of their research. Here, researchers refer their evolving analysis back to their co-researchers for confirmation: when the participant agrees with the researcher's assessment, it is seen as strengthening the researcher's argument.

Such confidence may, however, be misplaced. It needs to be remembered that participants have their own motives, needs and interests. They also have varying degrees of insight. Moreover, what may have been 'true' for them at the time of the interview, for instance, may no longer be the case. Their ability to put themselves back into the specific research context may well be limited. For all these reasons, processes of participant validation need to be engaged in carefully and with awareness of the complex conscious, unconscious and contingent dimensions which may lead a co-researcher to support or refute any one analysis. (Of course the researcher, too, is subject to their own complex conscious, unconscious and contingent elements: hence the need for researcher reflexivity.)

In his evaluation of participant validation, Ashworth (1993) supports it on moral-political grounds but warns against taking co-researchers' responses too seriously as it may be in their interests to protect their 'socially presented selves'. As he notes,

> Participant validation is flawed … since the 'atmosphere of safety' that would allow the individual to lower his or her defences … and act in open candour … is hardly likely to be achieved in the research encounter. (Ashworth, 1993, p. 15)

In the case of the research with Ann above, it could be argued that Ann's involvement in the co-production of the findings strengthens the trustworthiness and ethical basis of this research. This is not the same as saying that Ann has validated this study thereby ensuring its veracity. As relational-centred researchers we do not claim to seek a 'truth' which can be validated in this way. We recognize that findings are produced in a specific context. Rather than seeing the process of involving co-researchers in analysis as being about validating the 'correctness' of findings, we should emphasize that it is about empowering them to share in meaning-making processes (Haumann, 2005).

Concluding the Research

The end phase of research involves tying things up with co-researchers, and also writing up and disseminating the research. While the first process is conducted within the relational context, the second usually occurs away from co-researchers and is therefore outside the relational context. However, in all these stages the issue of reciprocity comes to the fore. Is there an opportunity to give something back?

The process of tying up the research with co-researchers usually involves some sort of debrief towards closure of the research relationship. When and how this is achieved varies enormously depending on the type of research involved. For some research, it may occur at the end of the interview/observation stage with researcher and co-researcher perhaps sharing their experiences of doing the research in an interactive summing up. Certainly, in whatever methodology adopted co-researchers should be given time to reflect on their experience and the space to discuss further issues.

In more collaborative types of research, closure may come with seeing a tangible, jointly produced end product. Co-researchers may, for instance, get a real 'kick' out of seeing their story in print. Others may appreciate the fact that the researcher is going on to write official reports which can 'make a difference' or they are planning to share the findings in some productive, constructive way.

After achieving some degree of closure of the research relationship, researchers will present their findings to the wider professional and academic community and here fresh ethical questions emerge. To begin with, there is the issue of how others may react to experiences that co-researchers have been willing to share. For example, in the Ellis, Kiesinger and Tillmann-Healy (1997) research on the experience of bulimia (described above in Example 11.5), the co-researchers needed to think very carefully about how they would be seen by others after telling their stories – particularly as they were about to apply for academic jobs. The research article they collaboratively wrote was to become part of their job application packets and clearly identified them as women with eating disorders if not other emotional vulnerabilities (Ellis, 2007).

Also pertinent is the impact of the research on the co-researchers themselves. In the following passage, Haumann (2005) discusses her discomfort about her participants having little say or power over her interpretations. In this research she was exploring psychodynamic psychotherapists' own experiences of personal therapy. Haumann was particularly concerned about her analysis of the issue of power and unresolved conflicts between her participants and their therapists. She describes herself as feeling on a 'slippery slope':

> On the one hand the participants were also therapists and should be able to
> know that my interpretations were not "truths", but only *my* interpretations,

and could be useful comments on their therapies. On the other hand, these interpretations could also invade the space of therapy, do real damage there and also undermine the participant's ability "to interpret his experience in his own way" (Hadjistavropoulos & Smythe, 2001, p. 164). (Haumann, 2005, p. 22)

Haumann's comments suggest that a more pernicious ethical challenge when writing up research is the sense of discomfort researchers may feel about treating co-researchers as *objects* to 'talk about' rather than as persons to 'talk with'. Put in Levinas' terms (1969), the power we can misuse is a function of the way we objectify others in relation and that we should choose to act to reduce such dominance. Josselson (1996, cited in McLeod, 2001) nicely expresses this discomfort of exploring the guilt and shame that go with writing about others in an objectifying way:

My guilt, I think, comes from my knowing that I have taken myself out of relationship with my participants (with whom, during the interview, I was in intimate relationship) to be in relationship with my readers. I have, in a sense, been talking about them behind their backs and doing so publicly. Where in the interview I had been responsive to them, now I am using their lives in the service of something else, for my own purposes ... I am guilty about being an intruder and them, to some extent, a betrayer ... And my shame is the hardest to analyse and the most painful of my responses. I suspect this shame is about my exhibitionism, shame that I am using these people's lives to exhibit myself, my analytic prowess, my cleverness. I am using them as extensions of my own narcissism and fear being caught, seen in this process. (Josselson, 1996, cited in McLeod, 2001, p. 198)

There are no easy ways to preclude such feelings of discomfort. However, being reflexively aware both of the nature of our research enterprise and of our ethical responsibilities is a good place to start. Just as in life, we have to make choices in difficult, uncertain circumstances, and cope with competing demands and responsibilities.

It also helps if you believe your research has the potential to benefit, at some level, your co-researchers even if your initial intention was to benefit a wider community. Pat made this point to Linda, for instance, at the conclusion of their research collaboration exploring Pat's lived experience of having a cochlear implant. Pat acknowledged how the research had helped her make sense of, and come to terms with, the trauma of her experience. Now Pat feels some satisfaction that her story has been told as it allows others to learn from her experience:

Use the experience we had together as much as you can. It is interesting and valuable. Remember it requires readiness and painful honesty; also respect for each other's skills. Not many people can handle this well. You could have roller-coasted me and you didn't. I respect you for that. You can be as open as you want. [I] wish more people did what you did; not everybody has the same skills. Without you my story might not have been told … What we did was fascinatingly difficult believe me …We ended up not only with the end product but many other things as well. (*Personal communication from Pat to Linda*)

Reflections

Ethical relational research practice involves much more than following rules and procedures. Instead, it is a process which begins with an idea and does not end until the research has been disseminated. Issues arise in inter-actions within research relationships and compromises may need to be made. Every research encounter brings up ethical challenges which, because context specific, need to be individually negotiated. Rather than rely on professional ethical codes to guide us through this process, we argue that it is essential that researchers grapple *reflexively* with the ethical problems and uncertainties that arise.

As ethical relational-centred researchers we celebrate efforts to embrace dialogical collaborative ethical research which listens to, and values, the other's 'voice' while we also acknowledge the complexities involved. The process of gaining informed consent and maintaining co-researchers trust and goodwill, particularly when the research involves sensitive subjects and/or vulnerable people, invariably challenges.

We appreciate, too, the complexity of the power relations involved where power is never one-way and always enacted in subtle and multi-layered ways. However, we believe that by giving up some of our control as research-ers, we open ourselves to new possibilities.

It behoves us to use our researcher power wisely and ethically while acknowledging both the limits of our research and its potential to broaden understanding and add to the sum of human knowledge. As Krüger (2007, p. 21) says,

> To live with this inherent power is to enter the realm of ethics. The only way of surviving as a true professional is to see, accept and live with the paradox: to behave ethically and exert power – simultaneously.

Notes

[i] The British Association of Counselling and Psychotherapy (BACP), for example, state their ethical framework is applicable to both practice and research. See <www.bacp.co.uk/ethical_framework/>.

[ii] Some researchers pay their co-researchers or recompense them in some way such as paying expenses.

[iii] This extract has been reproduced from Krüger (2007). An introduction to the ethics of gestalt research with informants, *European Journal for Qualitative Research in Psychotherapy*, 2, 17–22, with the kind permission of the Editor, Ken Evans.

[iv] This extract has been taken from Finlay (2006c), The embodied experience of multiple sclerosis: An existential-phenomenological analysis, *Qualitative research for allied health professionals: Challenging choices*, edited by Linda Finlay and Claire Ballinger, with the kind permission of Wiley-Blackwell.

Chapter 12

Becoming a Relational Researcher

In this brief final chapter in Part II, we take the opportunity to reflect on the process of becoming, and developing as, a relational researcher by seeking to answer four key questions:

- How should I start doing relational-centred research?
- Do I have to do relational centred research – What of other types?
- How can I develop as a relational-centred researcher?
- How can I learn more about doing relational-centred research?

How Should I Start Doing Relational-centred Research?

The hardest step to take when doing research is probably the first one. Not only are you stepping into the unknown, you are probably uncertain about your footing and unsure about whether or not you want to go on this expedition in the first place. It is not surprising that novice researchers (be they students or practitioners) struggle to start doing their research. We have spoken to many practitioners who express the urge to engage in research but, in practice, find taking that first step too daunting.

One of our main intentions in this book is to show how psychotherapists have an advantage compared to other novice researchers. You have skills,

Relational-centred Research for Psychotherapists: Exploring Meanings and Experience
Edited by Linda Finlay and Ken Evans

values, interests and understandings which are directly transferrable to the research world. You come equipped with the ability to enable and empathize with others, and a capacity for intuitive reflexive inferential interpretation. You also have the patience to deal with uncertainty and ambiguity, knowing something of value is likely to emerge eventually, however tentative. On the basis of just talking with people, you are able to reach profound insights. You are also used to reviewing and analysing sessions (the equivalent to 'data') and planning therapeutic strategy and interventions based on your evaluations. These professional skills embrace the abilities and qualities you need to be a competent qualitative and/or relational-centred researcher.

If you are struggling with that first step, we want to gently nudge you forward to give it a go. You might try one small expedition and see how you fare. For example, you could start by analysing a single therapy session (as Maria did in *Chapter 14*) or one client's special story (as Darren did in *Chapter 15*). Alternatively, you could ask yourself if there is a topic or research question that particularly interests or excites you? Virginia and Susan (in *Chapters 13* and *16*) both interviewed people about their experience. Maybe something similar would appeal to you? If you are seeking inspiration, check out the numerous examples of small-scale research offered in this book and just pick any topic or approach that catches your eye.

In whatever way you choose to begin, we advise you to keep your aims modest. If you are a first-time researcher, start by learning to do some basic research and producing academically respectable reports. Simply try a small project to get your feet wet! (*See Chapter 6: Setting Up Research* which provides more advice about setting up research.)

Do I Have to do Relational-centred Research – What of Other Types?

No, you do not have to do relational-centred research. Other forms of research – qualitative or quantitative – could be more appropriate for the kind of project you might have in mind and may well be less demanding. It depends on your inclination and your research question. What are you seeking to do?

We would advocate a relational-centred approach specifically if:

1) You want an approach which mirrors your practice, values and concerns as psychotherapists where you seek to engage positively with unconscious, emotional and/or relational processes.

2) You want to engage in small-scale research based firmly in clinical experience.

3) You are seeking to embrace a reflexive, dialogical approach and do research *with* as opposed to *on* participants.

4) You celebrate the co-creation of knowledge as arising in the embodied, dialogical encounter.

In our own approach to relational-centred research (which draws on gestalt, existential-phenomenological and relational psychoanalytic ideas) we emphasize the significance of the *between* and of surrendering to whatever emerges into moment-by-moment awareness. In *Chapter 2* we mention other qualitative research methodologies that are available which may or may not fit the relational paradigm. (*See* also p.27 footnote iv where we link methodology with psychotherapy modalities.) You may well prefer to use one of these methodologies without adopting a relational approach.

Relational-centred research is not for every researcher because many researchers lack the interest, skills and experience needed to tap into relational process. Also, not every topic requires a relational focus; not every research relationship offers rich layers to probe. It can also be argued that the relational route demands an unnecessary extra step when in the qualitative research territory.

That said, we maintain that relational-centred research can open up new vistas and allow you to experience multi-layered, nuanced and in-depth understandings. At its best, relational research can touch heart and soul, and has the potential to be transformative in all sorts of unlooked-for ways (Finlay, 2009, *Forthcoming*).

How Can I Develop as a Relational-centred Researcher?

Relational-centred researchers share a similar developmental process to that of psychotherapists. It takes time to learn the art of working as reflexive practitioners in the *between* of relationships. It is constructive to review the normal growth process of novice therapists and assume the need to return to, and renew, this growth process as a researcher.

Novice researchers will tend to draw on their own internalized 'shoulds'. In one way or another these convey the message you have to do research 'in the right way' or even that 'you have to do this perfectly'. Invariably such messages originate with significant others from our early environment, and as often as not, from our school days.

Gradually the novice grows away from the internalized 'shoulds and oughts' of their past, replacing them with their mentor's or supervisor's attitudes and knowledge via discussion and learning. At first the researcher-therapist internalizes this teacher relying more or less on their internalized 'voice' and working to their suggested established models or practices.

> At this stage the supervisee will be introjecting the supervisor as a "new" Parent and will tend to use the new Parent messages as though they are inviolate "rules". (Gilbert & Evans, 2000, p. 22)

Gradually we develop and grow our own internalized mentor/supervisor which includes our own independent thinking, autonomous judgment and a capacity for more spontaneity (Casement, 1985). At this stage of development the researcher-therapist will be able to monitor the extent of their presence while practising inclusion. They will be more alert to unconscious processes and able to keep in simultaneous view the Other, themselves and the dynamic between.

We believe that however experienced and knowledgeable the researcher (or therapist) becomes there will always be a need – and perhaps even an ethical requirement – to commit to supervision. Continued education and unfolding self-awareness are ongoing throughout our professional life. The process of supervision 'should develop into a dialogue between the external supervisor and the internal supervisor' (Casement, 1985, p. 32).

Put in more concrete terms, a novice researcher may feel less overwhelmed at the prospect of doing research if they can follow an established method involving relatively well-defined steps. For example, methodologies which have clearly demarcated stages will probably be preferred. If interviews are planned it will feel safer to follow pre-prepared questions, particularly as these could well be the most appropriate approach for the research. As these researchers grow in confidence and experience, they might feel more able to experiment with their methodology and approach, and perhaps engage in semi-structured interviewing. The more experienced a researcher, the more they are likely to feel comfortable with leaving structure and pre-established techniques behind. The most confident relational-centred researcher, who has grown sufficiently emotionally literate and developed an internal supervisor, will feel able to risk a more open engagement, as in the 'two-chair work' example of *Chapter 9*. These more experienced researchers will also, paradoxically, have the maturity to reach out for the support, stimulation and challenge that comes with supervision and with sharing their research more widely with peers.

In making links between developmental process, therapy and research, we are not in any way suggesting that the relational-centred researcher should engage in therapy or that therapists engaged in research should confuse the boundary between therapeutic purpose and research purpose.

What we are suggesting is that we can learn from therapy and that this learning will support, encourage and help you to access deeper levels of awareness in the research exploration.

The sharing that occurs with co-researchers can be transformative in all sorts of ways. While the research may help empower and, perhaps to some extent, heal your co-researcher, it also is likely to impact you, the researcher. Susan Morrow makes this point in *Chapter 16* (page 237) when she says the research helped her to make sense of her own experiences both in childhood and around being a therapist committed to the healing process with survivors of abuse:

> I learned to listen in a different way. Where as a counselor I had listened partly to make diagnostic meaning of my clients' distress, as a researcher I learned to listen for the real meanings that my participants made of their abuse, survival, coping, and healing. This has made me a different kind of therapist and a different kind of person.

How Can I Learn More About Doing Relational-centred Research?

The watch words are 'do', 'read' and 'share'.

There is no substitute for actually *doing* and practising the craft of research. Every research encounter will bring new learning as well as specific challenges and dilemmas which help us grow.

In addition to doing research, it is important to read around the subject – both about your methodology and your topic. Throughout this book we have offered references and suggestions for good source material. We also recommend that you take time to read actual accounts of research experiences in books and journals.[i] In this way you will learn from their experiences and about how to go about doing and writing up research.

The research voyage can be a lonely one and it is often best undertaken with other researcher-explorers. Opportunities for working with more experienced researchers can offer an invaluable apprenticeship and you are more likely to get your research results published, which is rewarding affirmation. If you choose to do research on your own then we recommend you find someone who can act as your research mentor or supervisor. (If you are short of contacts you might consider contacting a researcher or someone who has written about your subject, someone you respect, and asking that person to offer suggestions. Alternatively, try connecting with a local psychotherapy training institute and see what courses or contacts they might suggest.)

Sharing the research process in a collaborative team offers another possibility of support, as well as providing encouragement and challenge along the way. Teamwork can also be useful in highlighting different points of view and for allowing a productive division of labour. Barry (2003) notes these points when she discusses the research undertaken in her team of five practitioners/researchers looking at doctor–patient interactions:

> Through sharing common ground, enabling multiple voices to emerge and developing a productive dialectic, we believe we … improved the rigour and quality of our research. Communicating and negotiating our differences has broadened our views and increased the rigour of our theoretical thinking. Nothing is taken for granted: positions have to be thought through and weak arguments exposed. (Barry, 2003, p. 224)

Finally, sharing occurs when disseminating research through conference presentations and writing academic papers. Opening up your research to wider audiences is a key way to gain feedback, support, and to grow as others will challenge and stimulate you. We urge you to embrace and enjoy these opportunities to dialogue with peers whatever your level of experience.

Reflections

With the current and seemingly relentless march toward state regulation of psychotherapy across Europe, never in the history of the profession has there been a more important time to be thinking about doing research. Yet the gap between research and practice yawns wide. Practitioners finding research unhelpful, uninspiring or irrelevant to their practice may well simply ignore it. A pool of relevant, resonant research is growing but sadly many practitioners remain unaware and untouched by it – perhaps threatened by it(?)

We feel saddened and frustrated when we see colleagues doing excellent work and yet not taking the step to share their ideas more broadly. We are also saddened and frustrated to see much of the good and interesting research that has been written up as 'case studies' and 'research dissertations' languishing on practitioner and professional training centres/university shelves. What a waste!

Of course, carrying out and then disseminating research to wider audiences is challenging and can be a risk, particularly when our resistance(s) get in the way. But there are pay-offs too. As we share and offer our ideas to others in dialogue – in the relational spirit – we too grow and learn, and just possibly we can 'make a difference'.

We agree with Laurel Richardson when she argues that research needs to reach wide and diverse audiences:

> It seems foolish at best, and narcissistic and wholly self-absorbed at worst, to spend months or years doing research that ends up not being read and not making a difference to anything but the author's career. (Richardson, 1994, p. 517)

So step on board, batten down the hatches, set yourself a course, raise the sails and let the wind carry you forward. *Bon voyage!*

Note

[i] There are hundreds of journals which are relevant to psychotherapy though many cater for the academic market and their content may prove less accessible for novice practitioner researchers. We would recommend starting with journals developed with the reflexive practitioner in mind such as: *Counselling and Psychotherapy Research* and *the European Journal for Qualitative Research in Psychotherapy*.

Part III

Relational-centred Research in Action

Introduction

In this final section of the book, material from the preceding chapters is pulled together. Four accounts of relational-centred research in action are presented. These accounts show how relational work (including the use of presence, inclusion, intersubjectivity and reflexivity) can be engaged in practice across a range of methodologies.

In inviting these contributions, our aim is not to provide you with models of 'how to do' phenomenology, grounded theory or other methodologies. Instead, we hope these exemplar chapters will give you a feel for what is possible when you embrace relational-centred research and the kinds of issues, challenges and commitments which arise in the process.

We have invited our four authors to follow the same structure. After introducing their topics, each discusses their *Methodology* and *Findings*. In a final *Reflections* section, mirroring the structure of the previous chapters, the authors engage more personally and reflexively with the discomforts, rewards and excitements experienced when doing their research.

In *Chapter 13*, Virginia Eatough explores the lived experience of anger using a hermeneutic (i.e. involving interpretation) phenomenological approach. Virginia examines how the interview context resulted in compelling accounts from her women participants which brought their anger alive for her. Her participants' bodies resonated with her own body and anger experiences. Virginia underlines the way that findings involve multi-layered co-constructions.

In *Chapter 14*, Maria Luca similarly emphasizes the spontaneous embodied encounter in her account of a therapist's portrait of a clinical encounter with a 'somatizer'. Maria analyses a single therapeutic session and uses grounded theory to systematically chart and categorize the discourse of her client. She found that the client presented emotions in a disproportionately negative and intellectualized manner devoid of affect and, this in turn, impacted her own responses deeply.

Darren Langdridge, in *Chapter 15*, uses a critical narrative approach to research to investigate the life story of one of his clients – a middle-aged man struggling to live a 24/7 sadomasochistic (SM) life as a slave. The story draws attention to the 'everyday' nature of SM relationships and the difficulties that many of us have in giving up control and trusting that we are 'good enough' to warrant the love of someone we adore. Darren reflexively explores his relationship with his client and shifts in his emerging understandings.

In *Chapter 16*, Susan Morrow describes a slice of her broader collaborative, participatory feminist research study on how women, who had been sexually abused as children, constructed their experiences of abuse, and the survival and coping strategies used. She selectively features how evocative creative media (art, poetry and metaphor) can be employed to gather and analyse data, and to present the research. Susan brings to light how researchers might empower their co-researchers and contribute to their healing.

Chapter 13

'My Heart was Killing Me': A Hermeneutic Phenomenological Study of the Lived Experience of Anger

Virginia Eatough

Being angry is a profoundly relational experience. Typically, it occurs between people who share close intimate bonds (Averill, 1983). Understanding one's anger, especially if experienced as persistent and unremitting, can be arduous and distressing. From a phenomenological perspective anger speaks to the intentional relationship we have with the world; that is how our anger has directedness, unfurling and reaching out to others, to objects and to ourselves. Very simply, whatever the reasons for our anger, we are always angry with someone or about something. Anger is distinctly personal, involving judgments about ourselves, our place in the world, and our relationships with others. In a myriad of ways, anger binds us to other people.

In this chapter I describe and reflect upon a phenomenological psychology study which addressed the question of what it means to be angry. My interest was not in the ontological status of anger – I was not looking to establish what anger ultimately is – but rather to approach the question phenomenologically focusing on anger-as-experienced. For as Solomon says, 'Unlike "ontology", phenomenology encourages a healthy humility, an attention to detail, a wariness of flights of philosophical jargon substituting for insight and understanding' (Solomon, 1997, p. 289).

The chapter focuses on two aspects of the research which involved interviews with a small number of women who agreed to take part in a study

Relational-centred Research for Psychotherapists: Exploring Meanings and Experience
Edited by Linda Finlay and Ken Evans
Copyright © 2009 John Wiley & Sons, Ltd.

exploring how they resolved conflict in their adult intimate relationships. First, I will discuss how the women provided rich and compelling descriptions of their subjective experience of anger. Their portrayals were emphatically embodied drawing attention to how the body lies at the core of the emotional experience of anger, and they reminded me that meaning is rendered not only through our linguistic practices but through our bodily participation in the world. Relatedly, I will show how the women's spontaneous use of metaphor and image helped to reveal their embodied lived experience of anger.

Second, I will focus explicitly on how attempts to understand and give meaning to our anger are woven into the fabric of our relational worlds. Specifically, I will draw attention to how one of the women who was in counselling was struggling to create a new meaning for her anger in order to better manage it within her lifeworld. The counselling sessions were encouraging Marilyn (a pseudonym) to reflect on past and present relationships with significant others, how they were brought to bear on each other and how her anger might be understood as arising, at least in part, out of her relational past. In particular, I will consider how these emergent meanings brought considerable interpretive power to bear on my understanding of her anger as well as my attempts at subsequent theorizing.

Finally, I conclude this chapter by reflecting on how the findings of the study are a multi-layered co-construction of both the researcher's and the participants' making, as well as appraising the value of a phenomenological psychology approach and method for relationally oriented research.

Methodology

Interpretative phenomenological analysis (IPA) was the approach used in this study. It is one of a number of phenomenological psychology approaches within qualitative research and in this section I briefly describe its epistemological and philosophical underpinnings. In addition I sketch what is involved in actually doing the research. I hope to show how many of the core features and skills of phenomenological research are shared with psychotherapists and counsellors.

IPA is rooted in two clearly identifiable and compatible ways of knowing: phenomenological philosophy and hermeneutics. Moran and Mooney (2002) describe the phenomenological project as both a way of seeing and as a movement intended to herald in a new daring way of doing philosophy which avoid 'abstract metaphysical speculation wrapped up in pseudoproblems, in order to come into contact with the matters themselves, with concrete living experience' (Moran, 2000, p. xiii).

Phenomenology investigates in the words of its originator, Husserl, 'whatever appears as such', in the 'how' of its appearing. The project is to describe and understand phenomena as they are revealed to us in consciousness, as meaningfully lived experiences. The aim, as far as is possible, is to strip away our preconceptions, presuppositions, etc. – no matter if they are from folk psychology, science, common sense, social and cultural traditions – so that the phenomenon is revealed 'as it appears to our flesh-and-bone selves' (Varela, 1999, p. 267).

Yet, this is a self which is always a situated and holistic self-with-others. One of the most enduring phenomenological concepts is *Dasein*, the proposal that we are all a *Being-in-the-world* and that the world of *Dasein* is fundamentally relational; both a with-world (*Mitwelt*) and a world-with-others (*Mitsein*) (Heidegger, 1927/1962). Thus, our lived experiences are embedded in a shared intersubjective world and they come to be meaningful through the ebb and flow of our dialogues and relations. The holistic nature and mutuality of these concepts constitutes an outright rejection of Cartesian thinking which is pushed further by Merleau-Ponty and his ideas on embodied existence. Merleau-Ponty (1945/1962) dissolves the dualist distinction imposed on the mind and body arguing that there can be no separation between our body and our existence. The body is inextricably caught up with our sense of self, our world, and our relations with others: simply put, we are our body. In practice, a phenomenological way of seeing encourages qualitative researchers to recognize (and identify with) participants as embodied situated historical persons whose lifeworlds come to be understood through the intersubjective work of researcher and participant. Phenomenology thus, requires first-person accounts and an acceptance of subjectivity in the construction of knowledge.

Hermeneutics is the customary name used to describe the skills or art of interpretation, a practice which began with the interpretation of biblical texts. Much later, Enlightenment thinkers set about systematizing this practice into a general method of understanding (Moran, 2000). For Heidegger, hermeneutics was not simply a method; rather our mode of Being is as an 'illuminator and creator of one's world' (von Eckartsberg, 1998, p. 11). At the same time he recognized that understanding and reflection inevitably change the phenomenon being studied because of the impossibility of approaching it directly. Understanding is always mediated through our existing understandings; this is the hermeneutic circle whereby new understandings emerge from what we already know from our lived experiences. Thus, for Heidegger our existence is 'factical', it is 'particular, concrete, inescapably contingent, yet worldly' (Moran, 2000, p. 223) and understanding is always from a particular perspective.

This view of persons as self-interpreting beings (Taylor, 1985) is emphasized in hermeneutic phenomenological approaches such as IPA. Throughout the analytic process, the researcher explores the lived experiences told by the participants by being open to layers of meaning which in turn bring forth multiple possible interpretations. These are held up and interrogated for their ability to convince the reader that they are both evocative and consequential of a person's lifeworld.

This requires the researcher to move between different ways of being interpretive, working with multiple 'horizons of interpretation' (Garza, 2007, p. 321). For example, one might remain close to and identify with the lived experience, wanting it to feel and resonate for you in the way it does for your participant. Such empathic interpretations are intent on capturing the quality and mood of the experience as lived by the participant. Alternatively, one can be interrogative and imaginative, asking 'what if ... ?' This critical attitude is not faithful to the nature of the lived experience; rather it employs what has been called a hermeneutics of suspicion (Ricoeur, 1970). This looking behind the experience for lost or hidden meanings is closely aligned to psychoanalytic traditions. The phenomenological researcher will move between these empathic and suspicious dimensions striving for interpretive understandings which are multi-layered. Inevitably these understandings are always emergent and partial.

In practical terms, IPA is not a prescriptive approach; rather it provides a flexible set of guidelines which can be adapted by individual researchers in light of their research aims. Typically, IPA employs interviews as the primary method of data collection, and a carefully pre-planned interview schedule designed to answer the research question(s) is used to guide the interview. Questions aim to elicit the taken-for-granted and the details which flesh out the story being told. Good opening questions designed to elicit rich descriptions and which might provide the main dimensions of the phenomenon might be 'Can you tell me about ... ?'; 'Do you remember a time when ... ?'; 'Could you describe in as much detail as possible a situation when ... ?' It is possible to follow up with more specific questions such as 'What did you feel then?'; 'How did your body react?'; 'What did you do next?'

Yet, the underlying assumption is of the interview as a participant-led conversation, a dialogue understood in the original Latin meaning of conversation as 'wandering together with' (Kvale, 1996, p. 4). The researcher is both an attentive, active questioner/listener and one who respects research participants as the experiential experts of the phenomenon being studied.

If both these features are adhered to, then the interview becomes a site for the in-depth mutual exploration of the phenomenon as it appears and is understood from the perspective of the participant's lifeworld. Consequently, novel and unanticipated understandings can emerge enabling the complexity of phenomena to be acknowledged and examined in a fresh light by both researcher and participant.

Moreover, the material gathered will be a rich repository to be mined as the researcher moves through the various stages of analysis. These stages include several close and detailed readings of the material ensuring a holistic perspective is maintained; initial themes are identified, organized into clusters and checked against the material; themes are refined, condensed and examined for connections between them; a narrative account is produced which is created out of the interpretative activity of the researcher and the participants' account of their experiences in their own words (Smith & Osborn, 2003) (see Smith and Eatough, 2007 for a detailed discussion of the procedures of carrying out an IPA study). Thus, any narrative account of the research process will offer up knowledge for evaluation which is brought into being through the involvement of both participant and researcher's lifeworlds.

Hopefully, this section has provided a flavour and sense of how a hermeneutic phenomenological approach such as IPA engages research as a human science endeavour. This concern is shared by those in the therapeutic and counselling professions and both have been identified as humanizing forces in the search for knowledge (Todres, 2007). Equally, I hope it has highlighted how many of the qualities and competencies needed to be a successful therapist are the same ones that are required to undertake useful and convincing research.

Findings

Embodied anger

The following presents a brief account of some of the findings from my IPA study which looked at how women resolved conflict in their lives (for a more detailed account of the study see Eatough and Smith, 2006a, 2006b; Eatough, Smith and Shaw, 2008). I will show how hermeneutic phenomenological analysis aims to produce knowledge about what is being studied which is person- relational- and world-centred. The themes to be discussed include what it feels like to be angry and the ambiguity and complexity involved in making meaning of one's anger.

In this study, I was keen to capture the what-is-it-like dimension of being angry, to get close to the women's lived experience of it. In part, this was driven by my sense of how psychological research did not speak to my own anger experiences, how mostly my anger feels visceral and primal, and how it is always an engagement with others.

The women's descriptions of what it is like to be angry brought to the fore the body's involvement in our emotional experiences. They conveyed this through compelling images of heat, explosiveness and internal turmoil. Debbie says of a jealous altercation with another woman:

> I just remember like seeing dots in front of my face, in front of my eyes and everything just went red ... It was all this rage, I went red hot and it's like I was having a hot flush or something and I just felt that I'd got to hit her.

Similar to Debbie's dots in front of her eyes, Julie's vision is disrupted by a red glaze. Both suggest confusion and an inability to 'see' clearly:

> I see red you know when people do say they see red I did see red, red was in my eyes I could see a red glaze and I was sweating.
> I don't know what it is when I get angry it's like my head's going to explode. I, I see red, I really do see richly red before my eyes and, I don't know I get this extra energy from somewhere.

The heat felt by both women is evident in Marilyn's description also:

> But I can how I feel is, I can feel myself getting hotter and hotter and erm it's like I feel my blood pressure boiling and I can feel my face going up red and just hate, hate anything anybody that's in my way.

The colour red symbolizes that anger is experienced as dangerous and has a tangible quality to it. It can also feel overwhelming as when Julie describes her head about to explode. The explosive imagery, the heat and the visual disruption convey the instability of the anger experience. This is reinforced by how Alison feels her anger:

> I was thinking I want to get rid of this anger and I think what do I do, so I just lay in the bed and I could feel it building up and my heart was killing me.

Alison's anger seems to have a different temporal dimension from Julie and Marilyn in that the anger develops in a less immediate and more deliberate manner. It seems inexorable rather than volatile, centred in her heart rather than suffusing her entire body, yet her words 'I could feel it building up and my heart was killing me' point to how the anger is just as intensely and deeply felt.

The women's anger also exerted powerful effects on how they understood their sense of self and their relations with others. For example, Debbie tells us something about how she perceives herself in relation to significant others:

> I class myself as a twig. I bend for so long and then eventually I snap. Erm, it does take me a lot for my temper to go now. I mean, I could sort of like feel myself going as my temper gets worse during that day. It could start off with like little things like when the kids are shouting.

Interestingly, her depiction is in stark contrast to the rage she describes above and which made her want to hit out (an angry and jealous argument with another woman). Here, describing her anger in relation to her children, it would seem that she experiences herself as slow to anger, and instead of a rapid escalation of feeling, it is more like a steady drip. The difference lies in the relational context: always a self in relation to others her anger is lived and experienced through these relationships and has very real if diverse outcomes.

From a phenomenological perspective these descriptions of the lived experiences of anger point to how the body is always implicated in our understandings. Gendlin says, 'The body knows its situation directly' (Gendlin, 1997, p. 26) and it grounds our more fully articulated reflections. One way this grounding is achieved is through the use of images and metaphors as can be seen from the women's descriptions above. Both help to unfold and structure our pre-reflective and tacit bodily experience through the use of imagination and intuition.

Making meaning

The second aspect of the analysis I want to highlight is the often complicated and ambiguous nature of our meaning-making. Although not neglecting the pre-reflective, tacit knowledge derived from our lived body participation, IPA pays particular attention in the cognitive reflective self-interpretive dimension of sense-making.

Marilyn's attempts to understand her pervasive anger through counselling were encouraging her to challenge explanations which she had long relied on but which were becoming increasingly unsatisfactory. The search for new understandings can give rise to the possibility of alternative and more liveable ways of *Being-in-the-world*. For Marilyn, this involved an acknowledgement that her past relationships might be significant in understanding her present pervasive anger, although not in any straightforward determinative way. More specifically, this involved a painful wrestling with powerfully mixed emotions about her relationship with her mother:

> I do hate me mum. I've learned [that] through counselling. I do hate my mum but I love her for being, she's a symbol you know.

Marilyn makes direct reference to her mother being a symbol. Such symbols are enacted and acquire meaning through our individual lifeworlds. Typically, mothers are symbolic of selflessness, yet for Marilyn there is a lack of fit between her lived experience and what the culture she lives in has taught her to expect. This symbolic potency is further underlined:

> I really really hate her. I don't like saying it because she at the end of the day she is my mother but I hate her for what she's done. She's hurt me and it's not so much that she doesn't want to see me but he's her grandson you know what I mean. I can't understand any parent not wanting to see their children never mind their grandchildren or anything like that.

To admit hatred of one's mother transgresses socially prescribed norms and there is a sense that Marilyn experiences her hate as illegitimate because in spite of her mother's actions she is 'at the end of the day' her mother. Moreover it seems that this ambivalent relationship is further complicated for Marilyn now that she is a mother herself. It is possible that her son's birth has created a relational matrix in which the hurt that dominates Marilyn's relationship with her mother is now felt as a double whammy of rejection. Marilyn experiences rejection not only of herself but also through her son, who is part of herself.

   Although I asked no questions explicitly about Marilyn's mother, the relationship was 'live' for her because of her current counselling experiences. Marilyn's commitment to understanding her anger meant reflecting on her lived experiences of rejection. She relates how, as an adolescent, her mother compared her to her cousin:

> She wanted me to be there for her in a pretty pink dress with lovely pigtails and I was too big for that (laughs). And she used to think more of my cousin who was dainty, she was the same age as me, there were two weeks between us but she was small, she was petite you know, prettier looking and I think she was more with her, she was how can I say it, she showed her more emotion than she did me.

My analytic focus is on the phrase 'she was more with her' which suggests that Marilyn understands her mother and cousin as connected in a way she is not. The relational field is one of separateness and isolation for Marilyn because of the negative comparison she senses her mother makes between her and her cousin. The experience of rejection and feelings of disconnectedness pervaded Marilyn's talk about her mother.

The heavy presence of Marilyn's mother encouraged me to work at a more abstract conceptual level building on Marilyn's words in order to develop other interpretations which might be used to shed light on how the relationship with her mother might be implicated in her lived experiences of anger. This 'what if ... ?' phenomenological stance involves imagining alternative ways of seeing and thinking about phenomena which can bring to light unforeseen and novel understandings.

My early thinking and intuiting around notions of separation and connection were used to examine Marilyn's narratives in a more critical and probing way. In particular, her understandings of how the mother-brother-self bonds within the family were played out:

> My mum was always with my brother, he was always you know, he was the lad and my mum used to be like, say that I used to look like my dad and she didn't like my dad so I always thought she didn't like me. It was that type of relationship, not close at all.

A simple interpretation is that Marilyn believed her brother to be her mother's favourite. However, a more thoughtful interpretation is that the word with points to Marilyn's sense that her mother and brother are connected together with a shared identity which excludes Marilyn and places her on the outside. This possible meaning is strengthened by Marilyn's words elsewhere:

> She was always my brother [sic]. I mean my brother could never do anything wrong but I think that was because she was in two minds whether he was my stepfather's. She, I think she'd been having an affair with him and I think she might have thought he was my stepfather's and not my real dad's. She used to always compare me to my dad in my ways and my looks and my actions and that and it just wasn't, but I mean there was never any affection. I mean I can't remember ever her putting her arm around me and kissing me. My stepdad he used to, but my mum never. My dad was very loving, I remember that, he really was.

Marilyn's omission of with from her statement that 'She was always my brother' was a vital insight into how I came to understand Marilyn's anger, an understanding which emerged from Marilyn's own sense-making.

Elsewhere, I have proposed that from Marilyn's perspective the relationship between mother and brother is not simply one of close ties but, rather for Marilyn, they have psychologically 'fused' into 'one' person. Marilyn stands outside and separate from mother–brother, compelled to become 'one' with the father whom she looks like and whom her mother hates. Marilyn's understanding of these relational dynamics is suffused with separateness. It is possible that attempts to make meaning from this relational patterning play a part in Marilyn's adult intimate relationships (Eatough & Smith, 2006a).

Hopefully, this section has conveyed a sense of what can be achieved with a hermeneutic phenomenological approach such as IPA.

Reflections

The importance of attending to the lived body in order to develop rich and meaningful understandings of the women's anger became increasingly clear to me as I moved through the different stages of the research. It became evident even before I began to transcribe and analyse the women's account – in the interview context – during which the women's anger became alive for me through their bodies, resonating with my own body and my own anger experiences. For example, there was a shared recognition and shared participation when one of the women pressed her fist over her heart. I felt as if I was living and feeling the heartache in the moment she was reliving it. There was a pure quality to the experience, as if I had, for a moment, stepped into her life and understood what it was like to feel her pain and anger.

Finlay (2003c, 2005, 2006d) has written extensively about these embodied empathic moments describing them as a form of openness to a relational embodied intersubjectivity. These empathic embodied connections can be of an everyday sort such as when we see another person yawn and feel the desire to yawn ourselves. Or they can give rise to a profound sense of oneness with another. Finlay suggests that phenomenological researchers should acknowledge multiple levels of empathic engagement as they strive to understand the lifeworlds of others and contribute to hermeneutic phenomenological knowledge. Throughout the interviews I worked hard not to be simply a spectator of the women's lifeworlds but to be open to their experiences of anger and acknowledge moments of identification. The fist clenched over the heart was one such moment and is eloquently expressed by Finlay's notion of 'being with' rather than 'doing to' (Finlay, 2006d). It was a salutary reminder that the 'wisdom of the body' (Fuchs,

2001, p. 325) gives us an insight that our postmodern privileging of language often neglects.

The strength of all hermeneutic phenomenological approaches including IPA lies in their readiness to go beyond description and to develop understandings from a sustained interpretive engagement. These understandings are multi-layered: sometimes they are heavily rooted in the participant's lifeworld, staying close to the lived experience aiming to encapsulate something of its quintessential nature; other times they are more distant offering alternative narratives to the ones given by the women and which they might even reject. The empathic meaning-making of the anger experience theme (what it feels like to be angry) and the more abstract sense-making theme which foregrounds the voice of the researcher are examples of these different layers of interpretation. The former is an understanding rooted in my acceptance of the women's descriptions, an attempt to 'stand in their shoes' and convey their lived experience of anger in all its richness. In contrast, the latter illustrates how I was more interrogative developing understandings which opened up new ways of seeing and even new possibilities of being. In practice, this involved me assuming an imaginative and fluid stance. Just as in the interview I aimed to be both experiencing and reflective, in the analysis stage, the 'relational dance' (Finlay, 2006d) continued. I found this movement both back and forth, as well as in and through the data messy but not chaotic; challenging yet hugely rewarding. Reading 'how-to-do' guidelines did not (and could not) prepare me for the richly textured engagement with the material.

Reflecting on how this felt for me, I recognize it as involving processes of both immersion and retreat. The longer I dwelt in the women's words the more I realized I was moving back and forth between the two. When Marilyn said of her mother 'she petrified me just with a dirty look' my immersion in that experience enabled me to recall times when my mother gave me such looks, experiences which live with me to this day. Reliving and re-imagining those experiences brought me closer to Marilyn's and gave rise to a better understanding of how she felt. Retreating from both our experiences I reflected upon Marilyn's use of the word 'petrify' with its implications of being stunned or paralysed with terror. I thought about this in the context of the stormy relationships we had with our mothers. I theorized that Marilyn's sense of self was threatened with potential obliteration. This tentative interpretation might be something Marilyn would be unable or unwilling to consider. It is a result of my reflections from a distance, yet it was borne out of my empathic engagement with Marilyn's words.

In this chapter I have attempted to give a sense of what it is like to carry out a hermeneutic phenomenological study. I have tried to bring such a project alive, conveying something of the quality of its 'doing'. Examples from my work on anger experiences hopefully illustrate what can be achieved by assuming a phenomenological and relational stance to the things we want to understand. This sort of research has taught me that all understandings are created out of our way of being which is inherently relational, participatory and reciprocal. Our research endeavours are always projects entailing a mutual journey of exploration and understanding for all those involved.

Chapter 14

A Therapist's Portrait of a Clinical Encounter with a Somatizer

Maria Luca

The topic of this research is a client's relational pattern constructed through a therapy encounter. The client (whom I call Rebecca) was referred for somatization and presented initially with a range of somatic symptoms.[i] Somatizers are regarded as concrete thinkers with interpersonal difficulties, particularly when engaging and connecting emotionally with others. The profile of a somatizer is therefore a challenge to relational therapists and researchers alike. Studies on relational depth demonstrate the importance of 'co-presence' and therapist satisfaction obtained in an engaging and reciprocal therapy interaction (Cooper, 2005). However, little is known about the limitations of relational depth when the client/co-researcher is preoccupied with physical symptom reporting compromising the therapist's desire to relate psychologically.

Some of the content of this chapter originates from my larger doctorate thesis (Luca, 2007).[ii] I utilize my emergent researcher responses and observations from my encounter with Rebecca to show the impact of her demeanour on our intersubjective experience.

The choice of topic was influenced by many years of being a therapist exposed to clients whose stories focused on physiological symptoms. My experience gave rise to a series of questions about the phenomenon of somatization: How do somatizers present in therapy? What is their lived experience? How should/do therapists/researchers respond?

Relational-centred Research for Psychotherapists: Exploring Meanings and Experience
Edited by Linda Finlay and Ken Evans
Copyright © 2009 John Wiley & Sons, Ltd.

Clients diagnosed as somatizers are often told by medical professionals that the problem is 'in your head'. This attitude can perpetuate existing distress. My experience in therapeutic work with somatizers confirms that their worst fear is that professionals' attitude will be that either the pain is imagined or that the aetiology is psychological. Over the years I have learned the value of acknowledging the client's lived experience not only as a guide to understanding the depth of the experienced self but as an aid to a therapy of trust. Making the pain tangible, whether psychological, emotional or physical, by locating it in the body is not unusual. It is common in many cultures for people to locate their distress in physiological pain. Clients' conviction that the problem is indeed physiological is seen as key to difficulties in forming working alliances with these clients (Kirmayer & Robbins, 2005). In my experience, it is challenging to develop a relationship but believing that the client's pain is genuine fosters safety and nurtures the alliance.

In my practice as therapist/researcher I try to stay present in the spontaneous, embodied encounter. The feelings, intentions, desires and expectations of researcher/participant or therapist/client feature strongly in the embodied relationship. Unspoken (possibly implicit) agendas, may indeed be sensed in the quality of clients'/co-researchers' presence, as well as our felt sense. Individuals in interaction bring their horizons of understanding – horizons of personal histories and expectations – which together produce the relational, intersubjective construction of a shared, felt reality. These ideas were integrated into my grounded theory method used to analyse the data.

Methodology

The grounded theory method

Glaser and Strauss (1967) produced a grounded theory which came to be known as a systematic, disciplined way of theory building. I chose the revised grounded theory method of Strauss and Corbin (1990, 1998) to research this project for its bottom up and systematic way of deriving theory. Here the researcher does not begin with a hypothesis but looks within the data generated for observations and theory.

Strauss and Corbin (1998) recognized that the researcher is involved with – and actively constructs and interprets – the data throughout the process. This leads to the development of explanatory schemes and theoretical constructs capturing a lived world. This perspective rests on the principle that there is neither a logical universe, nor an ordered reality to be unravelled to get to the truth. Instead, people are seen to interact by exercising their agency to reach a negotiated understanding of reality. This philosophical stance is very much the *sine qua non* of postmodernity (Kvale, 1992) where truths are not fixed but are subject to historical change that demands new ways of situating identities congruent with existing realities (Foucault, 1988). This type of intersubjective research position reflects Husserl's idea of the 'life-worlds' where truth is 'a contingent creation of a particular intersubjective community' (Husserl, 1965, cited in Thompson, 1994) and is a valuable principle with the potential to enrich the meaning of research.

I adopt a postmodernist model of consciousness that is guided by human desire and intention, not one that passively mirrors the world. Human agency is central in my approach to studying human experience. This position removes the subject–object dichotomy of the positivistic paradigm and approaches research participants as co-researchers and not as objects of observation. I employ Patton's (2002) 'embracing-subjectivity' where all subjects party to the research are active agents in the construction of meaning and Lincoln and Guba's (1986) criteria of 'authenticity'. By giving due consideration to culture, context and agency, especially intentions, motivations and preconceptions of all participants, any emergent meanings are the products of an embodied investigation which is potentially enriching to understanding. Embodied inquiry carries within it these fundamental principles and postmodern researchers recognize that these criteria give quality and validity in qualitative research (Morrow, 2005; Polkinghorne, 1983; Polkinghorne, 1992; Rennie & Fergus, 2006).

The Researcher and Reflexivity

I am a UKCP registered psychotherapist integrating psychodynamic, existential/phenomenological and humanistic principles in my practice. My view that relationality in the therapy encounter fosters trust and a solid alliance on which to build understandings rests on emphasizing transparency of researcher agency. The researcher can learn from immersion into all aspects of the research without fear of contaminating the data and recognizing that reflection during analysis can provide a deeper understanding.

Reflexivity implies transparency and disclosure of researcher subjectivity. It is what gives research credibility and value. It is a revelation of identity including assumptions, beliefs and philosophical position as well as any prior knowledge on the subject of investigation giving the research trust-worthiness (Morrow, 2005). Reflexivity enables the investigator to be 'self-reflective and to express the returns of reflexivity' (Rennie, 2000, p. 495) rather than be involved in the painstaking task of bracketing subjectivity. As McLeod (2001, p. 157) states: 'The issue of the relationship between researcher and research participant/informant is of special significance to researchers ... because it mirrors debates surrounding the preferred relationship between therapist and client.'

Context of the study

The data used in this chapter comes from the transcript of a single session with a client who gave her consent to use material from her session for research purposes. Rebecca was referred for therapy via her GP with depression, anxiety and several physical symptoms that caused her disability and distress. The therapy took place once a week for one year.

Before Rebecca sought psychological treatment she was medically investigated for her symptoms and shown to have no organic aetiology. She received a brief psychological intervention of six sessions in a primary care setting and was referred for further, longer-term private psychotherapy. Whilst in psychological treatment she continued to receive invasive investigations and consulted specialist psychiatrists and physicians for the medically unexplained symptoms. Her motivation for seeking therapy was symptom relief.

Procedure

Once Rebecca gave ethical approval and consented to the use of excerpts from the session for research purposes, I audio-recorded the session and transcribed it soon after. The session lasted 50 minutes. The data from the text was systematically coded applying the 'constant comparative method'. Here the researcher checks and modifies derived categories against successive paragraphs of text (Rennie, 2000; Strauss & Corbin, 1998). By immersing myself in the text I was able to identify categories and sub-categories, and generate an over-arching model to form the portrait of the phenomenon of somatization. The writing up of the portrait was an opportunity to meta-reflect on my thoughts and feelings in response to the client's story and physical presence.

The analysis of the data was not concerned with internal validity or generalizability, concerns more appropriate for causal or explanatory case studies (Yin, 1994), nor with 'smoothing' of the data, an approach dominant in psychodynamic approaches where the researcher selects the material after a session is conducted (McLeod, 1999, p. 35). My aim was to identify how an individual's lived experience is presented in the language studied from a transcript of a session during the initial phase of a helping relationship. Valuing the role of embodiment, both verbal and implicit client language were analysed along with my own therapist/researcher experience.

The analysis of the data involved a 'circling of consciousness' using immersion in the data, engagement, constant abstraction and reflexivity. The coding procedure consisted of identifying meaning units, evaluating their relations to each other and deriving categories grounded in the data. The procedure led to the identification of a set of 14 lower order themes. These were analysed for connections to provide a framework for the development of a set of 6 higher order categories. I used words that best represented the meaning of codes. This process involved depth reflection and revision until I reached a place that fitted with the significant meanings in the text.

The descriptive categories underwent three separate audits to check for validity. My research supervisor and four postgraduate research students checked the coding and categorizing and discrepancies found led to adjustments at each stage.[iii] This process of checking the validity of the coding led to re-coding and re-arrangement of categories leading to the core categories. The frequency of coded responses was also analysed for weight and client preoccupation. The coding of the text produced a set of lower order themes; their frequency is shown in Table 14.1 below.

The constant comparative analysis procedure in grounded theory yielded themes which appeared related. These were then organized under higher order categories (see Table 14.2 below), for analysis and theory building (Rennie, 1998, 2000). Text fragments such as *'I'm getting physically worse'* (physical deterioration) and *'My muscles were clamming up as a result of what was going on'* (muscular aches and pains) came under the higher order category of: Bodily Preoccupation. This was the procedure used to arrive at the higher order categories.

Axial coding (Strauss & Corbin, 1998) enabled the analysis to look at common features in the categories and connections between them were made. Following the comparative method a hierarchical structure emerged. It consisted of one core category, 'Discourse of a somatizer' and three higher order categories, 'Affective orientation', 'Concrete orientation', 'Stress and struggle in the family' (see Figure 14.1). Figure 14.2 shows the frequency and preoccupation of the client discourse.

Table 14.1   Themes in client language and their frequency in the text. Lower order categories.

Themes	Frequency	%
Emotions	21	15.22%
Physical deterioration	2	1.45%
Muscular aches and pains	16	11.59%
Physical weakness	18	13.04%
Physical pain	4	2.90%
Physical stress	1	0.72%
Physical illness	2	1.45%
Health anxiety	1	0.72%
Complaining on treatment	8	5.80%
Medical treatment	20	14.49%
Medical diagnosis	6	4.35%
Early childhood problems	12	8.70%
Relationship issues	14	10.14%
Aha and Mmm sounds	13	9.42%
Total	**138 (100%)**	**100%**

Table 14.2   Themes in client language and their frequency in the text. Higher order categories.

Categories	Frequency	%
Emotions	21	15.22
Bodily preoccupation	44	31.88
Medical treatment focus	26	18.84
Stress factors in the family	26	18.84
Aha and Mmm sounds	13	9.42
Dissatisfaction with medical treatment	8	5.80
	138 (100%)	**100%**

Findings

Affective orientation

The affective category, capturing Rebecca's feelings, had the lowest frequency. As the therapist/researcher I had to use considerable probing to encourage the client to identify her feelings whilst telling her story. I sometimes used my own felt sense to achieve this, tentatively checking it with Rebecca. For example I would say: 'I have a sense of frustration, perhaps anger as you say that.' At times Rebecca appeared puzzled. At other times

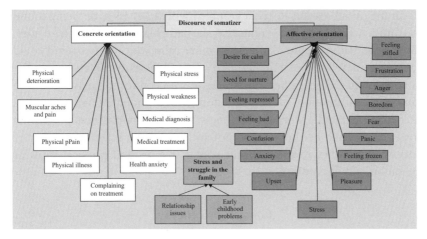

Figure 14.1 Discourse of a somatizer
Branches demonstrate the process of clustering fragments into meaning units. The core category is: Discourse of a somatizer. The three sub-categories are: Affective orientation, with 16 properties; Concrete orientation with 10 properties; and Stress and struggle in the family with 2 properties

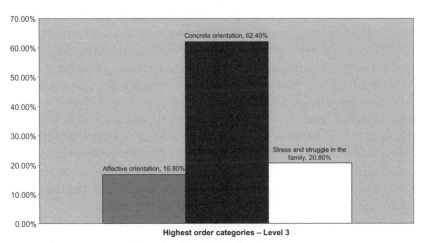

Note: The graph shows a quantitative demonstration. It is not a statistical analysis.

Figure 14.2 Language of somatizer

she resonated with the feeling, though quickly moving back to her physical symptoms again.

Rebecca's story made reference to cultural idioms of distress where physical illness received family attention. As a child of seven she had spent months in hospital after a road traffic accident. This earned her the 'little princess' label. Feelings on the other hand were dismissed and regarded as unimportant. She therefore learned to appease early on.

In the initial session Rebecca grappled with a key issue of 'being found out' for having lied to her parents that she had obtained her Masters degree. She feared being caught. She desired inner calm which in her mind could only be achieved if she could be cured of her illnesses, complete her studies and wrap up the lie. In her mind there was no connection between the lie and the exacerbation of her symptoms, even though these coincided. Rebecca inhabited a world of bleakness, fear and hopelessness poignantly revealed through her body. I had not anticipated the extent of her fear of emotion, at times revealed through long silences and physical signs of agitation and discomfort.

Concrete orientation

This category consisted of bodily focused descriptions as Figure 14.1 illustrates. Rebecca's story was told repeatedly through references to medical diagnosis and treatments, physical symptoms, dissatisfaction with medical treatments and a preoccupation with bodily functions, such as discomfort in sitting down, difficulty in feeding herself due to muscular weakness and other disabilities. She had several medical investigations and was seen by neurologists, rheumatologists, an orthopaedic surgeon, an osteopath, a chiropractor and a homeopath. Her symptoms included: irritable bowel syndrome, muscle pain and stiffness, muscle weakness, irregular periods, paralysis of the leg, limited movement, pins and needles, burning sensations and spinal pain. Some of the medical diagnoses for which various treatments had been administered included: a slipped disc two years before the onset of the paralysis and fibromyalgia. Medical treatment included Prozac and physiotherapy; both failed to alleviate the symptoms.

Rebecca's narrative was characterized by repeated references to physical sensations and bodily symptoms. Her concrete speech endorsed the self as 'ill' at various levels. Presenting to the medical profession with somatic symptoms legitimized Rebecca's self-perception of being ill and might have provided a secondary gain in receiving attention and justifying being off work.

Listening to a narrative full of these descriptions was no easy task. As her relentless symptom-focused narrative intensified I found myself unintentionally slipping into boredom.

Stress and struggle in the family

Childhood family conflict and current relationship issues were the two properties captured under this category of 'Stress and struggle in the family'. Her 'ill self' contained aspects of family conflict and culturally endorsed behaviours reported about the family which led to receiving nurture. With probing, Rebecca spoke of frustration, anxiety and fear in her relationships. She felt fearful, angry and obligated to appease and calm conflict-ridden situations. She felt useless in her studies and resorted to lying rather than risk rejection and humiliation. She was anxious that if she returned to work she would panic and physically deteriorate. Work and illness seemed inseparable in her mind. As far as she was concerned being ill provided the physical care and comfort she needed and legitimized the self-imposed label of being disabled.

Rebecca portrayed her early history and relationships without feeling. If she spoke of being upset or angry, or of threatening behaviours, she remained cool and disaffected. Talk about ailments, symptoms, medical diagnosis was animated. She came alive, spoke fluidly with a raised tone in her voice and had no qualms about giving lucid detail of the bodily theatre. This reminded me of what she had said during the assessment: '*As I was lying there in the hospital bed after the accident, I'll never forget this … well, my father came to visit and I was not able to speak then … it could've been the shock … I don't know … but he kneeled down by the bed and looked at me as if to say how sad and worried he was … I don't remember if he cried, but it seemed as if I saw him crying. Mmm … It was the only time I remember my father showing some sort of feeling. I'll never forget that.*' This was the only statement containing an open display of emotion throughout the session. The rest were devoid of aliveness and were spoken in a timid monotone or not spoken at all.

Non-verbal Observations[iv]

Rebecca's general demeanour was characterized by a couched, frozen and rigid bodily gesture. She sat lightly in her chair, giving the impression of someone in physical pain and discomfort. She appeared tense with arms tightly held above her shoulders indicating muscular tension. During moments of talk about bodily symptoms and medical treatments she became animated and assertive. It looked as if, in the midst of these symptoms, she had found a home. These concrete utterances were not empty and devoid of meaning. They formed the nucleus of Rebecca's ill self. It was obvious to me that – in contrast with the tension observed during feeling moments in the session – there was a satisfying ease as she spoke of her body, medical treatments and diagnoses.

The subtle changes in the sound of Rebecca's voice and the pauses as she described how she felt about herself in relation to her illness disclosed uneasiness. She looked unsure as she spoke, almost disembodied. In contrast to the intensity in Rebecca's description of bodily symptoms, she seemed disinterested and puzzled that we were thinking about how she felt. The changes in tone of voice during distinct moments of talk were noticeable. Rebecca seemed to have organized her self and her life in general around being ill. It took on enormous significance and became the cornerstone of her relationships with the world. Whenever I explicitly shared my sense of any of her feelings she became dismissive and confused. I became aware that in response to a world devoid of feeling, I was experiencing myself as barren and, rather than engaging, I was closing down.

Reflections

Therapist subjectivity

The consulting room was filled with a suffocating array of inert objects, mostly referring to a sick body. The concreteness and weight of this narrative became central in my own mind. This woman had been trying for years to draw attention to her pain. Yes, she felt it in her body. However, she did not display any ability to even consider any feelings that might be associated with the bodily experience. *Her sick body was her identity.*

Every muscle and every tendon in Rebecca's *body cried out loud*. At least that is how it seemed to me. Rebecca could not move her neck without the sensation that any moment it would come apart and she would end up without a head on her shoulders. Every tingling sensation, every movement was a catalyst of pins and needles, of immobility, of disability. Rebecca's body was the stage in the therapeutic theatre. The protagonist was the body communicating intense pain; Rebecca was the seeker of a valid explanation for this suffering. Out of several investigations and a multitude of diagnoses nothing seemed to fit, nor provide any relief from the symptoms. As the source of pain remained mystified Rebecca's body could not be set free and transformation into the longed for state of aliveness seemed an impossible dream.

At times I felt like a physician lost in a language of repetition, of symptoms and of ailments. I was bored. The narrative was animated yet incongruent with the deadness I experienced as the receiver of this apparently animated story. My mind returned to my therapist agenda. I was impelled to remove myself from the boredom and shift the therapeutic impasse away from deadness. By this stage I was beginning to doubt whether there was an affective life to access! My head was now full of Rebecca's language: a concrete, sensation-based language, devoid of an emotional life. There is an emotional deficit I thought, or un-modulated affect. If I could dig deeper I might be able to free this affective life and then the work will begin. The apparent lack of empathy in Rebecca toward herself and others, her self-preoccupation with concrete aspects of her life, the protracted detail of symptoms and medical diagnoses captured in her discourse, prompted me to begin to wonder whether there were autistic features. These diagnostic thoughts (which became more prominent when Rebecca left the room) might have been attempts to make sense of the experience or even live a life in my head to relieve the deadening impasse. Certainly I felt that a psychological formulation might help crystallize this thick fog in my mind.

My experience of boredom suggested an increasing lack of interest on my part in a story that turned me into a detached observer. I was clear in my own mind that the encounter lacked relational depth (Cooper, 2004).ᵛ Determined not to be disheartened by the stagnation I felt in this session, I assured myself that the work could be fruitful after all. No matter how disconcerting my thoughts and irrespective of my boredom, *the therapy had begun*. My own thoughts and feelings were in fact the beginning of an attempt to devise a psychological formulation and process Rebecca's predicament. This encounter with my own consciousness is otherwise described as the conceptualization of a given phenomenon; to achieve it the therapist enters into a reflective space, described by Fonagy et al. (2002) as the 'mentalization process'.

Researcher Subjectivity

In many qualitative methodologies there is emphasis on the value of participant language where researchers are exhorted to stay close to the meanings of the text. Less credence is given to the relational researcher/participant encounter. I sought to bridge both approaches.

Analysing the text my experience was that of leaping in and out of analytic systems. I was simultaneously inside and outside the text. I would step into the memory of listening to the text and then from immersion into hundreds of meaningless codes, I stepped into a heap of ideas in urgent need of reflection. I describe this as a leaping in and out of levels of unreflected experiencing. To be true to the grounded theory method the first step was to analyse the text but without losing sight of my own responses as a therapist. The leaping in and out of levels of experiencing was accompanied by thoughts and images that seemed to come out of this engagement with text analysis. Pondering for a moment on this experience of understanding the text, the best way to describe it is as an encounter with my subjectivity or a 'circling of consciousness'.

Whether the researcher applies a systematic method of analysis or claims objectivity, there is an inevitable encounter with subjectivity. Strauss and Corbin's (1998) maxim to postpone hypothesis making until after the grounded theory is developed to achieve verification (Rennie, 2000), becomes difficult. To postpone a hypothesis requires bracketing the thoughts that leap out of the research analyst's mind whilst immersed in the process. To postpone emergent thoughts (which are the hypotheses) risks losing the fluid understanding and theory building. It made better sense to me to allow these hypotheses to emerge, note them and re-visit them later for reflection and testing.

Back in the consulting room and away from the analysis of the text, my experience of the encounter as the therapist captured certain images which stayed in my mind throughout the coding, categorization and analysis of the transcript. It felt like stepping inside and outside the direct experience and then looking at it from the outside in. This inside and outside experiencing is linked by a space in between, like a thread that connects the two levels of consciousness. Inside, the experience is an immersion and engagement with consciousness; outside becomes an observation of consciousness, almost as if someone else was looking at it from the outside. This is the act of reflection.

When Rebecca described the experience of her 'sick' body, her effort to find meaning in her search for an effective medical treatment, she was describing a world of struggle to be visible and understood. For her, this was an ordinary and familiar world that she could recount fluently. It defined her identity. In the auspices of the therapy consulting room the story unfolding captured an experience far beyond that of the personal. I listened as the themes of physical symptoms crowded the room with pain. There was no space for anything else. If there was, I certainly had no access to it. As I accompanied Rebecca through her story, images of medical doctors appeared in sanitized hospital rooms. Thoughts of professionals rallying round, eager to understand the roots of this bodily pain took centre stage. Nothing worked according to Rebecca. Nothing made sense. As an outsider to Rebecca's story thus far, I was in a position to be one step removed and able to think about her emerging experience. The somatic descriptions formed the character of Rebecca's everyday life and the nexus of her preoccupations. Her body took centre stage in her worldview. This is how she chose to portray her identity to me. However, being the therapist I was also inside this experience, as I had opened myself to be affected by the contents of Rebecca's consciousness and empathize with her pain. Without empathy the therapeutic quest becomes an observational endeavour, removing the relational and indeed fundamental healing ingredients of therapy. Therefore as researchers and as therapists we are simultaneously experiencing and reflectively observing the process. We are in touch with emotion but also removed, thinking about the client's and our emotions. Both levels of experiencing influence and shape the research analysis, are worthy of consideration and valuable in the final understanding.

As the coding of utterances during the analytic procedure was well under way, my therapist subjectivity was captured in my thought, feeling and image responses during the session. Resolved to stay faithful to the grounded theory process, I postponed reflection and interpretation. However, my subjectivity was at play throughout and must have implicitly influenced the coding and categorization process. The activity of reflecting on my experience in order to process and organize it could not be entered into fully until the grounded theory method had reached saturation. However, this is not to say that reflection did not mediate and influence the coding and analysis of the data.

A Portrait of an Encounter with a Somatizer

My interaction with Rebecca produced images of sanitized rooms, hospital staff tending to her discomfort and Rebecca lost in her body. The image of: '*A mass of flesh and bones*' leapt out at me during the coding process. It seemed significant. On reflection I was struck by my image of Rebecca as 'flesh and bones' with no differentiated emotion. I felt disturbed and concerned with my apparent objectification of Rebecca. However, it seemed to parallel her own words which tended to be crowded with concreteness (presence) yet without emotional substance (absence). Rebecca was unable to think about her predicament in psychological terms except as a body in pain. She was not psychologically minded, I thought.

My own thinking troubled me. In my effort to make sense of my thought processes I often reached an impasse, got stuck on my own dislike of my thoughts, challenged these and found myself engaged in a 'circling of consciousness'. Rebecca's somatic presentation entailed no reflection or linking of feelings with her distress and certainly no consideration or understanding that the symptoms could have a psychological basis or relationship with flare-ups of the condition.[vi] To help organize my own thinking I focused on 'absence' and 'presence' in terms of what I would expect of ordinary encounters in order to arrive at a description of one type of person in comparison to another. The idea of a 'robotic existence' seemed to encapsulate the sense of inertness and absence of thought present in the client's language. The concreteness was indeed very present in Rebecca's presentation of being in the world.

My clinical encounter suggested that emotions talked about in the session were disproportionately negative and presented in an intellectualized manner devoid of affect. Reflection and the capacity to organize internal states in a meaningful and coherent manner were altogether absent. This lack of 'mentalized affectivity' draws attention to a difficulty in discovering meanings of one's own affect states. Fonagy et al. (2002) argue that without these characteristics the individual is unable to mentalize. Rebecca's language showed indication of an impoverished psychological life found in dissatisfaction in interpersonal relationships, in the sphere of work and lack of capacity to exercise her agency. The latter was represented in the emphasis unduly given to physiological causes, rejecting the possibility of psychological factors playing a part in the sick body, as well as almost entirely resting her hope in a medical cure.

The phenomenon of somatization is found in all cultures. It is a physiological and a psychosocial process. Irrespective of the universality of the phenomenon, the meaning attributed to symptoms by the individual concerned and their reaction to the illness are shaped by past experiences, personality and coping styles, familial and cultural norms and current interpersonal interactions. The expression of pain, whether physical or psychological, is unique to the individual concerned. The client in this encounter chose, habitually, to express herself in a concrete, symptom-oriented language. The somatic method of expression of pain was not only taken seriously by Rebecca's family, it legitimized the level of attention and care she received. This was parallel to my experience of Rebecca's use of me as a therapist and might have been unconsciously motivated to indirectly draw attention to her psychological pain.

Evaluation

It would be premature to suggest that the finding of a lack of emotional content and mentalization in the text drawn from a single session analysed, equips us with a clear understanding of the subjectivity of the individual studied or of the phenomenon of somatization. Neither would the meaning constructed around researcher and co-researcher/client interpersonal interaction provide a crystallized understanding of the client's lived world. Nevertheless, it is fair to suppose that the absence of articulation of feeling, the lack of reflection on the meaning of symptoms and their autobiographical influence, provide a portrait of somatization as one where reflection on the inner self is problematic or indeed deficient. This type of lifeworld is 'disembodied'.

Reflection my therapist/researcher subjectivity both during the process of therapy and the meta-analysis of the research, constitute meaningful components. The process of writing up the chapter itself helped raise awareness of the limitations in some of the micro-processes involved in the research, such as 'bracketing' of the spontaneous flow of researcher/clinician subjectivity. The mere fact that analysis of a spontaneous thought – though registered and memoed – is postponed, does not preclude it from entering the theorization process, irrespective of whether the order in which this had been developed is inductive.

The value of the analysis of a single session[vii] lies in the understanding it can provide regarding the phenomenology of the language of a somatizer presented at the early phase of therapy. As Broom (1997, p. 1) put it, 'The patient's story is, amongst many other things, a woven tapestry – of events, of perceptions of events, and of highly idiosyncratic responses to events. Many of the very significant events have to do with the vicissitudes of the patient's relationships with the world, and with other significant persons.' For Rebecca, family and cultural idioms of distress played an important role in the experience and communication of illness. The reality of the body was contingent upon the individual's experience of the world around her which provided legitimacy for her behaviour. The meaning of being ill consisted of a reality of gain, of 'being let off the hook', and of not having to answer for perceived failure, but be nurtured for being ill.

Undoubtedly, researcher subjectivity and relationality influence psychological formulations. The notion of a human being as intrinsically relational and inter-relational has underpinnings in philosophical phenomenology (Heidegger, 1927/1962; Merleau-Ponty, 1945/1962) as well as in psychoanalysis (Bowlby, 1988; Fonagy et al., 2002; Stern, 1985). Phenomenology presents humans as 'intentional' 'cultural' and 'embodied', qualities intrinsic to the human condition, and psychoanalysis presents humans as 'attachment-seeking individuals'. My own professional training, theories and concepts of somatization, are also influencing factors in the meanings and interpretations I have attributed to the client discourse.

It should be noted that the exploration of therapeutic discourse from a single session limits the scope of this study. Had the study embraced the complete therapeutic cycle as some studies have done (Rennie, 1990, 1992) and studied further units of language, more scope could be given to comparing changes in language units of meaning over time and how and to what extent psychotherapy could be effective in enabling the client to transform her/his 'lifeworld'. But that would be another study. This analysis was intended to describe what Berger and Luckman (1966) define as the 'home world'. A world consisting of one session and reflections of the therapist/researcher on that session is meaningful in itself.

Notes

[i] Somatization is described as high levels of medically unexplained symptom reporting in multiple physiological systems (Kirmayer & Robbins, 1991).

[ii] This larger project employed grounded theory. My use of grounded theory rests on postmodern principles denouncing the belief in an objective reality and advocating that researchers are subjects relating to other subjects. Philosophically this position embraces the notion that researchers are intentional beings exercising agency and relationality in our encounters with participants.

[iii] On subsequent reflection I would argue that such audits serve the requirements of positivistic research and do not necessarily increase validity. Other researchers' observations can be limited, whereas the researcher's involvement in the data produces more in-depth observations.

[iv] Transcripts reflect the literal contents of a session and are therefore limited in capturing the full essence of communication. Pauses, intonation, quality of voice expression and non-verbal bodily communication are important aspects in interaction. These merit some reflection.

[v] Responses in therapists are given due consideration in studies attempting to measure alexithymia (difficulty in describing and/or coping with emotions). Parker and Taylor (1997) cite studies supporting the idea that feelings of boredom and dullness in therapists point toward 'a deficiency in the interest affect system of these patients, as low interest is contagious' (pp. 79–80).

[vi] This landscape of concreteness is described by Pierre Marty and the Paris Group of psychosomatics as *la vie operatoire*, 'wherein the subject is bereft of virtually all higher level mental functioning, and reduced to going through the motions of a highly constricted, concrete and more or less robotized existence where the only focus is upon the actuality and factuality of life' (Lefebvre, 1988, p. 46).

[vii] Choosing to analyse a single session from the first therapeutic encounter would, I felt, provide the foundation and understanding on which to build a larger research project, especially in comparing clinicians' portraits of somatizers. A single transcript minimized the amount of data to analyse and provided the space for a more systematic line by line coding. This type of research venture could be enhanced by the method of *sampling by type* (Lepper & Riding, 2006), where more cases of diagnosed somatizers' use of language could be compared and contrasted and more in-depth results developed.

Chapter 15

Relating through Difference: A Critical Narrative Analysis

Darren Langdridge

This chapter demonstrates a critical narrative approach to research (Langdridge, 2007, 2008) for psychotherapists based on an investigation of the life story of one of my clients – Brian – a middle-aged man struggling to live a 24/7 sadomasochistic (SM) life as a slave. Previous literature on SM has for the most part been grounded in psychopathology with only recent writing approaching this topic from a non-pathological perspective (Barker & Langdridge, 2005; Langdridge & Barker, 2007). More recent research has sought to identify and examine discourses around SM and work phenomenologically to understand the appeal of this much maligned sexual practice/identity (see, for instance, Beckmann, 2001; Langdridge and Butt, 2004, 2005; Langdridge, 2005a; Taylor and Ussher, 2001). To date, however, there has been little work examining – in a non-pathologizing way – the individual life stories of people engaging in these practices and the struggle 'SMers' may have to realize their identities. This chapter presents one of the first systematic narrative analyses of the journey into SM for one man. That this research has emerged out of my therapeutic relationship with Brian raises a number of important and quite subtle ethical issues to do with boundaries and power.

Permission to do this research was gained at the end of a therapeutic session with me explaining the nature of the work in detail, handing Brian an information sheet and consent form and asking that he think about this

Relational-centred Research for Psychotherapists: Exploring Meanings and Experience
Edited by Linda Finlay and Ken Evans
Copyright © 2009 John Wiley & Sons, Ltd.

outside the session before letting me know whether he would like to participate. I emphasized the fact that whether he chose to participate or not would not influence his therapy but of course the impact of this unusual intervention needs considerable thought.

I decided to ask Brian to participate as he was a client I had seen for some time and I felt our relationship was secure enough to withstand the intervention. Brian was in a position to say 'no' and that was crucially important. Asking him about this research at the end of a therapy session seemed more appropriate to me as I absolutely did not want the research to intrude on the centrality of the therapy to our relationship. But even with this forethought when I initially planned to ask Brian to participate I felt that given the nature of the session (with discussion of particularly difficult issues, which I had not expected) I found myself deciding not to ask about participation on that occasion. Instead, I waited a few weeks until the atmosphere was less charged. (This was challenging as I had a writing deadline to meet but the priority must be the client and their needs rather than that of the researcher, whatever the circumstances.)

Below I discuss the reasons for choosing a critical narrative analysis (CNA) in the context of psychotherapeutic research, outline the methodology and then briefly present the findings from this particular study. The chapter ends with a reflexive evaluation of the use of CNA for counselling/psychotherapeutic research along with discussion of a number of issues that arise from conducting such research with one's own clients.

Methodology

Rationale

There is no single correct way of carrying out research and that is as true for narrative research as any other method. Different narrative methods have different strengths and weaknesses and so decisions about which to use must be guided by the questions the researcher seeks answers for. The form of CNA being described here includes aspects of other methods and much will be familiar to those schooled in other phenomenologically informed narrative methods. There are some differences, however, and these need to be noted. What is unusual is the way in which often disparate components are philosophically grounded and practically combined into one analytic approach whilst still remaining grounded in the phenomenological tradition (see Langdridge, 2008).

The key distinguishing feature between this form of narrative analysis and others, however, is the inclusion of a 'critical moment', where an attempt is made to interrogate the text using aspects of social theory as a *hermeneutic of suspicion*, albeit one modified from that of Ricoeur (1970).[i] This makes the method particularly suitable for researchers interested in conducting work on topics which are clearly and directly inflected with issues of power and politics. The focus of this study, the often pathologized sexuality of sadomasochism, is an ideal topic for research given the difficult history of psychotherapy and marginalized sexualities. Sadomasochism has occupied a particularly troubled/troubling position in counselling/ psychotherapeutic theory from Freud onwards (see Taylor, 1997) and many therapists continue to struggle to understand, acknowledge and accept SM practices/identities as a normal and healthy way to have sex, live and love.

CNA methodology

CNA is idiographic (a focus on studying the individual) with a strong emphasis on understanding the life story as presented, bounded by the research focus of the study. Case study work from this perspective is, in many ways, ideal but not the only possibility. It is perfectly possible to collect data from a number of participants in order to identify general patterns of narrative with regard to the topic being investigated. It is worth distinguishing here what is meant by 'case study research' versus a psychotherapeutic 'presentation of a case study'. Although there are clearly many similarities between the two activities, they can – and arguably ought – to be distinguished. Psychotherapeutic research involves the systematic application of a research methodology, such as CNA, with the relationship changing – albeit temporarily in many cases – from therapist-client to researcher-participant. This shift in relationship is important as it offers up the possibility of some critical distance and the opportunity to generate findings that may provide insights into the topic being investigated (and possibly the therapeutic process itself).

There are six stages in a critical narrative analysis, none of which should really be seen as discrete since one of the aims of CNA is the synthesis of a variety of analytic tools, to better enable the analyst to work critically with their data and shed light on the phenomenon being investigated. The stages are:

(1)   a critique of the illusions of subjectivity;
(2)   identifying narratives, narrative tone and rhetorical function;

(3)   identities and identity work;
(4)   thematic priorities and relationships;
(5)   destabilizing the narrative;
(6)   synthesis.

More detail on these stages is given in Langdridge (2007) but I will briefly outline them here. The first stage involves the researcher subjecting him- or herself to critique using the 'hermeneutic' (method of interpretation) that is most appropriate to the study being conducted. In the case of this study with Brian, my analysis is partly filtered through the lens of the latest thinking in sexuality studies, notably queer theory (see, for instance, Seidman, 1996).[ii] Queer theory involves re-thinking the very normality of 'everyday' sexuality and in the process highlighting the myriad assumptions which underpin such an understanding: issues such as hetero-normativity, mono-normativity, gender and power and so on. Applied to this case study, sado-masochism is not simply treated as different from 'everyday' sexual practice (whatever that might be!); it is seen as acceptable and demands a non-pathologizing perspective.

Stage 1 of my study involved me in considerable reflexive evaluation of my own position with regard to sexuality and normality. This requires more work than may at first be thought. I am a gay man who has spent many years researching issues in sexualities (including sadomasochism from a non-pathological perspective) but even so I needed to think (and feel) through my responses to sadomasochism as it related to this particular client-participant. This involved me reflecting on questions of gender and power (Brian is heterosexual and visited female 'Pro-Domme' prostitutes), issues of race and ethnicity (Brian is white and English and preferred black dominant women), and issues of age (Brian was in his sixties and I am much younger and much more familiar with younger SM participants) amongst other things. There is no simple setting aside of one's preconceptions but rather I needed to carefully and reflexively evaluate my relationship with my client-participant[iii] and his world. Given the relational context, this was something I needed to do at every stage of the research. In particular, I needed to take considerable care not to project my own subjectivity on to Brian and his narratives. I needed to revel in our differences and the rich detail of his lifeworld.

The second stage is more straightforward and involves identifying distinct narratives in the text (in short, the number and form of any stories with a beginning, middle and end), and then working through these to identify the 'tone' and 'rhetorical function'. The *tone* refers to the emotional character of the story (whether it is a happy one or a sad one, a triumphant tale or a story of loss and regret, for instance). The *rhetorical function* is where the story is engaged in argumentation, often with an invisible other which is frequently a dominant counter-narrative. So, for instance, a client may speak to us about feeling like an object when discussing their mental health problems with a medical professional and through this implicitly argue against a (dominant) medical model of mental health in favour of a more holistic view of the person and their experiences.

The third stage is where the researcher tries to see what kind of person is being conjured up in the narrative being told. What narrative identity is the client-participant constructing through the telling of a particular story? The concept of narrative identity comes from the work of the French philosopher Paul Ricoeur and emphasizes the idea that our conception of selfhood comes about from the stories we tell of ourselves and others. That is, there is no fixed or essential notion of self (or personality if you will) with our identity (or more correctly, identities, given that different identities may be constructed at different times and in different social contexts) instead being conjured up by us when we work through language (story telling) to link the episodes of our lives into a coherent story.[iv]

Stage 4 involves an analysis of the common themes underpinning a narrative though this should not involve systematic coding of the text (that is, breaking it down into its constituent parts) as that would result in the loss of the narrative form but rather identification of key themes emerging from the stories being told. This involves a close reading of the text looking for recurring ideas and themes and the analyst identifying links and connections (much as the therapist does in practice).

Stage 5 involves a return to Stage 1 but here the critical analysis is turned on the narratives told by the client-participant rather than the researcher. This is not an archaeological process where the hermeneutic is used to dig into the past to uncover hidden causes (as one might find in psychoanalysis) but rather a future-focused one with the goal of opening up other possible ways of telling the story. The critique is therefore not turned on the participant by projecting some superior understanding onto their experience but rather used to facilitate the researcher in identifying ways in which narratives might block future possibilities rather than open them up (offering a new perspective with which to view the focus of investigation). A queer hermeneutic is thus appropriate and valuable in the context of my research with Brian as this radically different way of viewing sex, gender and sexuality enables an opening up of possibilities for viewing things from a new perspective. In other research, other hermeneutics would be more appropriate (such as those from critical social theory on class, race and ethnicity or dis-ability) and the choice must always be grounded in the topic being investigated.

Method

A biographical interview (see Langdridge, 2007) was conducted with one of my clients, Brian.[v] The interview began with just one question asking him to tell me his story of SM in as much detail as possible. (This beginning marked a distinction of our work in therapy which was more broadly focused.) I also explained that I would mostly listen and not interrupt too much though I might ask clarifying questions occasionally. I had a series of more standard interview questions designed to encourage Brian to elaborate different aspects of his story if necessary. Brian began to tell his story with great gusto and the interview lasted three hours with very few interventions from me and no need for most of the follow-up questions.

The client-participant, Brian, is an older white British heterosexual man (61 years) who – following his marriage breakdown – has only recently begun to fully explore his interests in SM. Brian first presented in therapy with me by talking about how he met a dominatrix and quickly entered into a full-time (24/7) slave relationship with her. This led to a number of problems for him that ultimately led to the breakdown of the relationship. He came into therapy with me aware of a long-standing need to address a number of relationship issues, which came to a head with this particular relationship – in part due to the way in which such SM relationships involve the explicit negotiation of power (Langdridge & Butt, 2004). In the research interview Brian began by talking about his earliest recollections of an interest in SM and his gradual exploration of this through his encounters with professional dominatrices. What emerged at a relatively early stage of the research interview is how many of the presenting issues are – in very many ways – 'everyday' issues of concern for people in SM and non-SM relationships alike. Our work has, to date, focused on exploring Brian's ways of relating and how he might find new ways of relating to allow him to live his life in the way that he wishes. At the time of the interview Brian had been coming to see me for approximately 14 months, once weekly for the first year and then once a fortnight for the later months.

Findings

Two distinct narratives emerged from my research interview with Brian: the first telling of his 30-year history of visiting Pro-domme prostitutes (professional dominatrices) and the second sharing his recent love affair with one Pro-domme (Mistress K) and his experience of a 24/7 slave lifestyle with her. The first narrative (made up of a series of eight sub-

narratives) detailed particular moments in his history, most often relationships with significant Pro-Dommes. The second narrative consisted of five
sub-narratives, four of which were sub-plots in the story of his relationship
with his Mistress and the final one a reflection on his experience of psychotherapy, which was initiated by me. This structure was – in itself –
highly informative as it showed his life story in two halves: before and after
meeting Mistress K, and the discovery of the life he had always wished to
live. In many ways, his therapy has been about re-narrating his history,
accepting the need for change and how this might be realized in the future
through a loving relationship in which his identity might be fully realized.
That is not to say that success – in Brian's terms – will be judged through
him living happily with Mistress K who he loves but rather that he comes
to understand his own desire and the implications this has for how he
might understand himself better and realize a satisfactory future relationship. This story was reprised in the research.

One of the themes of the first narrative was Brian's 'search for perfection'
and this was constructed as a search for sexual perfection in his visits to
professional dominatrices.

> Erm, the funny thing is though, with the, when a man goes to, well no,
> when this man goes to pro-dommes, it's like you're always kind of seeking
> perfection …

In many ways this theme represented his own desire for control through
financial exchange for sexual pleasure. Brian talked of ticking off his
requirements on a form and/or discussing his preferences with the professional dominatrices he visited in his efforts to find sexual satisfaction. At
times he found sexual satisfaction in these encounters for an hour or two
but then always returning to his 'normal' life in between and thus frustration at not realizing his sexual identity fully.

It was only when he found love with Mistress K that he actually found
what he was looking for, a connection and route into a fulfilling and permanent realization of his sexual identity. Perhaps ironically, this was not
particularly sexual perfection, though there was obviously sexual compat-
ibility, but rather love and acceptance. He discovered the possibility of a
lifestyle with Mistress K, a way of living in which he was accepted totally.
He had previously been married and was content for while, having a daughter together with his wife who he loves dearly, but his wife was never totally
accepting of his submissive nature and therefore of him as a submissive
man. The narrative of his encounter with Mistress K is one of 'romance
and discovery'. The story of romance is classic with them coming to love
each other through everyday activities and in the process what emerges

from him is the discovery of the possibility of a permanent 24/7 lifestyle, something that was hitherto unknown and indeed unknowable.

In meeting and developing his relationship with Mistress K he moved beyond a financial transaction for a moment of pleasure to the possibility of a mutually satisfying lifestyle.

> I saw her every day during the day and escorted her round London, and that, was as good as the session for me, being with this person … just being with her was wonderful …

But finding this perfection led to anxiety and doubt about his ability to meet her perfection and he 'lost' himself. That is, his own lack of confidence in her desire for him, and his doubt about the possibility of realizing his dream, led to his own downfall when he went to live with Mistress K. This was almost certainly allied to a loss of control, which was initially at least unfamiliar and emotionally troubling. At first, things went well but very quickly he found himself doubting everything, worrying about doing things wrong as he thought it was necessary for him to be as perfect as he perceived his Mistress to be. His anxiety led to insecurity – 'Am I good enough?' – which in turn led to conflict.

> When you go and see a pro-domme, the big difference is you, the client, me, I am actually in charge. I want to be a slave but in actual fact I am dictating the terms. Very often you'll be given a 'erm almost a tick sheet of activities, so 'do you want to be caned?', you tick … So it's almost a reverse of being, wanting to be a slave but actually saying 'right, I want this, but I don't want that': it's like a menu. And that's how it is when a man visits a pro-domme and so that's, and I mention that because that's one of the big changes from when I went in, with a lifestyle domme.
>
> I got bound up in wanting to do things right and making cock-ups of fairly simple things.

This second narrative moved from a classic story of 'romance' to one of 'tragedy' (where what could be called his fatal flaws lead to an inevitable downfall) and much of our therapeutic work together since this time has been concerned with him coming to understand his own role in these events. Moving from limited sexual encounters circumscribed by the financial transaction (indeed, guaranteed by the financial transaction) to a full-time relationship which required a confidence and certainty of him that he was not yet ready to give, whilst offering elements of the domination and submission he loved. It seemed to be a case of too much, too soon, with his lack of knowledge, lack of self-esteem, and most importantly, lack of belief that this was really realizable leading to his increasingly irrational and unpredictable behaviour. His attempts to gain some control led to him reverting to familiar behaviours such as gift giving and financial exchange. He bought Mistress K a house which was offered 'without strings' but which he acknowledged later was almost certainly an attempt to secure a foundation for himself in her affections. Prior to his relationship with Mistress K, Brian had always exchanged money for sex and affection even whilst maintaining and managing complex relationships (friendships) with a number of professional dominatrices. This could not sustain this relationship, however, which was grounded in a different mode of relating, one that was much less instrumental and as a result much more fragile.

Different identities are constructed through the different narratives being told. In his 30 years visiting pro-dommes he tells a story of an 'explorer', albeit a naive one searching for sexual perfection. He presents a series of sub-narratives highlighting his own sexual discovery and in the process a very human story of relationality. In the second narrative there is the story of romance and learning to live *with* his sexuality, rather than simply satisfying his sexual desire. He presents as a determined man who, having had a taste of what life might be, wants to work hard to realize his identity and live his dream. This too is recounted in a somewhat naive way but becomes more insightful upon reflection and his developing understanding of his own role in the downfall of his dream.

Brian's narrative served a number of rhetorical functions (within the broader context of simply telling his story) and interestingly not those that I first assumed might be relevant. There was little engagement (and resistance) with traditional narratives of pathologization, with him fighting against a perception that his desire is 'unnatural'. Instead, his story set up his desire as 'natural', as ever present. This is in line with other published accounts of BDSM identities (see, for instance, Langdridge & Butt, 2004). His story was not without *shame*, however, and his first major narrative was heavily inflected with guilt and shame. He stressed the infrequency of his visits and how these encounters were much more than simply an instrumental transaction of money for sex. The rhetorical move here seemed to be his attempt to resist others' judgment.

> She didn't have a great deal but she was very clever and 'erm, I did get turned on and 'erm ... I went back there quite a few times, but, not kind of regularly like every week or every month, but it was sporadic, me going back. And she kind of, she got on well with me 'cos I'd come down and she'd say 'oh look, here's a pound; go and get me some cigarettes from the shop and little, running errands where she just trusted that I was not going to walk off with the money.

There was also a sense of Brian speaking rhetorically to a feminist audience and a perception that his actions might have been seen as exploitative of women. His rhetoric here is perhaps not surprising given his left-wing political views and active participation in the emancipatory politics of the Left and demonstrates some recognition of possible tensions between feminism and SM (see Ritchie & Barker, 2005). This was, however, subtle and never explicitly articulated but still recognizable as resistance to a 'canonical narrative' (Bruner, 1990) – that is, one that is dominant within a particular culture – which necessitated a rhetorical (and I would argue also, personal) struggle within the narrative to avoid the telling of an anti-feminist story.

> I was almost passive and 'erm, which is a very unfair relationship really, between two people in that respect.
>   There'd be girdles and corsets ... that would excite me and for me that's always been, that's a woman's power in a ways, this 'I', 'erm 'I put this round me' and, you know, I kind of recognize that and bow to it; I see that as a power thing. Other people see the opposite; they see it as a woman being restricted; I don't at all.

In the second major narrative much of his guilt and shame was lost. Indeed, he began to realize his potential and to revel in his identity when he met Mistress K and began to fall in love with her.

> I said 'you know I wanted to kiss your boots when you arrived'; 'go ahead (laughs)', so I knelt down in front of everybody and kissed her boots and thought 'I don't mind this at all' and sat back and we'd talk and we laughed and I told her a bit about myself and she ... we just had a wonderful time.

Whilst the stories told are Brian's they are also inflected with therapeutic reflection as they have been produced in an encounter with me – his therapist. Upon examining the interview, I could identify times when I may have shifted the dialogue, for instance, and perhaps encouraged Brian's moves to resist judgment from me. Most of my interventions were minimal but towards the end of the interview I asked about the present and Brian's decision to enter therapy and choosing to see me. This moved the story in a different direction, which is not to suggest that there was anything false in his account but rather that it was co-constructed in a very particular way, emerging out of my intervention and speaking to me as a therapist in this moment.

To conclude, in this analysis we can see a split in Brian's story and a need to move from control through uncertainty (with the consequence of anxiety and self-doubt) to belief in the possibility of realizing his identity and dream. This has echoes of other 'coming-out' stories, such as those of gay men and lesbians (Plummer, 1995), and suggests that for some people, at least, who are exploring SM as an identity and lifestyle it may be necessary to work through such a complex process. Whilst this story may appear unusual, in many ways it highlights the 'everyday' nature of SM relationships and the difficulties that many of us have in giving up control and trusting that we are 'good enough' to warrant the love of someone we adore such that we may realize our dreams.

Reflections

I believe CNA is a method ideally suited to psychotherapeutic case study research, though it is not of course restricted to this. In this small study I found my narrative research informing the therapy (and vice versa) in particularly helpful ways. Because psychotherapy is – in most cases, at least – a dialogue involving one party revealing stories of their life, a narrative research process mirrors this. It is also, in a number of ways, a distinct enterprise providing an opportunity for distance and reflection. This can of course feed back into the therapeutic process if the therapy is ongoing and this happened in this case with me discussing my analysis with Brian. This proved particularly fruitful as our work was nearing its end and such an overview provided an excellent opportunity for us both to reflect on and review both progress in therapy and also his life more generally. Having a transcript which was subjected to close analysis enabled me to bring back otherwise lost material in the latter stages of our work, which was helpful in enabling Brian to recognize quite how much progress he had made.

The impact of the therapy itself on the content and type of narratives produced must also be reflected upon. I interviewed Brian after approximately 14 months of therapy and this had led to a shift in the content and form of the narrative. When Brian first came to see me he told me how he had visited two other counsellors, both of whom had 'diagnosed' him with sexual addiction and would 'treat' him for this problem. This left him puzzled and confused. It did not make sense for him and he, therefore, did not return to either counsellor but it left its mark on him. In the first session with me he started by telling me what the other counsellors had determined with regard to his 'pathological sexuality' and that 'if you also say that I guess I will have to believe it'. I found this deeply troubling and representative of the dangers of the therapist imposing their subjectivity on to the client. His early story was, therefore, one in which he spoke to pathology much more than in his interview, which was produced some 14 months later after an encounter with me, working knowingly and deliberately to resist any notion of pathologization: not through force of will but rather through a respectful though critical phenomenology which honoured Brian's desire. My own existential psychotherapeutic practice continues to be as informed by this method of critical narrative analysis as is my research and so engaging in a process of critique with therapist and client acting as co-critics on a pathologizing social world is a familiar element in all my work with sexual minority clients.

Further to this, it is important to reflect on the relationship between myself and Brian within the therapy and research interview itself as this has implications for the research process and analysis. As I have come to know Brian I have been touched by his honesty and courage and this obviously forms the backdrop to the analysis I have presented here. His indefatigability and quest to grow at this later stage in his life are remarkable and have been an inspiration to me. This should not be seen as undermining the work, as all research is inevitably enmeshed in interpersonal dynamics but is instead reflexively significant when I (and you) consider my investment in the research process and analysis. More than this, I have found myself transformed through this encounter with new possibilities opening up for me as I story my own life. The possibility of pursuing a dream whatever one's age has always been available to me intellectually but in my encounter with Brian I have now connected with this possibility in a much more direct and embodied way. I am reminded of the work of the existentialist Martin Buber and his emphasis on the need to go beyond the conditions of classic humanistic theory and 'allow myself to be called out of myself by the other' and become 'available for communion instead of just for communication' (van Deurzen-Smith, 1997, p. 75) in an 'I-Thou' dialogue (Buber, 1923/2004) with another. This intensity in the interpersonal (communicative) context is invaluable for relational depth in psychotherapy and should therefore be reflexively acknowledged in the research process too.

All research involves a mutuality in which there is a 'fusion of horizons' (Gadamer, 1975/1996) of client-participant and therapist-researcher. That is, as I have argued elsewhere 'the therapeutic encounter becomes a dance where therapist and client form a unity, a synchronous back and forth of embodied mutuality' (Langdridge, 2005b, p. 96) and whilst this is often ameliorated by methodology it is present – as either therapeutic background or research presence – in the research process too. In my research interview with Brian it was background but could still be experienced then and in my analysis through our shared history of the therapeutic encounter. This work requires considerable care and much more honesty than may be usual in other forms of research but a critical awareness of self and other in relation can only benefit the research process, especially when the research builds on or is grounded in a prior therapeutic encounter.

Engaging in a critical narrative analysis needs considerable care and attention paid to ethical dimensions, however. This is a notion of 'care' as our condition for being responsible human beings, human beings who are always in relation with others and thus always inclined to care about the other. Engaging in 'suspicious critique' (i.e. being critically analytical and/ or interpretive) must always be secondary to an understanding of the lived world of the client-participant, with a sense of humility in the presence of the story of another human being. Employing external (critical and/or suspicious) theoretical frameworks in clumsy ways when engaged in therapy or research will only lead to the imposition of the therapist/ researcher's subjectivity onto the client. Critique must always be focused on the narrative and not the narrator, whose story must always be heard and respected as a faithful account of their experience.

Notes

[i] Hermeneutics of suspicion are external theoretical frameworks employed to critically interrogate meaning, revealing new layers of understanding. Perhaps the best known hermeneutic of suspicion is psychoanalytic theory where we can see the therapist using theory to identify unconscious dynamics in their search for meaning.

[ii] Queer theory offers a radical challenge to dichotomous ways of thinking about sexuality and as such offers a particularly valuable way of enabling the researcher to make a perspectival shift so that different possibilities for the narratives being told are opened up. In this case, for example, a queer take on sexual psychopathology might involve a challenge to taken-for-granted assumptions of normality and abnormality. Instead of simply avoiding pathologization, however, this involves the dissolution of such binaries themselves for they invariably foreclose on possible ways of understanding self and other.

[iii] I am using the conjunction 'client-participant' here deliberately to remind us of the dual nature of the relationship: for whilst there is a shift in the relationship from therapist-client to researcher-participant, this is necessarily complex and the need for care on the part of the therapist must not be forgotten when making such a shift into a research mode.

[iv] The process of therapy itself is probably the best example of two people coming together to tell/hear a story and then work to facilitate the telling of other possible stories which might better enable the client to reconcile their past with the present and find new ways of understanding their situation for the future.

[v] Brian is a pseudonym and indeed other elements of his life story have been changed where necessary to protect his anonymity. However, where such changes have been made all attempts have been made to maintain the heart of the story as told by Brian himself.

Chapter 16

A Journey into Survival and Coping by Women Survivors of Childhood Sexual Abuse

Susan L Morrow

The amount of, just, honor and respect – it's just not like anything I've ever experienced, Sue. The research is also ... it rings true. ... You have done something really extraordinary. It's so much more than a dissertation. ... Honor and respect. That's what we all lost. ... It's touching the place I've been protecting, I think – the place I'm afraid to open up, even to myself. It's the place that believes I'm honorable, worth knowing. It's the place that's protected by thick spiraling cords coiled like a snake around a core that's truly loved and honored. It's the place that yearns to be told in a voice that resonates with foreverness, "I love you."

With these words, Danu, one of the 11 research participants in my dissertation research on the ways in which women who had been sexually abused as children survived and coped, described her experience of the research process in which we had engaged for 18 months. As powerful as this research experience was for the women in the study, it impacted me as well, helping to make sense of my own experiences in childhood and as a therapist who was committed to the healing process with survivors of abuse. In this chapter, I explore this experience with a particular focus on this study as a feminist, relational, participatory project in which I hoped to empower and even contribute to the healing of the women I invited to take part in the research. I hope to take you, the reader, on a journey where you will experience – in at least a small way – how powerful it was for me

Relational-centred Research for Psychotherapists: Exploring Meanings and Experience
Edited by Linda Finlay and Ken Evans
Copyright © 2009 John Wiley & Sons, Ltd.

to share this experience with my participants. I will give you an overview of the study itself and what I found, with a particular focus on some of the more alternative kinds of data such as art, poetry and metaphor. And I will conclude with a gift from one of my participants, her poem called 'A Voice, My Voice'.

Methodology

This feminist relational research investigated the ways that women who had been sexually abused as children constructed their experiences of abuse, available resources, and survival and coping strategies, both at the time of the abuse and throughout their lifetimes.

Feminist relational participatory research

As a feminist qualitative researcher, I believe it is critical to share with you, the reader, my particular positioning as the 'instrument' of the research. At the time I conducted this research, I was completing my doctoral work in the field of counseling psychology. I had been a Masters' level therapist for a number of years, specializing in work with women who had been sexually and physically abused as children. My passion for this work drove my research quest, and I very much wanted to better understand how women like my clients had survived and coped with what was often indescribable abuse when they were babies, toddlers and little girls. As a feminist therapist, I believed that the 'symptoms' borne by adults that are often viewed as pathology had meaning; and my work with my clients supported this view. I was witness to the stories of countless women who, as children, had created amazing strategies to survive and keep the best parts of them alive, from self-inflicting physical pain to drown out the intolerable anguish they felt at being hurt by people who were supposed to be their caregivers, to creating parts of themselves in their minds to compartmentalize their trauma and preserve their creativity and loving spirits. This research would shine a light into some of the darkest places that humans experience.

What made this a feminist, relational project? To begin, my underlying assumptions were strengths-based, that children who were being abused found the best possible ways to cope given the resources – internal and external – that were available to them at the time. I implemented this perspective in the wording that I used in my interviews and in my interpretations that I made to participants, such as saying, when a participant shared that she had become anorexic because she learned that the physical pain of starvation would block the emotional pain she experienced, 'That was an amazing way of coping!'. My perspective as a feminist researcher was that I deeply believed in conducting my research from an egalitarian, relational model where I worked to equalize the power in my relationship with participants as well as forming a genuine, self-disclosive relationship with them. Thus, I shared with them my own traumatic experiences and became, as much as possible, a participant with them in my own research. I invited them to become not traditional research participants, but participant co-researchers who would work with me, according to their own time and willingness, to guide the project, to raise new questions for investigation, and ultimately to co-analyse the data. Above all, I wanted this research to be empowering of my co-researchers.

Participant co-researchers and generating data

To begin, I contacted therapists in agencies and private practice who were known to work with sexual abuse survivors with an introductory letter explaining the study and asking them to pass an attached recruitment flyer on to women clients, aged 18 and older, who would be appropriate for the study. Eleven women responded by phone, and I arranged initial interviews with them. The women's ages ranged from 25 to 72. One was African-American, one West Indian, and the remainder Caucasian. Two identified as lesbians, one as homosexual ('a lesbian is someone from the Isle of Lesbos'), one bisexual and the remainder heterosexual. Two women had disabilities, one experienced multiple physical illnesses and disorders, and the remainder were able-bodied. The participants came from a variety of socioeconomic statuses, educational backgrounds, occupations and spiritual/religious orientations. This diversity was important in this study, as I hoped to create a space for the voices of marginalized and silenced women to be heard.

All 11 women took part in individual (in-person) interviews lasting from 45 to 105 minutes. They responded to two questions: 'Please tell me everything you are comfortable telling me at this time about what happened to you surrounding your abuse', and 'How did you survive and cope with what happened to you?' All interviews were audio-taped; additionally, two were video-taped because one of the participants had 'told her story' in the form of art – paintings and drawings – throughout her life. I video-taped the pages of her many portfolios as she talked about her abuse, her healing process, and gave me evidence of how she had survived and coped. Another participant, who had survived by creating various 'personalities' or selves, was open to being video-taped so that I would better see the physical transitions that took place as various selves talked with me.

In addition to the individual interviews, I asked participants to share with me any writings or art that they had produced in the past that might help me to understand how they survived and coped. Two women shared art they had created; several brought poetry, some written prior to and some composed during the course of the research project. Amaya, who had formed a number of different 'selves' in response to her abuse, wrote:

> Today I got in touch with *mi otro yo (my other me)* …
> And I felt her, she was alive inside of me.
> I have always been afraid to get to know her.
> I thought that if I felt her I would die.
> I have been running away from her, not knowing
>
> That she was me and I was her …
> Today I got in touch with *mi otro yo* …
> Yes, I felt nervous, but I was not afraid
> like I had anticipated to be.
> I did not die like I thought I would when I felt her.
>
> Today I got in touch with *mi otro yo* …
> She is so powerful, so sure of herself, so strong, so real, so alive.
> I did not die like I thought I would when I felt her.
> Instead, I got in touch with the missing part of my inner power and
>   wholeness.
>
> Today I got in touch with *mi otro yo* …
> She felt warm and gentle as the early midnight summer breeze
> I did not die like I thought I would when I felt her.
> Instead, for the first time in my life, I touched my warm body without
>   shame.
>
> Today I got in touch with *mi otro yo* …
> She was loving and nurturing like a mother's breast
> Feeding her child for the very first time.
> I did not die like I thought I would when I felt her.
> Instead, I was able to feel and love my entire self without crying and
>   hurting.
>
> Today I got in touch with *mi otro yo*…
> She felt so fine like an eagle feather
> slowly falling down from the great blue sky
> to the palm of my hand.

I did not die like I thought I would when I felt her.
Instead, for the first time in my life, I felt freedom and life inside of me.

Today I got in touch with *mi otro yo*. ...
She is beautiful and wise like our mother earth.
I did not die like I thought I would when I felt her.
Instead, I felt the beautiful connection between all of us.

Today I felt *mi otro yo* ...
and I did not die when I felt her like I thought I would.
She told me that I would not die when I felt her.
I was she and she was me.
Today I am whole
Today I am alive
Today I am my self
Today I am free
Today I am love
Today I am *mi otro yo* ...

Of the 11 women whom I interviewed, 7 opted to take part in a 9-week focus group, which was explained as a support group for the purpose of better understanding how women had survived and coped. This group was held weekly and video-taped, and the questions that I asked the group to discuss began with questions I had after reading the interview transcripts and conducting some preliminary analysis. Although I already had established a trusting and supportive relationship with each of the participants, it was important to me to help them experience safety and connection in the group. Therefore, the first sessions focused on helping the participants get acquainted and tell their stories. I modelled the kind of response I hoped the group members would take, where they would become empathic listeners who supported one another but did not try to 'rescue' each other when they expressed pain or anger. Also, I had established a clear boundary about my own role in the group: (a) Although I was a therapist, I would not be doing therapy with this group; (b) The purpose of the group was to better understand how the participants made sense or meaning of their experiences; and (c) Where necessary, I would intervene in the discussions to manage crisis and keep the group on focus. Given these clear boundaries, I believe the participants were clear that they were not participating in a therapy group; they provided amazing support for one another; and they became co-investigators as they asked one another how they made sense of their experiences. I also asked the co-investigators to generate their own questions for the focus groups, which they did. Some of the questions they asked the group to consider included: 'How did we survive all these years without killing someone or ourselves?' 'How has the process of healing changed you?'

As part of the focus groups, I asked co-researchers to journal between our meetings and to bring their journals to me, either in written/typed format or on audio-tape (which I provided). I hoped to make the journal-writing process as comfortable as possible by providing format options. I also invited the women to write, draw, or express their experiences in whatever modality suited them best. About halfway through the group sessions, Paula brought her art, created in ink, paints and pastels since childhood, forming a pictorial account of her experiences of abuse, survival and coping. Paula and I, along with several group members, stayed after group to delve more deeply into the meaning of the paintings. One of her most powerful pieces was an intricate pen drawing, coloured with water colours, of a great, fierce dragon lying atop a huge pile of coins and jewels. When asked what the meaning was of the dragon, Paula responded, 'The dragon is my anger ... you don't fuck with the dragon!'

Findings: Co-analysis and Making Meaning of the Data

At the conclusion of the focus groups, I invited any women who wished to do so to join me as co-analysts of the data we had gathered. At that time, I envisioned that we would meet for perhaps two additional sessions to generate preliminary results of the study. I had yet to understand how deeply committed to this process some of the participants were. Four women decided to continue in the study as co-researchers.

I had begun data analysis immediately after the first individual interview and continued to analyse data throughout the interviews and focus groups using a grounded theory approach (Glaser & Strauss, 1967; Strauss & Corbin, 1990) as the core of the formal analysis. This approach engages the investigator first in assigning code or concept names to meaning units found in the data (words, phrases, or sentences that describe a construct in a meaningful way), then grouping these codes to form categories and superordinate categories until a hierarchical model is constructed that illustrates the meanings made by participants of their experiences. Ultimately a core category is identified that subsumes and explains all of the data, and the relationships among all of the categories are explained as a conceptual framework or 'grounded theory'.

I explained the grounded theory process in which I was engaged to the four co-researchers, and I gave them an overview of my coding and categorizing process thus far. In addition, I asked them to analyse the data in whatever way made the most sense to them. After meeting for two sessions, the co-researchers were clear that they wanted to be involved over time with me, and we began a series of regular meetings that were to last for over a year. These meetings lasted two to three hours and were characterized by sharing food, tears, anger, joy, support and love. Following the 'instructions' laid out by Strauss and Corbin (1990), I strove to find a single core category; however, the participant co-researchers would not allow me to 'settle' on an analysis that did not fully reflect their experience.

As we analysed the data, two overarching themes emerged: '*Keeping from being overwhelmed by threatening and dangerous feelings*' and '*Managing helplessness, powerlessness and lack of control*'. In my efforts to come up with a single core category, I kept trying to subsume the second theme within the first; and each time I brought my attempts to the group, they vetoed it. Thus, the two themes stand separate in the final analysis, as they should. The strategies that participants used to keep from being overwhelmed by threatening and dangerous feelings were: (a) reducing the intensity of the feelings, (b) escaping or leaving, (c) overriding, substituting, or distracting from the feelings, (d) releasing the feelings, (e) finding comfort, (f) not knowing, and (g) dividing. They managed helplessness, powerlessness and lack of control by (a) using resistance strategies, (b) reframing the abuse to create an illusion of control or power, (c) attempting to master the trauma, (d) attempting to control other areas of life besides the abuse, (e) seeking confirmation or evidence from others, and (f) rejecting power.

These strategies had great *practical relevance* to the research participants. Meghan, for example, told a story one week about how understanding these strategies was having a positive impact on her relationship with her husband. The couple had been having conflicts as Meghan had been in therapy dealing with her abuse. Her husband had felt he could never do anything right in relation to the feelings Meghan was having; she felt that he was letting her down. As we analysed the data and began to understand some of the strategies she was using, it became clear that, when she was distressed, her husband wanted to comfort her; but when he did so, she was unable to avoid the intensity of her feelings and would push him away. When he backed off, she experienced him as not providing the comfort she so desperately needed. As they began to understand the dilemma in which they found themselves, they were able to communicate more clearly about what Meghan needed in the moment and stop a downward cycle in their relationship. Meghan also spoke of the impact that participating in this research had on her:

> Your interest and invitation to be in that role (of co-researcher) communi-
> cated to me that you liked me and respected me ... As I thought about what
> was important about it all, I think the thing that was so powerful in terms
> of empowerment was participating in the grounded theory-generating
> process. That was the key to the empowerment. It wasn't really the [nine]
> weeks. It was really the five of us ... I am an individual voice in all other
> settings. The group provided some support, but was still a collection of
> individual voices ... [But this process] was a shared voice, a shared para-
> digm. It provided a system into which my experience fit that I had a part in
> creating. That creates the experience of being understood.

A final addition to the analysis consisted of the use of narrative and metaphors to understand participants' stories. We looked for the metaphors that
participants used to describe their abuse (dirt or mud), coping (flying
away), and healing (cleansing fire); the meanings that were imbedded in
participants' stories; and the societal 'story' of child sexual abuse. I examined popular magazines from the times that the youngest and eldest participants had been abused, finding that Paula's abuse was a replay of a
cartoon feature in the *Playboy* magazine that her father and brother read,
and that stories in *Saturday Evening Post* and *Ladies' Home Journal* set a
norm for tacit acceptability of abuse of women and children as well as
sexualizing little girls in 1925 when Barbara was first abused.

Sexual abuse survivors and their therapists have, over time, found my
research to be very relevant to their healing; many times therapists have
shared the published articles (Morrow, 2006; Morrow & Smith, 1995) with
their clients, who in turn have gone to university libraries to obtain the full
dissertation (Morrow, 1992). Because the themes are explained in depth in
these publications, I will not go into detail here, but I would like to illustrate
some of the themes with quotes from my own participants, particularly in
the form of their poetry and metaphors.

Danu describes her metaphoric vision of her birth into a life in her
abusive family:

> A small girl struggles in the waters of a raging river.
> Foul water, green and brown and putrid, pours over her head,
> stings her eyes, churns around her neck,
> fills her mouth and nostrils.
> Choking, she pushes upward, gasping for breath –
> The water quickly pulls her under again ...
>
> She lived in that river for many years,
> absorbing the filth through her skin,
> swallowing the pain,
> seeking nurture in the percolating waters.

Ananda painted mud in many of her dream journals to symbolize her abuse. In one, she is pictured in a green dress stained with mud. She says, 'And here I see myself, the mud again … it's a symbol of my abuse. I have muddy footprints.'

Referring to being overwhelmed by threatening and dangerous feelings, Meghan wrote:

> Being overwhelmed would be like being in a car crash, ripping, screaming metal, screaming people, bodies pierced by shards of hot metal, blood, anguish, ongoing, ongoing anguish … pain that goes on and on and on and never stops.

One way to escape was to hide, as Danu illustrated:

> I didn't want to be
> "miss smarty pants".
> I tried to be quieter
> more secret and private.
> I knew it would be safer
> if no one noticed me.

Some participants took control of their lives and tried to gain mastery by helping, saving and rescuing others. As Barbara illustrated, 'I'm a savior. I ride a white horse, rescue. I rescue.'

Participants' metaphors of healing were stunning revelations of the power of the therapy process and of their own resilience:

> Then one day, life began to change.
> The child felt a bank of sand beneath her feet.
> Tentatively, she tried to stand.
> The sands shifted, tumbling her, and she was frightened –
> little had changed in her years in the river.
> But she kept trying, again and again,
> until finally she found a balance.
>
> She stood, strong and powerful,
> a wise woman.
>
> I am the wise woman.
>
> I step from the water, singing,
> gathering the small girls and young woman:

"How could anyone ever tell you
   you were anything less than beautiful?
How could anyone ever tell you
   you were less than whole?
How could anyone fail to notice
   that your loving is a miracle?
How deeply you're connected to my soul?"
            Danu, with quoted song by Libby Roderick (1990)

Danu also wrote of her decision to include her husband in her healing process:

... it was time
to let David visit us on this journey.
I built a fire, and cooked some food,
and sat with him, and drank some wine,
and told our story.

In the telling, some of the fog lifted
and I became more alert.

I thanked him for listening,
and felt comfort and delight
as our bodies responded in love,

"You may come and be with me,
from time to time," I said.

"You may ask to join me,
or I may ask you.
But it is my journey.
I must find my way alone,
guided by my wisdom,
fueled by my strength."

Sexual abuse survivors and their therapists have, over time, found this research to be very relevant to their healing. This reflective process took me to the depths of my own experience, and I was able to gain awareness of my very human tendency to view my participants' experiences through my own lens. I began to understand more clearly the ways in which my unexamined assumptions and biases could negatively affect my research, and I further reflected on the implications of this experience for me as a therapist. Conducting this study removed most of my lingering remnants of the tendency that we therapists have to think of distress as disease, as pathology.

Reflections: Self-reflection as Researcher and Therapist

Clearly, the women who participated in this research had healed and changed during their therapy experiences as well as by engaging in this research. I found myself changed as well. I had asked my participants to self-reflect, deeply. I, too, was committed to a process of self-reflection as I conducted this research. This reflective process took me to the depths of my own experience, and I was able to gain awareness of my very human tendency to view my participants' experiences through my own lens. I began to understand more clearly the ways in which my unexamined assumptions and biases could negatively affect my research, and I further reflected on the implications of this experience for me as a therapist. Conducting this study removed most of my lingering remnants of the tendency that we therapists have to think of distress as disease, as pathology. Although I had articulated a strengths-based approach to my endeavour as a feminist researcher, I became aware that as a therapist I had not always been clear in this regard. I learned to listen in a different way. Where as a counselor I had listened partly to make diagnostic meaning of my clients' distress, as a researcher I learned to listen for the real meanings that my participants made of their abuse, survival, coping and healing. This has made me a different kind of therapist and a different kind of person.

As I revisit this research experience, I recall the many evenings spent with women who started as research participants, became co-researchers, and are now friends. I am still in contact with three of them and hear from them about others. Lauren, with whom I now have the most regular contact, was present with several other co-researchers at my dissertation defence. After our group had stopped meeting, I laboured to create the final dissertation myself. In the process, I became aware how pervasive the metaphor of 'voice' had been throughout the research, from my earliest conceptualizations through the words of the participants. However, none of the participants knew of the importance of this metaphor to me, and none knew, until the day of the defence, that I had titled my dissertation *Voices: Constructions of Survival and Coping by Women Survivors of Child Sexual Abuse*. But after the defence, at our celebration back at my home, Lauren gave me a gift, a framed poem that she had written:

> A Voice, MY Voice
>
> A Voice
> Rings loud and strong
> Not my voice
> That of a man; or should I say boy

Mean, rough
Don't move, Don't tell, Don't cry
He yelled!

Another voice
Quiet, frightened
Smothered with a hand
Still screaming, silent
Help me!
Why can't anyone hear me?
My voice?
Not a voice at all.

He hurt me more
Each time I cried
The pain lay deep inside
A knife, a strange fire.

I learned not to cry
Not to speak
Shh … don't bother
Who the hell knows
Where's my mother or father?

Silence became easier
Years pushed memories
Deeper and deeper inside
Left in a room
Echoing darkness
Feelings too, are stored, abandoned
Seemingly left a mystery …

She came along
No coincidence, I'm sure
Some sort of incest survivors group
Me involved?
Why should I care?

With her pen in hand
Eyes kind and compassionate
I heard a voice
Soft and reassuring
Determined, motivated
A Voice, Her Voice.

After a while
My silence was lifted
Anger, sadness and pain surfaced
Not his voice; MY VOICE
Louder and stronger.

No more, will I be silent
My tears
Now flow freely
A gift from a woman
Inspiring, moving.

A Voice, My Voice
No longer a mystery.

The thought of the noise
What power, how precious
Both yelling and crying
Sadness – reality
More joy – freedom
As you share with others
Your gift, Your voice.

Softly I Thank You
With deep love
In MY Voice.

References

Abrahams, H. (2007). Ethics in counselling research fieldwork, *Counselling and Psychotherapy Research*, 7, 240–244.

Angus, L.E. and McLeod, J. (Eds) (2003). *The Handbook of Narrative and Psychotherapy: Practice, Theory and Research*. London: Sage.

Aron, L. (1996). *A Meeting of Minds: Mutuality in Psychoanalysis*. Hillsdale, NJ: The Analytic Press.

Arvay, M. (2003). Doing reflexivity: A collaborative, narrative approach. In L. Finlay and B. Gough (Eds), *Reflexivity: A practical guide for researchers in health and social sciences*. Oxford: Blackwell Publishing.

Ashworth, P.D. (1993). Participant agreement in the justification of qualitative findings, *Journal of Phenomenological Psychology*, 24, 3–16.

Ashworth, P.D. (2003). An approach to phenomenological psychology: The contingencies of the lifeworld, *Journal of Phenomenological Psychology*, 34, 145–156.

Atkinson, J.M. and Heritage, J. (Eds) (1984). *Structures of Social Action: Studies in conversation analysis*. New York: Cambridge University Press.

Atwood, G.E. and Stolorow, R.D. (1994). *Structures of Subjectivity: Explorations in psychoanalytic phenomenology*. Hillsdale, NJ: The Analytic Press.

Averill, J.R. (1983). Studies on anger and aggression: Implications for theories of emotion, *American Psychologist*, 38, 1145–1160.

Baker, B.L. and Benton, C.L. (1994). The ethics of feminist self-disclosure. In K. Carter and M. Presnell (Eds), *Interpretive Approaches to Interpersonal Communication*. New York: SUNY.

Relational-centred Research for Psychotherapists: Exploring Meanings and Experience
Edited by Linda Finlay and Ken Evans
Copyright © 2009 John Wiley & Sons, Ltd.

Ballinger, C. and Wiles, R. (2006). Ethical and governance issues in qualitative research. In L. Finlay and C. Ballinger (Eds), *Qualitative Research for Allied Health Professionals: Challenging choices.* Chichester, West Sussex: John Wiley & Sons, Ltd.

Banister, P., Burman, E., Parker, I., Taylor, M. and Tindall, C. (1994). *Qualitative Methods in Psychology: A research guide.* Buckingham: Open University Press.

Barker, M. and Langdridge, D. (Eds) (2005). Special issue: contemporary perspectives on S/M, *Lesbian and Gay Psychology Review, 6*(3).

Barry, C.A. (2003). Holding up the mirror to widen the view: Multiple subjectivities in the reflexive team. In L. Finlay and B. Gough (Eds), *Reflexivity: A practical guide for researchers in health and social sciences.* Oxford: Blackwell Publishing.

Beckmann, A. (2001). Deconstructing myths: The social construction of 'sado-masochism' versus 'subjugated knowledges' of practitioners of consensual 'SM', *Journal of Criminal Justice and Popular Culture, 8,* 66–95.

Benjamin, J. (1992). *The Shadow of The Other: Intersubjectivity and gender in psychoanalysis.* New York, NY: Routledge.

Berger, P. and Luckmann, T. (1966). *The Social Construction of Reality* (Reprinted 1991). London: Penguin Books.

Bochner, A.P. (1984). The functions of communication in interpersonal bonding. In C. Arnold and J. Bowers (Eds), *The Handbook of Rhetoric and Communication* (pp. 544–621). Thousand Oaks, CA: Sage.

Bochner, A.P. (2000). Criteria against ourselves, *Qualitative Inquiry, 6,* 266–272.

Bochner, A.P. (2001). Narrative's virtues, *Qualitative Inquiry, 7,* 131–156.

Bohart, A.C. (2000). The client is the most important common factor: Clients' self-healing capacities and psychotherapy, *Journal of Psychotherapy Integration, 10,* 127–149.

Bolton, P., Bass, J., Betancourt, T. et al. (2007). Interventions for depression symptoms among adolescent survivors of war and displacement in northern Uganda: A randomized controlled trial, *Journal of the American Medical Association, 298,* 519–527.

Bourdieu, P., Accardo, A., Balazs, G., Beaud, S. et al. (1993). *The Weight of The World: Social suffering in contemporary society* [trans. By P.P. Ferguson]. Stanford, CA: Stanford University Press.

Bovasso, G.B., Williams, W.E. and Haroutune, K.A. (1999). The long-term outcomes of mental health treatment in a population-based study, *Journal of Consulting and Clinical Psychology, 67,* 529–538.

Bowlby, J. (1988). *A Secure Base.* London: Routledge.

Braud, W.G. and Anderson, R. (Eds) (1998). *Transpersonal Research Methods for the Social Sciences: Honoring human experience.* Thousand Oaks, CA: Sage.

Braun, V. and Clarke, V. (2006). Using thematic analysis in psychology, *Qualitative Research in Psychology, 3,* 77–101.

Braverman, B., Helfrich, C., Kielhofner, G. and Albrecht, G. (2003). The narratives of 12 men with AIDS: Exploring return to work, *Journal of Occupational Rehabilitation, 3,* 143–157.

Broom, B. (1997). *Somatic Illness and the Patient's Other Story*. London: FAB.

Brown, J. (2006). Reflexivity in the research process: Psychoanalytic observations, *International Journal of Social Research Methodology*, 9, 181–197.

Bruner, J. (1990). *Acts of Meaning*. Cambridge, Mass: Harvard University Press.

Bryan, L., Dersch, C., Shumway, S. and Arredondo, R. (2004). Therapy outcomes: Client perception and similarity with therapist view, *American Journal of Family Therapy*, 32, 11–26.

Buber, M. (1923/2004). *I and Thou* [Trans. W. Kaufman]. London: Continuum.

Buber, M. (1958). *I and Thou* [Trans. R.G. Smith]. New York: Charles Scribner's Sons. (Original work published 1937)

Buber, M. (1967). *The Knowledge of Man*. New York: Harper and Row.

Bunge, M. (1993). Realism and anti-realism in social science, *Theory and Decision*, 35, 207–235.

Cartwright, D. (2004). The psychoanalytic research interview: Preliminary suggestions, *The Journal of the American Psychoanalytic Association*, 52, 209–242.

Casement, P. (1985). *On Learning from the Patient*. London: Routledge.

Charmaz, K. (2000). Experiencing chronic illness. In G.L. Albrecht, R. Fitzpatrick and S.C. Scrimshaw (Eds), *The Handbook of Social Studies in Health and Medicine*. London: Sage.

Christians, C. (2005). Ethics and politics in qualitative research. In N. Denzin and Y. Lincoln (Eds), *Handbook of Qualitative Research* (pp. 139–165). Thousand Oaks, CA: Sage.

Churchill, S.D. (2000). Phenomenological psychology. In A.D. Kazdin (Ed.), *Encyclopedia of Psychology*. Oxford: Oxford University Press.

Clandinin, D.J., and Connelly, F.M. (1994). Personal experience methods. In N.K. Denzin and Y.S. Lincoln (Eds), *Handbook of Qualitative Research*. Thousand Oaks, CA: Sage.

Conway, S., Audin, K, Barkham, M., Mellor-Clark, J. and Russell, S. (2003). Practice-based evidence for a brief time-intensive multi-modal therapy guided by group-analytic principles and method, *Group Analysis*, 36, 413–435.

Cooper, M. (2004). Viagra for the brain: Psychotherapy research and the challenge to existential therapeutic practice, *Existential Analysis*, 15, 2–14.

Cooper, M. (2005). Therapists' experiences of relational depth: A qualitative study. *Counselling and Psychotherapy Research*, 5(2), pp. 87–95.

Cresswell, J.W. (1998). *Qualitative Inquiry and Research Design: Choosing among five traditions*. Thousand Oaks, CA: Sage.

Cutcliffe, J.R. and Ramcharan, P. (2002). Leveling the playing field? Exploring the merits of the ethics-as-process approach for judging qualitative research proposals, *Qualitative Health Research*, 12, 1000–1010.

Dahlberg, K., Dahlberg, H. and Nystrom, M. (2008). *Reflective Lifeworld Research* (2nd edition). Lund, Sweden: Studentliteratur.

Dallos, R. (2004). Attachment narrative therapy: Integrating ideas from narrative and attachment theory in systemic family therapy with eating disorders, *Journal of Family Therapy*, 26, 40–66.

Dallos, R. and Vetere, A. (2005). *Researching Psychotherapy and Counselling.* Maidenhead, Berkshire: Open University Press.

Davies, K. (2001). Silent and censured travellers? Patients' narratives and patients' voices: Perspectives on the history of mental illness since 1948, *Social History of Medicine, 14*, 267–292.

Denzin, N.K. and Lincoln, Y.S. (1994). Introduction: Entering the field of qualitative research. In N.K. Denzin and Y.S. Lincoln (Eds), *Handbook of Qualitative Research.* Thousand Oaks, CA: Sage.

Denzin, N.K. and Lincoln, Y.S. (Eds) (2005). *Handbook of Qualitative Research* (3rd edition). Thousand Oaks, CA: Sage.

Department of Health (2001). *Research Governance Framework for England.* London: Department of Health.

De Walt, K.M. and De Walt, B.R. (2002). *Participant Observation: A guide for fieldworkers.* New York: Altamira.

DeYoung, P. (2003). *Relational Psychotherapy: A primer.* New York: Brunner-Routledge.

Donmoyer, R. (2001). Paradigm talk reconsidered. In V. Richardson (Ed.), *Handbook of Research in Teaching* (pp. 174–197). Washington DC: American Educational Research Association.

Du Plock, S. (2004). What do we mean when we use the word 'research'? *Existential Analysis, 15*, 29–37.

Eatough, V. and Smith, J. (2006a). "I was like a wild wild person": Understanding feelings of anger using interpretative phenomenological analysis, *British Journal of Psychology, 97*, 483–498.

Eatough, V. and Smith, J.A. (2006b). I feel like a scrambled egg in my head: An idiographic case study of meaning making and anger using interpretative phenomenological analysis, *Psychology and Psychotherapy, 79*, 115–135.

Eatough, V., Smith, J.A. and Shaw, R. (2008). Women, anger and aggression: an interpretative phenomenological analysis, *Journal of Interpersonal Violence, 23*, 1767–1799.

Edley, N. (2002). The loner, the walk and the best within: Narrative fragments in the construction of masculinity. In W. Patterson (Ed.), *Strategic Narrative: New perspectives on the power of personal and cultural stories.* Lanham, MD: Lexington Books.

Ekman, P. (1985). *Telling Lies.* New York: Norton.

Elliot, S., Loewenthal, D. and Greenwood, D. (2007). Narrative research into erotic counter-transference in a female therapist-male patient encounter, *Psychoanalytic Psychotherapy, 21*, 233–249.

Elliott, R. (2001). Hermeneutic single case efficacy design (HSCED): An overview. In K.J. Schneider, J.F.T. Bugental and J.F. Fraser (Eds), *Handbook of Humanistic Psychology* (pp. 315–324). Thousand Oaks, CA: Sage.

Ellis, C. (1991). Emotional sociology, *Studies in Symbolic Interaction, 12*, 123–145.

Ellis, C. (1999). Heartfelt autoethnography, *Qualitative Health Research, 9*, 669–683.

Ellis, C. (2007). Telling secrets, revealing lives: Relational ethics in research with intimate others, *Qualitative Inquiry, 13*, 3–29.

Ellis, C. and Bochner, A. (2000). Autoethnography, personal narrative, reflexivity: Researcher as subject. In N. Denzin and Y. Lincoln (Eds), *Handbook of Qualitative Research* (2nd edition, pp. 733–768). Newbury Park, CA: Sage.

Ellis, C., Kiesinger, C.E. and Tillmann-Healy, L.M. (1997). Interactive interviewing: Talking about emotional experience. In R. Hertz (Ed.), *Reflexivity and Voice*. Thousand Oaks, CA: Sage.

Etherington, K. (2004). *Becoming a Reflexive Researcher: Using our selves in research.* London: Jessica Kingsley.

Evans, K. (2007). Relational-centred research: A work in progress, *European Journal for Qualitative Research in Psychotherapy*, 2, 42–44.

Evans, K.R. (2009). *Contributing to the Development of the Profession of Psychotherapy in the United Kingdom and Europe 1987 to 2008*, Unpublished Doctorate of Psychotherapy by Public Works. London: Metanoia Institute, University of Middlesex.

Evans, K. and Finlay, L. (2009). *To be, or not to be … registered:* A relational-phenomenological exploration of what State Registration means to psychotherapists, *European Journal for Qualitative Research in Psychotherapy*, 4, 4–12.

Evans K.R. and Gilbert, M. (2005). *An Introduction to Integrative Psychotherapy.* Basingstoke, Hampshire: Palgrave Macmillan.

Everall, R.D. and Paulson, B.L. (2002). The therapeutic alliance: Adolescent perspectives, *Counselling Psychotherapy Research*, 35, 131–143.

Fairbairn, W.R.D. (1952). *An Object-relations Theory of the Personality.* New York: Basic Books.

Finlay, L. (1998). *The life world of the occupational therapist: Meaning and motive in an uncertain world.* Unpublished PhD thesis. Milton Keynes: The Open University.

Finlay, L. (2002a). "Outing" the researcher: The provenance, principles and practice of reflexivity, *Qualitative Health Research*, 12, 531–545.

Finlay, L. (2002b). Negotiating the swamp: The opportunity and challenge of reflexivity in research practice, *Qualitative Research*, 2, 209–230.

Finlay, L. (2003a). The reflexive journey: Mapping multiple routes. In L. Finlay and B. Gough (Eds), *Reflexivity: A practical guide for researchers in health and social sciences.* Oxford: Blackwell Science.

Finlay, L. (2003b). The intertwining of body, self and world: A phenomenological study of living with recently diagnosed multiple sclerosis, *Journal of Phenomenological Psychology*, 34, 157–178.

Finlay, L. (2003c). Through the looking glass: Intersubjectivity and hermeneutic reflection. In L. Finlay and B. Gough (Eds), *Reflexivity: A practical guide for researchers in health and social sciences.* Oxford: Blackwell Publishing.

Finlay, L. (2004). From 'gibbering idiot' to 'iceman' – Kenny's story: A critical analysis of an occupational narrative, *British Journal of Occupational Therapy*, 67, 474–480.

Finlay, L. (2005). Reflexive embodied reflexivity: A phenomenology of participant-researcher intersubjectivity, *The Humanistic Psychologist*, 33, 271–292.

Finlay, L. (2006a). 'Going exploring': The nature of qualitative research. In L. Finlay and C. Ballinger (Eds), *Qualitative Research for Allied Health Professionals: Challenging choices*. Chichester, West Sussex: John Wiley & Sons, Ltd.

Finlay, L. (2006b). Mapping methodology. In L. Finlay and C. Ballinger (Eds), *Qualitative Research for Allied Health Professionals: Challenging choices*. Chichester, West Sussex: John Wiley & Sons, Ltd.

Finlay, L. (2006c). The embodied experience of multiple sclerosis: An existential-phenomenological analysis. In L. Finlay and C. Ballinger (Eds), *Qualitative Research for Allied Health Professionals: Challenging choices*. Chichester, West Sussex: John Wiley & Sons, Ltd.

Finlay, L. (2006d). Dancing between embodied empathy and phenomenological reflection. *The Indo-Pacific Journal of Phenomenology*, 6, 1–11.

Finlay, L. (2006e). The body's disclosure in phenomenological research, *Qualitative Research in Psychology*, 3, 19–30.

Finlay, L. (2006f). 'Rigour', 'Ethical integrity' or 'Artistry': Reflexively reviewing criteria for evaluating qualitative research, *British Journal of Occupational Therapy*, 69, 319–326.

Finlay, L. (2008). A dance between the reduction and reflexivity: Explicating the "phenomenological psychological attitude", *Journal of Phenomenological Psychology*, 39, 1–32.

Finlay, L. (2009 Forthcoming). Ambiguous encounters: A relational approach to phenomenological research, *Indo-Pacific Journal of Phenomenology*.

Finlay, L. and Ballinger, C. (Eds) (2006). *Qualitative research for Allied Health Professionals: Challenging choices*. Chichester, West Sussex: John Wiley & Sons, Ltd.

Finlay, L. and Gough, B. (Eds) (2003). *Reflexivity: A practical guide for researchers in health and social sciences*. Oxford: Blackwell Publishing.

Finlay, L. and Molano-Fisher, P. (2008). 'Transforming' self and world: a phenomenological study of a changing lifeworld following a cochlear implant. *Medicine, Health Care and Philosophy*, 11, 255–267. (Online version available from 2007.)

Finlay, L. and Molano-Fisher, P. (2009). Reflexively probing ethical challenges, *QMP Newsletter*, 7, 30–34.

Fischer, C.T. (Ed.) (2006). *Qualitative Research Methods for Psychologists: Introduction through empirical studies*. Amsterdam: Elsevier.

Fitzpatrick, N. and Finlay, L. (2008). 'Frustrating disability': The lived experience of coping with the rehabilitation phase following flexor tendon surgery, *International Journal of Qualitative Studies on Health and Well-being*, 3, 143–154.

Fonagy, P., Gergely, G., Jurist, E.L. and Target, M. (2002). *Affect Regulation, Mentalization, and the Development of the Self*. New York: OTHER Press.

Fonow, M. and Cook, J.A. (Eds) (1991). *Beyond Methodology: Feminist scholarship as lived research*. Bloomington, Indiana: Indiana University Press.

Foskett, J. (2001). What of the client's-eye view? A response to the millennium review, *British Journal of Guidance and Counselling*, 29, 345–350.

Foucault, M. (1988). *Politics, Philosophy, and Culture: Interviews and other writings, 1977–1984* [M. Morris and P. Patton (Eds)]. New York: Routledge.

Frank, A.W. (1998). Just listening: Narrative and deep illness, *Families, Systems and Health, 16,* 197–212.

Frank, A. (2000). *Venus on Wheels: Two decades of dialogue on disability, biography, and being female in America.* California: University of California Press.

French, S. (1993). "Can you see the rainbow?" The roots of denial. In J. Swain, V. Finkelstein, S. French and M. Oliver (Eds), *Disabling Barriers – Enabling Environments.* London: Sage.

Friedman, M. (1985). Healing through meeting and the problematic of mutuality. *Journal of Humanistic Psychology, 25,* 7–40.

Fuchs, T. (2001). The tacit dimension. *Philosophy, Psychiatry, and Psychology, 8,* 323–326.

Fuhr, R. (1992). Beyond contact processes: Ethical and existential dimensions in Gestalt therapy. *The British Gestalt Journal, 2,* pp. 53–60.

Gadamer, H.-G. (1975/1996). *Truth and Method.* London: Sheed and Ward. [Second revised edition originally published in German 1965.]

Garza, G. (2007). Varieties of phenomenological research at the University of Dallas: An emerging typology, *Qualitative Research in Psychology, 4,* 313–342.

Gendlin, E.T. (1996). *Focusing-oriented Psychotherapy: A manual of experiential method.* London: Guilford Press.

Gendlin, E.T. (1997). *Experiencing and the Creation of Meaning.* Evanston, IL: Northwestern University Press.

Gendlin, E.T. (1978). Befindlichkeit: Heidegger and the philosophy of psychology. *Review of Existential Psychology and Psychiatry, 16,* 43–71.

Gerson, S. (2004). The Relational Unconscious: A Core Element of Intersubjectivity, Thirdness and Clinical Process, *Psychoanalytic Quarterly,* LXXIII.

Gershefski, J.J., Arnkoff, D.B., Glass, C.R. and Elkin, I. (1996). Clients' perspectives of treatment for depression: Helpful aspects, *Psychotherapy Research, 6,* 233–248.

Gilbert, A. (2006). A phenomenological exploration of the impact of a traumatic incident (death of a child) on Social Services staff, *European Journal for Qualitative Research in Psychotherapy, 1,* 1–9.

Gilbert, M.C. and Evans, K. (2000). *Psychotherapy Supervision: An integrative relational approach.* Buckingham: Open University Press.

Giorgi, A. (Ed.) (1985). *Phenomenological and Psychological Research.* Pittsburgh, PA: Duquesne University Press.

Glaser, B.G. and Strauss, A.L. (1967). *The Discovery of Grounded Theory Research: Strategies for qualitative research.* Chicago: Aldine.

Goffman, E. (1959). *The Presentation of Self in Everyday Life.* New York: Penguin.

Goldfried. M.R. (1995). *From Cognitive-behavior Therapy to Psychotherapy Integration.* New York: Springer Publishing Company.

Gough, B. (1999). 'Subject positions within discourse anlaysis: some reflexive dilemmas'. Paper given at *International Human Science Research Conference,* Sheffield Hallam University, July.

Gough, B. (2003). Shifting research positions during a group interview study: A reflexive analysis and re-view. In L. Finlay and B. Gough (Eds), *Reflexivity: A practical guide for researchers in health and social sciences*. Oxford: Blackwell Science.

Grafanaki, S. (1996). How research can change the researcher: The need for sensitivity, flexibility and ethical boundaries in conducting qualitative research in counselling/psychotherapy, *British Journal of Guidance and Counselling, 24*, 329–338.

Granek, L. (2006). What's love got to do with it? The relational nature of depressive experiences, *Journal of Humanistic Psychology, 46*, 191–208.

Green, J. and Thorogood, N. (2004). *Qualitative Methods for Health Research*. London: Sage.

Greenall, P.V. and Marselle, M. (2007). Traumatic research: Interviewing survivors of 9/11, *The Psychologist, 20*, 544–546.

Greenberg, J.R. and Mitchell, S.A. (1983). *Object Relations in Psychoanalytic Theory*. MA: Harvard University Press.

Guba, G.G. and Lincoln, Y.S. (1989). *Fourth Generation Evaluation*. Thousand Oaks, CA: Sage.

Hadjistavropoulos, T. and Smythe, W.E. (2001). Elements of risk in qualitative research, *Ethics & Behavior*, Vol. 11, pp. 163–174.

Halling, S. (2008). *Intimacy, Transcendence, and Psychology: Closeness and openness in everyday life*. New York: Palgrave Macmillan.

Halling, S. and Leifer, M. (1991). The theory and practice of dialogal research. *Journal of Phenomenological Psychology, 22*, 1–15.

Halling, S., Leifer, M. and Rowe, J.O. (2006). Emergence of the dialogal approach: Forgiving another. In C.T. Fischer (Ed.), *Qualitative Research Methods for Psychologists: Introduction through empirical studies*. Amsterdam: Elsevier.

Hammersley, M. and Atkinson, P. (1983). *Ethnography: Principles in practice*. London: Routledge.

Haumann, H.J. (2005). *An intersubjective perspective on the role of personal therapy in being a psychotherapist*. Unpublished PhD thesis. Rhodes, SA: Rhodes University.

Heidegger, M. (1927/1962). *Being and Time*. Oxford: Blackwell. [1962 text trans. J. Macquarrie and E. Robinson.]

Heron, J. (1996). *Co-operative Inquiry: Research into the human condition*. London: Sage.

Hoffmann, E.A. (2007). Open-ended interviews, power, and emotional labor: The complex dynamics of interviewer/interviewee power, *Journal of Contemporary Ethnography, 36*, 318–346.

Holloway, I. and Todres, L. (2003). The Status of Method: Flexibility, consistency and coherence, *Qualitative Research, 3*, 345–357.

Hollway, W. (2007). Methods and knowledge in social psychology. In W. Hollway, H. Lucey and A. Phoenix (Eds), *Social Psychology Matters*. Milton Keynes, Buckinghamshire: Open University Press.

Hollway, W. and Jefferson, T. (2000). *Doing Qualitative Research Differently: Free association, narrative and the interview method*. London: Sage.

Hubble, M.A., Duncan, B.L., Miller, S.D. (Eds) (1999). *The Heart and Soul of Change: What works in therapy.* Washington DC: American Psychological Association.

Hunt, J.C. (1989). Psychoanalytic aspects of fieldwork. *Qualitative Research Methods* (Vol. *18*). Newbury Park: Sage.

Husserl, E. (1965). *Phenomenology and the crisis of philosophy*, cited in Thompson, D.L. (1994), Rorty and Husserl on Realism, Idealism and Intersubjective Solidarity. Accessed February 2006 from: <www.ucs.mun.ca/~davidt/Rorty.html #III.%20INTERSUBJECTIVE%20SOLIDARITY%20AND%20UNIVERSAL>

Hycner, R.H. (1991). *Between Person and Person: Toward a dialogical psychotherapy.* Highland, NY: Gestalt Journal Press.

Hycner, R. and Jacobs, L. (1995). *The Healing Relationship.* New York: The Gestalt Journal Press.

Jacobsen, C.H. (2007). A qualitative single case study of parallel processes, *Counselling and Psychotherapy Research, 7*, 26–33.

Janesick, V.J. (1994). The dance of qualitative research design: Metaphors, methodology and meaning. In N.K. Denzin and Y.S. Lincoln (Eds), *Handbook of Qualitative Research* (pp. 209–219). Thousand Oaks, CA: Sage.

Johnson, K. and Scott, D. (1997). Confessional tales: An exploration of the self and other in two ethnographies, *The Australian Journal of Social Research, 4*, 2.

Josselson, R. (1996). On writing other people's lives: Self-analytic reflections of a narrative researcher. In R. Josselson (Ed). *The Narrative Study of Lives, Vol. 1.* London: Sage.

Josselson, R. (2003). The space between in group psychotherapy: Application of a multidimensional model of relationship, *Group, 27*, 203–219.

Junker, B.H. (1960). *Field Work. An introduction to the social sciences (with an introduction by Everett C. Hughes).* Chicago: University of Chicago Press.

Kellogg, S.H. (2007) Transformational chairwork: Five ways of using therapeutic dialogues, *NYSPA Notebook, 19*, 8–9.

Kelly, G.A. (1955). *The Psychology of Personal Constructs* (Vol. *I*). New York: Norton.

King, N., Finlay, L., Ashworth, P., Smith, J.A., Langdridge, D. and Butt, T. (2008). "Can't really trust that, so what can I trust?": A polyvocal, qualitative analysis of the psychology of mistrust, *Qualitative Research in Psychology, 5*, 80–102.

Kirmayer, J.L. and Robbins, J.M. (Eds) (1991). *Current Concepts of Somatization: Research and clinical perspectives.* Washington, DC: American Psychiatric Press. (Reprinted 2005)

Kirmayer, L.J. and Robbins, J.M. (Eds) (2005). *Current Concepts of Somatization.* Washington, DC: American Psychiatric Press.

Kiser, S. (2004). An existential case study of madness: Encounters with divine affliction, *Journal of Humanistic Psychology, 44*, 431–454.

Klein, M. (1952/1993). The origins of transference. In *Envy and Gratitude: Collected works* (Vol. III). London: Karnac Books.

Kohut, H. (1984). *How Does Analysis Cure?* Chicago: University of Chicago Press.

Krüger, A. (2007). An introduction to the ethics of gestalt research with informants, *European Journal for Qualitative Research in Psychotherapy, 2*, 17–22.

Kvale, S. (1992). Postmodern psychology: A contradiction in terms? In S. Kvale (Ed.) *Psychology and Postmodernism*. London: Sage.

Kvale, S. (1996). *Interviews: An introduction to qualitative research interviewing*. London: Sage.

Lambert, M.J. (1992). Implications of outcome research for psychotherapy. In J.C. Norcross and M.R. Goldstein (Eds), *Handbook of Psychotherapy Integration*. New York: Basic Books.

Landy, R.J. and Hadari, A. (2007). Stories of destruction and renewal: A drama therapy experience, *Journal of Humanistic Psychology, 47*, 413–421.

Langdridge, D. (2005a). Actively dividing selves: S/M and the thrill of disintegration. *Lesbian and Gay Psychology Review, 6*, 198–208.

Langdridge, D. (2005b). The child's relations with others: Merleau-Ponty, embodiment and psychotherapy, *Existential Analysis, 16*, 87–99.

Langdridge, D. (2007). *Phenomenological Psychology: Theory, research and method*. Harlow: Pearson Education.

Langdridge, D. (2008). Phenomenology and critical social psychology: Directions and debates in theory and research, *Social and Personality Psychology Compass, 2*, 1126–1142.

Langdridge, D. and Barker, M. (Eds) (2007). *Safe, Sane and Consensual: Contemporary perspectives on sadomasochism*. Basingstoke: Palgrave Macmillan.

Langdridge, D. and Butt, T. (2004). A hermeneutic phenomenological investigation of the construction of sadomasochistic identities, *Sexualities, 7*, 31–53.

Langdridge, D. and Butt, T. (2005). The erotic construction of power exchange, *Journal of Constructivist Psychology, 18*, 65–73.

Latner, J. (2000). The theory of Gestalt therapy. In E. Nevis (Ed.), *Gestalt Therapy: Perspectives and applications*. Cambridge, MA: Gestalt Press.

Lebow, J. (2006). *Research for the Psychotherapist*. London: Routledge.

Lefebvre, P. (1988). The psychoanalysis of a patient with ulcerative colitis, *International Journal of Psycho-Analysis, 69*, 43–53.

Lepper, G. and Riding, N. (2006). *Researching the Psychotherapy Process*. London: Palgrave.

Levin, D.M. (1985). *The Body's Recollection of Being: Phenomenological psychology and the deconstruction of nihilism*. London: Routledge & Kegan Paul.

Levinas, E. (1969). *Totality and Infinity* (Trans. A. Lingis). Pittsburgh, PA: Duquesne University Press.

Lewis, I. (2008). With feeling: Writing emotion into counselling and psychotherapy research, *Counselling and Psychotherapy Research, 8*, 63–70.

Lincoln, Y.S. and Guba, E.G. (1985). *Naturalistic Inquiry*. Beverley Hills, CA: Sage.

Lincoln, Y.S. and Guba, E.G. (1986). But is it rigorous? Trustworthiness and authenticity in naturalistic evaluation. In D.D. Williams (Ed.), *Naturalistic Evaluation* (pp. 73–84). San Francisco: Jossey-Bass.

Lipson, J. (1997). The politics of publishing protecting participants' confidentiality. In J. Morse (Ed.), *Completing a Qualitative Project: Details and dialogue* (pp. 39–58). Thousand Oaks, CA: Sage.

Luborsky, L., Singer, B. and Luborsky, L. (1975). Comparative studies of psycho-therapy: Is it true that everyone has won and all will have prizes? *Archives of General Psychiatry*, *32*, 995–1008.

Luca, M. (2007). *Working with the Phenomenon of Somatisation: Psychodynamic and cognitive behavioural therapists' conceptualisations and clinical practices.* Unpublished PhD Thesis. Kent: Kent Institute of Medicine and Health Sciences, University of Kent.

Lutz, C.A. (1988). *Unnatural Emotions: Everyday sentiments on a Micronesian atoll and their challenge to Western theory.* Chicago/London: University of Chicago Press.

Madill, A. (2009). Construction of anger in one successful case of psychodynamic-interpersonal psychotherapy: Problem (re)formulation and the negotiation of moral context, *The European Journal for Qualitative Research in Psychotherapy*, *4*, 20–29. (<www.europeanresearchjournal.com>).

Mahrer, A.R. and Boulet, D.B. (1999). How to do discovery-oriented research, *Journal of Clinical Psychology*, *55*, 1481–1493.

Marcus, G.E. (1998). *Ethnography Through Thick and Thin*. Princeton, New York: University of Princeton Press.

Margison, F., Barkham, M., Evans, CMcGrath, G., Melllor-Clark, J., Audin, K. and Connell, J. (2000). Measurement and psychotherapy: Evidence based practice and practice based evidence, *British Journal of Psychiatry*, *177*, 123–130.

Maroda, K. (1991). *The Power of Transference*. New York: John Wiley & Sons, Inc.

Mason, J. (2002). *Qualitative Researching* (2nd edition). London: Sage.

McGuire, A. (1999) cited in Moodley, R. (2001). (Re)Searching for a client in two different worlds: Mind the research-practice gap, *Counselling and Psychotherapy Research*, *1*, 18–23.

McLeod, J. (1999). *Practitioner Research in Counselling*. London: Sage.

McLeod, J. (2001). *Qualitative Research in Counselling and Psychotherapy*. London: Sage. (Reprinted, 2006.)

Macran, S., Ross, H., Hardy, G.E. & Shapiro, D.A. (1999). The importance of con-sidering clients' perspectives in psychotherapy research, *Journal of Mental Health*, *8*, 325–337.

Mellor-Clark, J. and Barkham, M. (2003). Bridging evidence-based practice and practice-based evidence: developing rigorous and relevant knowledge for the psychological therapies, *Clinical Psychology and Psychotherapy*, *106*, 319–327.

Melnick, J. and Nevis, S.M. (1992). *Gestalt Therapy: Perspectives and applications.* New York: Gestalt Institute of Cleveland, Gardner Press.

Menzies-Lyth, I. (1988). *Containing Anxiety in Institutions: Selected essays.* London: Free Association Books.

Merleau-Ponty, M. (1962). *Phenomenology of Perception* [Trans. C. Smith]. London: Routledge & Kegan Paul. (Original work published 1945.)

Merleau-Ponty, M. (1964). *Signs* [Trans. R.C. McCleary]. Evanston, IL: Northwest-ern University Press. (Original work published 1960.)

Merleau-Ponty, M. (1968). *The Visible and the Invisible* [Trans. A. Lingis]. Evanston, IL: Northwestern University Press. (Original work published in 1964.)

Milloy, J. (2005). Gesture of absence: Eros of writing, *Janus Head, 8*, 545–552.

Moodley, R. (2001). (Re)Searching for a client in two different worlds: Mind the research-practice gap, *Counselling and Psychotherapy Research, 1*, 18–23.

Moran, D. (2000). *Introduction to Phenomenology*. London: Routledge.

Moran, D. and Mooney, T. (2002). *The Phenomenology Reader*. London: Routledge.

Morgan, S. (2004). Practice based evidence. In P. Ryan and S. Morgan (Eds), *Assertive Outreach: A strengths approach to policy and practice* (pp. 247–267). London: Churchill Livingstone.

Morrow, S.L. (1992). *Voices: Constructions of survival and coping by women survivors of child sexual abuse*. Unpublished Doctoral Dissertation. Arizona State University, December 1992.

Morrow, S.L. (2005). *Quality and Trustworthiness in Qualitative Research in Counseling Research*. New York: Aldine.

Morrow, S.L. (2006). Honor and respect: Feminist collaborative research with sexually abused women. In C.T. Fischer (Ed.), *Qualitative Research Methods for Psychology: Introduction through empirical studies*. Amsterdam, Elsevier.

Morrow, S.L. and Smith, M.L. (1995). Constructions of survival and coping by women who have survived childhood sexual abuse, *Journal of Counseling Psychology, 42*, 24–33.

Mottram, P. (2000). Toward developing a methodology to evaluate the effectiveness of art therapy in adult mental illness. Accessed March 2008 from: <www.baat.org/taoat/mottram2html>

Moustakas, C. (1990). *Heuristic Research: design, methodology and applications*. Newbury Park: Sage.

Myers, S. (2000). Empathic listening: Reports on the experience of being heard, *Journal of Humanistic Psychology, 40*, 148–173.

NICE (2004/7). *Guidelines on depression*. Accessed July 2008 from: <www.nice.org.uk/Guidance/CG23>

Norcross, J.C. (Ed.) (2002). *Psychotherapy Relationships That Work: Therapist contributions and responsiveness to patients*. London: Oxford University Press.

Orange, D.M. (1995). *Emotional Understanding: Studies in psychoanalytic epistemology*. New York: Guilford Press.

Parker, I. (1992). *Discourse Dynamics: Critical analysis for social and individual psychology*. London: Routledge.

Parker, J. and Taylor, G. (1997). Relations between alexithymia, personality, and affects. In G.J. Taylor, R.M. Bagby and D.A. Parker (Eds), *Disorders of Affect Regulation – Alexithymia in medical and psychiatric illness*. Cambridge: Cambridge University Press.

Patton, M.Q. (2002). *Qualitative Research and Evaluation Methods* (3rd edition). Thousand Oaks, CA: Sage.

Perls, F.S., Hefferline, R. and Goodman, P. (1951/1994). *Gestalt Therapy: Excitement and growth in the human personality*. Highland, NY: The Gestalt Journal Press.

Plummer, K. (1995). *Telling Sexual Stories: Power, changes and social worlds*. London: Routledge.

Polkinghorne, D.E. (1983). *Methodology for the Human Sciences*. Albany, NY: SUNY.

Polkinghorne, D.E. (1992). Postmodern epistemology of practice. In S. Kvale (Ed.), *Psychology and Postmodernism*. London: Sage.

Polkinghorne, D.E. (1999). Traditional research and psychotherapy practice, *Journal of Clinical Psychology*, 55, 1429–1440.

Polster, E. (1987). *Every Person's Life is Worth a Novel*. New York: W.W. Norton & Co.

Ponterotto, J.G. (2005). Qualitative research in counseling psychology: A primer on research paradigms and philosophy of science, *Journal of Counseling Psychology*, 52, 126–136.

Potter, J. (1997). Discourse analysis as a way of analysing naturally occurring talk. In D. Silverman (Ed.), *Qualitative Research: Theory, method and practice* (pp. 144–160). London: Sage.

Potter, J. (2003). Discourse analysis and discursive psychology. In P.M. Camic, J.E. Rhodes and L. Yardley (Eds), *Qualitative Research in Psychology: Expanding perspectives in methodology and design* (pp. 73–94). Washington DC: American Psychological Association.

Potter, J. and Wetherell, M. (1994). *Discourse and Social Psychology: Beyond attitudes and behaviour*. London: Sage.

Qualls, P.A. (1998). On being with suffering. In R. Valle (Ed.), *Phenomenological Inquiry in Psychology: Existential and transpersonal dimensions*. New York: Plenum Press.

Rao, R. (2006). Wounding to heal: The role of the body in self-cutting, *Qualitative Research in Psychology*, 3, 45–58.

Rawlins, M. (2008). *RCTs "placed on an undeserved pedestal" – Head of NICE*. Accessed January 2009 from: <http://homeopathy4health.wordpress.com/2008/10/17/rcts-placed-on-an-undeserved-pedestal-head-of-nice/>

Reason, P. (1988). Experience, action and metaphor as dimensions of post-positivist inquiry, *Research in Organizational Change and Development*, 2, 195–233.

Reason, P. (1994). *Participation in Human Inquiry*. London: Sage.

Reissman, C.K. (1993). *Narrative Analysis*. Thousand Oaks, CA: Sage.

Reissman, C.K. (2003). Performing identities in illness narrative: Masculinity and multiple sclerosis, *Qualitative Research*, 3, 5–33.

Rennie, D.L. (1990). Toward a representation of the client's experience of the psychotherapy hour. In G. Lietaer, J. Rombauts and R. van Balen (Eds), *Client-centered and Experiential Therapy in the Nineties* (pp. 155–172). Leuven, Belgium: Leuven University Press.

Rennie, D.L. (1992). Qualitative analysis of the client's experience of psychotherapy: The unfolding of reflexivity. In S.G. Toukmanian and D.L. Rennie (Eds), *Psychotherapy Process Research: Paradigmatic and narrative approaches* (pp. 211–233). Thousand Oaks, CA: Sage.

Rennie, D.L. (1998). Grounded theory methodology: The pressing need for a coherent logic of justification, *Theory and Psychology*, 8, 101–119.

Rennie, D.L. (2000). Grounded theory methodology as methodical hermeneutics – Reconciling realism and relativism, *Theory and Psychology*, 10, 481–502.

Rennie, D.L. and Fergus, K.D. (2006). Embodied Categorizing in the Grounded Theory Method, *Theory and Psychology*, 16, 483–503.

Richardson, L. (1994). Writing: A method of inquiry. In N.K. Denzin and Y.S. Lincoln (Eds), *Handbook of Qualitative Research*. Thousand Oaks, CA: Sage.

Ricoeur, P. (1970). *Freud and Philosophy: An essay on interpretation* [Trans. D. Savage]. New Haven, CT: Yale University Press.

Ritchie, A. and Barker, M. (2005). Feminist SM: A contradiction in terms or a way of challenging traditional gendered dynamics through sexual practice?, *Lesbian & Gay Psychology Review*, 6, 227–239.

Roderick, L. (Songwriter) (1990). *If You See A Dream*. Anchorage: Turtle Island Records.

Rogers, C.R. (1951). *Client-Centred Therapy*. Boston MA: Houghton Mifflin.

Rogers, C.R. (1975). Empathic: An unappreciated way of being, *The Counseling Psychologist*, 5, 2–10.

Rowan, J. and Cooper, M. (1999). *The Plural Self: Multiplicity in everyday life*. London: Sage.

Rowland, N. and Goss, S. (2000). *Evidence Based Counselling and Psychological Therapies*. London: Routledge.

Rucker, N.G. and Lombardi, K.L. (1998). *Subject Relations: Unconscious experience and relational psychoanalysis*. London: Routledge.

Saakvitne, K.W. and Pearlman, L.A. (1996). *Transforming the Pain: A workbook on vicarious tramatization*. New York: Norton.

Sartre, J.-P. (1969). *Being and Nothingness* [Trans. H. Barnes]. London: Routledge. (Original work published 1943.)

Savin-Baden, M. and Fisher, A. (2002). Negotiating 'honesties' in the research process, *British Journal of Occupational Therapy*, 65, 191–193.

Schmitt Freire, E. (2006). Randomised Controlled Clinical Trials in Psychotherapy Research: An Epistemological Controversy, *Journal of Humanistic Psychology*, 46, 323–335.

Seale, C. (1999). *The Quality of Qualitative Research*. London: Sage.

Seidman, S. (Ed.) (1996). *Queer Theory/Sociology*. Oxford: Blackwell.

Seligman, M.E.P. (1995). The effectiveness of psychotherapy: The consumer report study, *American Psychologist*, 50, 965–974.

Shaw, R. (2003). *The Embodied Psychotherapist: The therapist's body story*. Hove, East Sussex: Routledge.

Shepherd, I.L. (1992). Teaching Therapy through the Lives of the Masters: A Personal Statement. In E. Smith, *Gestalt Voices*. New York: The Gestalt Journal Press.

Shields, L. (1998). Integrated, feminist writing. In W. Braud and R. Anderson (Eds), *Transpersonal Research Methods for the Social Sciences: Honoring human experience*. Thousand Oaks, CA: Sage.

Silverman, D. (1993). *Interpreting Qualitative Data: Methods for analysing talk, text and interaction*. London: Sage.

Smith, M.L. and Glass, C.V. (1977). Meta-analysis of psychotherapy outcome studies, *American Psychologist, 32*, 752–760.

Smith, J.A. (Ed.) (2003). *Qualitative Psychology: A practical guide to research methods.* London: Sage.

Smith, J.A. and Eatough, V. (2007). Interpretative phenomenological analysis. In A. Coyle and E. Lyons (Eds), *Analysing Qualitative Data in Psychology: A practical and comparative guide* (pp. 35–50). London: Sage.

Smith J.A. and Osborn, M. (2003). Interpretative phenomenological analysis. In J.A. Smith (Ed.), *Qualitative Psychology: A practical guide to research methods.* London: Sage.

Social Research Association (2003). *Advancing the Conduct, Development and Application of Social Research since 1978: Ethical guidelines.* Accessed November 2008 from: <www.the-sra.org.uk/ethical.htm>.

Solomon, R.C. (1997). Beyond ontology: ideation, phenomenology and the cross-cultural study of emotion, *Journal for the Theory of Social Behaviour, 27*, 289–303.

Staemmler, F.M. (1997). Cultivating uncertainty: An attitude for Gestalt therapists, *British Gestalt Journal, 6*, 40–48.

Stanley, M. (2006). A grounded theory of the wellbeing of older people. In L. Finlay and C. Ballinger (Eds), *Qualitative Research for Allied Health Professionals: Challenging choices.* Chichester, West Sussex: John Wiley & Sons, Ltd.

Stern, D. (1985). *The Interpersonal World of the Infant. A view from psychoanalysis and developmental psychology.* London: Basic Books.

Steward, B. (2006). Strategic choices in research planning. In L. Finlay and C. Ballinger (Eds), *Qualitative Research for Allied Health Professionals: Challenging choices.* Chichester, West Sussex: John Wiley & Sons, Ltd.

Stiles, W.B., Barkham, M., Twigg, E., Mellor-Clark, J. and Cooper, M. (2006). Effectiveness of cognitive-behavioural, person-centred and psychodynamic therapies as practised in UK National Health Service settings, *Psychological Medicine, 36*, 555–566.

Stolorow, R.D. and Atwood, G.E. (1992). *Contexts of Being.* Hillsdale, NJ: The Analytic Press.

Strauss, A. and Corbin, J. (1990) *Basics of Qualitative Research: Grounded theory procedures and techniques.* Newbury Park: Sage.

Strauss, A. and Corbin, J. (1998). *Basics of Qualitative Research – Techniques and procedures for developing grounded theory* (2nd edition). London: Sage.

Strickland-Clark, L., Campbell, D. and Dallos, R. (2000). Children's and adolescents' views on family therapy, *Journal of Family Therapy, 22*, 324–41.

Sullivan, H.S. (1953). *The Interpersonal Theory of Psychiatry.* New York: Norton.

Symington, N. (1986). *The Analytic Experience.* London: Free Association.

Taylor, C. (1985). Self-interpreting animals. *Philosophical Papers: Human Agency and Language* (Vol. 1, pp. 45–76). Cambridge: Cambridge University Press.

Taylor, G.W. (1997). The discursive construction and regulation of dissident sexualities: the case of SM. In J.M. Ussher (Ed.) *Body Talk: The material and discursive regulation of sexuality, madness and reproduction.* London: Routledge.

Taylor, G.W. and Ussher, J. (2001). Making sense of S and M: A discourse analytic account, *Sexualities*, 4, 293–314.

Thériault, A. and Gazzola, N. (2008). Feelings of incompetence among experienced therapists: A substantive theory, *European Journal of Qualitative Research in Psychotherapy*, 3, 19–29.

Todres, L. (2007). *Embodied Enquiry: Phenomenological touchstones for research, psychotherapy and spirituality*. Basingstoke, Hampshire: Palgrave Macmillan.

UKCP (2009). *Code of Ethics.* Accessed January 2009 from: <www.psychotherapy. org.uk/c2/uploads/copy%20of%20copy%20of%2014402_codeethics_lflt.pdf>

UKCP (2008). *Report following the UKCP March 2008 AGM – The current picture regarding statutory regulation*, by Katherine Murphy. Accessed January 2009 from: <www.metanoia.ac.uk/OneStopCMS/Core/CrawlerResourceServer.aspx? resource=0acd6b05c24148e88a0e18e18492e951&mode=link&guid= a3c16bdc73fa4955874b8841e6982dab>

van Deurzen-Smith, E. (1997). *Everyday Mysteries: Existential dimensions of psychotherapy.* London: Routledge.

van Manen, M. (1990). *Researching Lived Experience: Human science for an action sensitive pedagogy.* New York: State University of New York Press.

van Manen, M. (2002). *The Heuristic Reduction: Wonder.* Accessed November 2007 from: <www.phenomenologyonline.com/inquiry/11.html>

Varela, F.J. (1999). The specious present: The neurophenomenology of time consciousness. In J.-M. Roy, J. Petitot, B. Pachoud and F.J. Varela (Eds), *Naturalizing Phenomenology* (pp. 266–314). Stanford, CA: Stanford University Press.

Vetere, A. and Gale, A. (1987). *Ecological Studies of Family Life.* Chichester, West Sussex: John Wiley & Sons, Ltd.

von Eckartsberg, R. (1998). Introducing existential-phenomenological psychology. In R. Valle (Ed.), *Phenomenological Inquiry in Psychology: Existential and transpersonal dimensions* (pp. 3–20). New York: Plenum Press.

Walsh, R. (1995). The study of values in psychotherapy: A critique and call for an alternative method, *Psychotherapy Research*, 5, 313–326.

Wampold, B.E., Mondin, G.W., Moody, M., Stich, F., Benson, K. and Hyun-nie Ahn (1997). A meta-analysis of outcome studies comparing bona fide psychotherapies. Empirically, all must have prizes, *Psychological Bulletin*, *123*, 203–216.

Wampold, B.E. (2001). *The Great Psychotherapy Debate.* New Jersey: Lawrence Erlbaum Associates.

Wertz, F. (2005). Phenomenological research methods for counseling psychology. *Journal of Counseling Psychology*, *52*, 167–177.

Westen, D., Novotny, C.M. and Thompson-Brenner, H. (2004). The empirical status of empirically supported psychotherapies: Assumptions, findings and reporting in controlled clinical trials, *Psychological Bulletin*, *130*, 631–663.

Wheway, J. (1997). Dialogue and Intersubjectivity in the Therapeutic Relationship, *British Gestalt Journal*, 6, 16–28.

Willig, C. (2001). *Introducing Qualitative Research in Psychology: Adventures in theory and method.* Buckingham: Open University Press.

Winnicott, D.W. (1965). *The Family and Individual Development*. London: Tavistock Publications.

Winter, D. and Viney, L.L. (Eds) (2005). *Personal Construct Psychotherapy: Advances in theory, practice and research*. London: John Wiley & Sons, Ltd.

Yalom, I.D. (1986). *Theory and Practice of Group Psychotherapy*. New York: Basic Books.

Yin, R. (1994). *Case Study Research: Design and methods* (2nd edition). Beverley Hills, CA: Sage.

Yontef, G. (1993). *Awareness, Dialogue and Process. Essays on Gestalt therapy*. Highland, NY: The Gestalt Journal Press.

Yontef, G. (2002). The relational attitude in Gestalt theory and practice. *International Gestalt Journal*, *25*(1), pp. 15–35.

Zahm, S. (Fall 1995). Self disclosure in Gestalt therapy, *The Gestalt Journal*. New York: The Gestalt Journal Press.

Zinker, J. and Nevis, S. (1994). The Aesthetics of Gestalt Couples Therapy. In G. Wheeler and S. Backman (Eds), *On Intimate Ground: A Gestalt approach to working with couples*. San Francisco: Gestalt Institute of Cleveland Press.

Zvelc, M. (2008). Working with mistakes in psychotherapy: A relational model, *European Journal for Qualitative Research in Psychotherapy*, *3*, 1–9. <www.europeanresearchjournal.com>

Index